Christmas 1992

Brother Mel,

Insightful ideas from one of the wisest heads —

Thanks for another great year at Saint Mary's!

PAX

Bill

COMMUNITY
OF LEARNING

COMMUNITY OF LEARNING

*The American College and
the Liberal Arts Tradition*

F R A N C I S   O A K L E Y

New York   Oxford
OXFORD UNIVERSITY PRESS
1992

Oxford University Press

Oxford   New York   Toronto
Delhi   Bombay   Calcutta   Madras   Karachi
Kuala Lumpur   Singapore   Hong Kong   Tokyo
Nairobi   Dar es Salaam   Cape Town
Melborne   Auckland

and associated companies in
Berlin   Ibadan

Published by Oxford University Press, Inc.,
200 Madison Avenue, New York, New York 10016

Oxford is a registered trademark of Oxford University Press

Library of Congress Cataloging-in-Publication Data
Oakley, Francis.
Community of learning : the American college and the liberal arts
tradition / Francis Oakley.
p. cm.
Includes index.
ISBN 0-19-505199-8
1. Education, Humanistic—United States.   2. Education,
Humanistic—History.   I. Title.
LC1023.015   1992
370.11'2—dc20   91-38855   CIP

9 8 7 6 5 4 3 2 1

Printed in the United States of America
on acid-free paper

To the greater
Williams Community
1793–1993

PREFACE

I did my first teaching in September 1953 as a twenty-one-year-old foreign student at the University of Toronto who oddly assumed that his background in medieval history somehow fitted him to instruct Canadian freshmen in the rudiments of their own governmental system. A subsequent (and, in its own way, highly educative) period of service in the British Army confirmed in me the aspiration to become an academic. Since the late 1950s, then, I have pursued a full-time career in teaching, research, and (increasingly) academic administration, first at Yale University and then, since 1961, at Williams College. There, blessed by first-rate students, and in a truly splendid academic setting distinguished by strong intellectual values and a high degree of collegiality, I have been fortunate enough to be able to pursue a calling that has never lacked in variety of challenge. Over the years, certainly, while pursuing my primary vocation as teacher and scholar, I have spent more time than I would care to compute in matters pertaining to the governance of the College, to its curriculum, to student admissions and campus life, to the recruitment, retention and intellectual sustenance of its faculty, to its management as a complex corporate enterprise with several hundred employees, and to the building and stewardship of the financial resources needed to sustain it in its mission.

This little book is grounded in the bedrock of that experience. Far from purporting to be a work of scholarship or, alternately, some sort of exercise of "emotion recollected in tranquillity," it simply reflects my own rather harried attempt, while working with and among colleagues and students whom I both like and admire, and *in medias res* as president of a college to which I am deeply attached, to come to terms with the American undergraduate experience. An attempt also to make some sense of the current wave of discontent about that experience, to peer into the fog of uncertainty that lies ahead, and to chart a course for the future that will speak to the very particular strengths of that quintessentially *American* contribution to the vitality of higher education—the free-standing, undergraduate liberal arts college. By temperament, historians are prone to glance backward before moving forward and, as befits a medieval historian, my own backward glance understandably reaches out to encompass a rather distant past. That I myself should find such an exercise illuminating is only to be expected. That others should do so is not as readily to be assumed. If I take the liberty of sharing these reflections with others, I do so in the hope that an historically conditioned approach to the present discontents, while providing no obvious or simple solutions to the problems of the day, may nonetheless afford a perspective on those problems delivered at least in part from the dyspeptic presentism characteristic of a good deal of the recent writing on the subject.

Of that, however, I must permit the reader to be the judge, mindful of how much I myself owe to the promptings and advice of my colleagues. I would be remiss if I did not express an especial gratitude to David Booth, Stephen Fix, Michael McPherson and Frederick Rudolph, who were all kind enough to read the manuscript in whole or in part and to give me the benefit of their help, criticism, and advice; to Deirdre Oakley and Jeff Urdang '89, for research assistance at critical moments; to my wife, Claire-Ann, for continued encouragement and support when the hours available for writing and research began to seem well nigh non-existent; and to Donna Chenail and her staff in our faculty secretarial office for their excellent work preparing the manuscript for the press. I must express my gratitude also to Peter S. Willmott and my other colleagues on the Williams Board of Trustees for giving me the timely minisabbatical in the spring of 1991 which enabled me to finish the book, and to the Trustees of the Braitmayer Foundation for the grant-in-aid that made it possible for me to go about that task in the splendid scholarly setting provided by the National Humanities Center, Research Triangle, North Carolina. For the numerous and characteristic kindnesses extended to me by W. Robert Connor, the Center's Director, and by the members of his wonderfully supportive staff, I am also most deeply grateful. As is only fitting, the book is dedicated to the greater Williams Community — students, faculty, staff, alumni, parents, friends.

Williamstown, Massachusetts F.O.
January 1992

CONTENTS

COMMUNITY
OF LEARNING

INTRODUCTION

The important thing is to realize that the American college is deficient, and unnecessarily deficient, alike in earnestness and in pedagogical intelligence; that in consequence our college students are, and for the most part emerge, flighty, superficial and immature, lacking, as a class, concentration, seriousness and thoroughness.

Abraham Flexner (1908)

... [B]eyond cavil is the fact that, as in Aristotle's time, there is little agreement about what liberal education should be. Both theory and practice are confused and contradictory.

Thomas Woody (1951)

What we have on many of our campuses is an unclaimed legacy, a course of studies in which the humanities have been siphoned off, diluted, or so adulterated that the students graduate knowing little of their heritage.

William J. Bennett (1984)

The genre is quasi-apocalyptic; the mood, in best American fashion, resolutely masochistic; the cumulative message, in disappointing degree, quite myopic. About the recent collective jeremiad of reports, articles and books focused on American higher education in general and the state of the liberal arts and the undergraduate course of study in particular, there is little enough to rejoice; in their contents still less to encourage.[1] The line of march generally pursued is drearily familiar; in its overall direction and the staging points that punctuate it, by now almost canonical. A golden age of educational coherence and curricular integrity is evoked or implied. If its precise location is no more than foggily determined, that it has been succeeded by a more or less catastrophic fall from grace is not left in doubt. The recent history of undergraduate education in the United States emerges as a deplorable descent from the realms of gold to our current age of iron—an age distinguished by declining academic standards, curricular incoherence,

3

creeping consumerism, rampant vocationalism and wavering sense of mission.

"The undergraduate college," we are told, "is a troubled institution," often "more successful in credentialing than in providing a quality education" for its students.[2] As for the undergraduate degree, "evidence of decline and devaluation is everywhere." In our day "a profound crisis" has overtaken undergraduate education.[3] We are beset, in effect, by nothing less than a "crisis of liberal education" itself— a crisis reflecting (variously) the distortion of our universities and colleges by the research ethos and a concomitant neglect of teaching, the fragmentation of knowledge and the growth of hyperspecialization in the academic disciplines, the corrosive inroads of cultural relativism,[4] the intrusion of a marketplace philosophy into the curriculum,[5] its politicization and the subordination of "our studies [accordingly] to contemporary prejudices."[6] Coupled with a "collective loss of nerve and faith on the part of both faculty and administrators during the late 1960s and early 1970s," as well as an abandonment of the old commitment to mediate to successive generations of students the richnesses of the Western cultural tradition,[7] these developments have eventuated, alas, in "the decay of the humanities" and the dissolution of the curriculum.[8] In sum, our "educational failures" as a nation are lovingly caressed,[9] a sense of time running out is evoked in the manner formerly made fashionable by the denizens of the Club of Rome, and the compelling need to respond to the challenge thus posed is urged with a vigor redolent of other, less cerebral, realms of discourse.

In all of this, despite the pervasive sense that somewhere and at some time things used surely to be better, the golden age evoked remains, historically speaking, remarkably elusive. Few of the recent critics of the American undergraduate experience seem disposed to seek the interpretative leverage afforded by a comparative perspective, either by looking back in time beyond the provincial simplicities of the curriculum dominant in the American colonial colleges[10] or by examining the texture of higher education in other regions of our own contemporary world. Little is made, accordingly, of the central role played by professional needs in the origin and development of the university itself.[11] And, in our own era, little attention is drawn to the comparatively greater commitment of some of the European systems of higher education (those, for example, of Sweden, the German Federal Republic and the Soviet Union) to specialized and vocational studies.[12] Eyes are discreetly averted, moreover, from the truly enormous gap (evident from the ancient world down to our own day) between ringing theoretical affirmations of commitment to the plentitude of liberal arts instruction and the more humdrum realities of what has actually been going on amid the day-to-day confusions and disruptions of educational life as it has usually been lived in the pedagogic trenches.[13] Still less does one detect the presence of any historically informed sense of the range, looseness, variability and flexibility of the liberal arts tradition itself across the course of its longer history, or of the tensions which have wracked it for centuries and may well account for much of its enduring vitality and strength. That tradition, after all, still bears the mark left by the fateful decision of the early Christian communities in the Graeco-Roman world not to establish their own schools but rather to adapt to their purposes a pagan educational tradition of essentially Hellenistic provenance. As the history of Plato scholarship well exemplifies, this helped set up a tension that was still making its presence felt in Europe as recently as the late nineteenth and early twentieth century.[14] Similarly, historians have detected the continued presence in the tradition of an even more enduring tension, that between the rhetorical vision of liberal education as pivoting on the cultivation of the ancient classics or their derivatives and the philosophical-scientific model driven by the urge for critical originality and advancing via the overthrow of received assumptions. The former has traditionally been directed to the development of the skills pertinent to public expression and legal and political persuasion, as well as to the inculcation in those destined for lives of public service of the hallowed values and traditions inherited from the past. The latter, instead, has persistently been targeted on the advancement of knowledge and understanding and on the development of critical rationality.[15] Between the hammer and the anvil of these competing approaches little peace over the centuries has been able to grow.

About such things our critics say next to nothing.[16] Nor, perhaps more surprisingly, do they allude at any great length to the impact on our colleges and universities of the cultural and demographic factors that loomed so large in the world of higher education in the 1960s and 1970s. And three of these loomed very large indeed. First, the growing and wholly unprecedented diversity (in terms of gender, race, age, ethnicity and social class) of our undergraduate population during the years since the Second World War. Second, the understandable push given to a cautious vocationalism among college students by uncertain job prospects amid the turbulent economic conditions of the 1970s. Third, and above all, the truly enormous pressures brought to bear on the whole apparatus of higher education by the G.I. bill, the baby-boom of the postwar years and the entry into college of a higher percentage of the young adult cohort, and then, in the 1980s and 1990s, by the progressive dwindling of that cohort—leading, among the less secure institutions, to a competitive scramble for students, a reduction in the number of liberal arts courses required, and the addition of a growing array of purely vocational majors.

The willingness to slight the impact of such demographic factors on the academic vitality of our colleges and universities is the more surprising at a time when historians of higher education in Europe have been quick to emphasize "the importance of the rise and fall of student numbers in affecting the quality of life at the universities," insisting (in relation to the early-modern period) that "so widespread were these movements and so dramatic in their impact on the universities, that in the future much of the history of higher education is going to have to be articulated around them."[17] Certainly, the comparative success of the much-maligned American system of higher education in adjusting to the enormous growth in undergraduate population since the Second World War (and without the swamping of existing institutions by students of differing expectations and capacities so evident in parts of Europe) might be taken to suggest that, despite the unevenness in academic quality that is their inevitable concomitant, there is something healthy and praiseworthy about the characteristics of independence, autonomy and sheer institutional variety which distinguish that system from systems of higher education abroad.[18]

Of such thoughts, however, we find little trace in the recent spate of gloomy commentary on the college experience in America. "Rather than explain, [their] authors have chosen to condemn the incoherence of undergraduate programs and requirements and to discuss the kind of courses students should take in order to become well-rounded persons fit for contemporary life."[19] Something comparably unflattering, it must be conceded, has to be said about the tone of more than one of the academic responses to those critiques, especially to those focused on the current state of the humanities and its impact on the quality of the education we are offering to our students. While I would judge unwarranted Roger Kimball's charge that *Speaking for the Humanities,* a multiauthored and mildly bewildered response issued under the aegis of the American Council of Learned Societies, conveys an attitude of "generalized arrogance,"[20] his claim that former Secretary of Education William J. Bennett's 1984 report, *To Reclaim a Legacy,* "occasioned paroxysms of rage" within the academy comes depressingly close to the mark.[21] In fact, the overall impression conveyed by the multitudinous exchanges on the subject in recent years is one of tendentious claims, overheated charges and rhetorical excess.

Interestingly enough, less of this is evident when the critics turn from proscription and denunciation to prescription and remedy. At that point the confidence and reasonably high degree of agreement which distinguish the diagnostic phase rapidly evaporate. For some, salvation is to be found by placing the emphasis not so much on the "what" of knowledge as on the "how"—"how that knowledge has been created and what methods and styles of inquiry have led to its creation."[22] For others, the reverse is the case and the remedy proposed is a shift in the educational goals being pursued from "inquiry" and "skills" to "knowledge" and "content."[23] About this and other related disagreements in the current debate there is, of course, nothing particularly surprising. The issues involved are complex and intricate. It would be too much to expect them to yield readily to resolution. Nor is there anything particularly novel about the shape of such disagreements. During the course of the present century, the writing of national reports on the status of liberal education in America has been endemic. So, too, has been the criticism of such reports, as well as the emasculation or rejection of their findings. Almost fifty years ago, J. Hillis Miller noted that those who set out to study and report on the matter were in the habit, perhaps necessarily so, of asking "age old questions which continue to defy satisfactory answers."[24]

The outcome, as a result, has been a sort of educational war of attrition. It is a war in which the contending sides surge back and forth across a desolate Great War-style battleground, terrain dominated by the same enduring set of issues, punctuated by the rubble of earlier high-minded experiments, and strewn with the remnants of discarded curricular equipment. It is also a war whose monotony is relieved by the introduction of few strategies not already tried, and whose long-established course, marked by an almost liturgical predictability, suggests the unwisdom of expecting, however intense the fighting, that any permanent victories are likely in the future to be won. Even if one were to be tempted accordingly to seek refuge in a stance of war-weary detachment, one would confront the chastening fact that such a temptation has itself, over the years, become an integral part of the script. Some thirty years ago, in the wake of another era of intense debate about higher education and the undergraduate course of study, President Conant of Harvard described the "sense of distasteful weariness" aroused in him by debates about the meaning of the word "education." "I feel," he said, "as though I were starting to see a badly scratched film of a poor movie for the second or third time."[25]

But as one of Conant's distinguished successors has done well to remind us, "the fact that curricular debates are inconclusive does not mean that they are unimportant."[26] And detachment is hardly an option today for those charged with the stewardship of the nation's institutions of higher education. Those debates hold, I believe, a particular importance for those of us who pursue our calling at one or other of the nation's free-standing liberal arts colleges, by their very nature committed to vindicating the importance of undergraduate education. Especially so, I would argue, for those fortunate enough to be affiliated with the small sub-group of those colleges usually designated as "highly selective." If the colleges of that sub-group constitute no more than a tiny fraction of the nation's institutions of higher education,[27] nonetheless they are a group exceptionally favored by the quality of their students and faculty, the clarity of their mission, and the strength of their financial resources.

Such advantages impose, I believe, certain obligations. And, not least among them, a cheerful willingness to enter the curricular arena, or to do so at least to the extent necessary to reflect on the educational mission appropriate to the free-standing liberal arts college if it is to discharge its responsibilities at this particular juncture in our educational history and in the intellectual and institutional climate now prevailing.

The task is neither easy nor straightforward. But it may be eased somewhat if, eschewing the rhetorical shortcuts, tiresome stereotyping and argumentative excess that have marred the current debate, one attempts to do two things. First, to bring to the task the peripheral intellectual vision and generosity of perspective which, at its best, a broad education in the liberal arts aspires itself to afford. Second, and more particularly, to bring to it also that liberation from temporal or regional provincialism which an appropriately comparative historical approach can make possible.

The objectives I propose for myself in writing this book, then, are at once both modest and ambitious. They are reasonably modest in that I do not aspire to legislate, in anything other than the most indirect and general way, a set of goals for a liberal arts education applicable to the full and extraordinarily varied range of institutions devoted to undergraduate education in the United States, still less to stipulate for all such institutions—community and junior colleges, free-standing four-year colleges and the undergraduate colleges within our universities—a uniform set of curricular instrumentalities for attaining those goals. I will be content instead if I can point, in reasonably persuasive fashion, to a set of directions for the future congruent with the traditional mission of our liberal arts colleges in general and pertinent especially to the strengths of the more highly selective among them.

At the same time, my objectives are quite ambitious in that I aspire to bring to an appraisal of the present discontents concerning undergraduate education in the United States a reasonably (if not exhaustively) informed sense of the long and broad history of higher education seen, to some degree, in cross-cultural perspective. A sense, accordingly, of the distinctiveness and complexity of the liberal arts tradition as it emerged from the womb of classical antiquity and developed, first in Europe and then in North America, across the centuries stretching down to the present. A sense, likewise, of the institutional singularity of the Western mode of organizing higher education around universities and university-colleges. That mode of educational organization, itself a creative deliverance of Europe and of the once-despised Middle Ages, has exerted a formative influence in the modern era, not only here in the New World but also in every region of the globe.

In setting myself these objectives, then, I respond in part to the claim that Max Weber, the great pioneer of historical sociology, advanced with such clarity and force. Namely, that our characteristically Western modes of life and thought do not represent any natural or inevitable culmination towards which all civilizations strive or have striven, that they represent, instead, only one very particular line of development, one possibility out of several radically different ones. In reflecting about our educational traditions and institutions then, as about our other most cherished assumptions, beliefs, customs and attitudes, we would do well to resist the temptation, so powerfully felt in the past, to assume that there is anything *natural* or universal about them. In some of their most creative and important dimensions they may, instead, be the product of our own peculiar cultural history here in the West.[28]

Such, certainly, is the claim I would make about those familiar academic institutions which have served as the bearers across time of the liberal arts tradition, institutions which we tend to take utterly for granted as we worry away at our essentially provincial disagreements about the current state of the curriculum and the health of the undergraduate college today. To those institutions we will now turn, proceeding in straightforward historical fashion, and taking the opportunity to erect the basic chronological framework upon which subsequent, less historical, chapters may safely depend.

CHAPTER I

INSTITUTIONAL:
The Bearers of the Tradition in Europe and America

No nobler institution came out of the Middle Ages [than the university].
Robert Nisbet (1971)

The longer history of our institutions of higher education is an extremely tangled one. As we edge up to an appraisal of our present educational discontents, we need to be conscious of that fact. In general, we need to be aware of the singularity, historically speaking, of our current institutional arrangements for higher education. In particular, we need to be disabused of three common misconceptions about those arrangements. First, that the specific distinction we are accustomed to make today between university and college is anything other than an American contribution, and a comparatively recent one at that. Second, that the history of higher education, in all eras and all parts of the world, is synonymous with the history of universities. Third, and even more fundamental, that without the existence of the *school*, more or less as we know it, there could be no higher education. These misconceptions I propose to take up in turn, beginning with the last and ending with the first.

1. The School: Hellenistic, Roman, Monastic, Cathedral

Despite the exclusion of "the godless 'science of the Ancients'"[1] from the curriculum of the *madrasas*, or schools of higher learning in Islam, the intellectual achievement of the great Muslim philosophers and scientists of the tenth, eleventh and twelfth centuries was an extraordinary one. It should serve to disabuse us of any notion that organized

11

institutional arrangements akin to those with which we are familiar are necessary in a culture for the development among small coteries of individuals of a very high level of learning and scholarship. A similar lesson can be extracted from the history of higher education in China across the fourteen centuries and more during which a national examination system focusing on the canon of Confucian texts held sway. That system served as a vehicle for selecting the imperial bureaucracy, and it stemmed from an attempt by the Sui emperors (589–618 C.E.) to assert their own imperial authority at the expense of the hereditary aristocracy which had come to dominate Chinese political life. It was originally independent of the schools.[2] Over the course of time, however, the examination system came itself to absorb the governmental system of higher education provided (at least from the Sung period— 960–1279) by the district, departmental and prefectorial schools and capped by the Imperial or National College in the capital. From the Ming period (1368–1644) onward, entrance to the crucial series of civil service examinations was barred to those who lacked *sheng-yüan* (licentiate or student) status. It was necessary, then, first to acquire that status by competing successfully in the round of entrance examinations given for the government schools. There was no age-limit imposed on candidacy for these latter examinations, the status conferred on those who competed successfully in them was the important thing (rather than access to collective modes of instruction), and the number of licentiates grew with time. As a result, the government schools—including the National College itself—gradually ceased to offer instruction. Although they survived into the modern era, they did so, oddly enough, not as institutions of learning but as bureaucratic institutions with some ritualistic functions.[3]

In the world of Graeco-Roman antiquity, on the other hand, the direction of educational development was less counter-intuitive.[4] It moved from aristocratic arrangements for individual tutoring of the young prevalent at Athens in the sixth century B.C.E., via schools offering a more collective mode of instruction intended for all free men which, along with the democratization of Athenian life, began to appear in the fifth century, down to the Hellenistic crystallization of its classical form in the wake of the stabilization of the Greek world after the death of Alexander the Great (323 B.C.E.). Adopted by the Romans during the second century B.C.E. after their conquest of the Greek-speaking territories to the East, the Hellenistic system of schooling was later drawn into the orbit of Roman imperial policy and financing, so that by the fourth century C.E. there was a network of municipal schools all over the Graeco-Roman world. Schools pursuing advanced studies came into existence in such great urban centers as Carthage, Naples, Milan, Athens, Alexandria, Antioch and Beirut, and Constantinople joined their ranks in 425 C.E., when the Emperor Theodosius II founded what Henri Marrou refers to as "a State University." As we shall see later on, he does so improperly but perhaps understandably, for the school was granted "a complete monopoly of the city's higher education." And though it had "many ups and downs, periods of decline and even temporary disappearances," that great "Imperial University" was to remain the true central support for the secular classical tradition in education right down to the Turkish conquest of Byzantium in 1453.[5]

It would be all too easy for us to read into such institutional arrangements much that was alien to them or was to become characteristic of the organization of higher education only after centuries of subsequent development. We talk blithely of "schools" and instinctively assume a measure of specialization, a cooperation among instructors working within the framework of an agreed curriculum supported, probably, by examination. But, for the ancients, while the existence of a school implied the presence of a group of teachers, it meant coexistence rather than cooperation. For them "a school was merely a geographical expression. It was [simply] a place where several teachers found it convenient to teach."[6] We should also be aware of the fact that in the culture of late antiquity the study of philosophy, in particular, meant less the pursuit of an intellectual discipline than the commitment to a vocation at odds with the normal way of life. Such philosophic "schools" as the Platonic Academy had not, in our terms, been schools at all. Instead, they were confraternities or "sects"—juridically speaking, that is to say, they were religious associations. And commitment to the philosophic path was something extraordinary, reached, indeed, by a process in our terms akin to religious conversion.[7] Despite the extraordinary nature of the Greek philosophic achievement, then, the philosophic commitment was quite uncommon among the Greek intelligentsia. And among the Romans, later on, it was even more unusual. In the imperial age Rome itself may have been the only place in the western provinces of the Empire where any organized instruction in philosophy could be found. By that time, Rome and several other great cities had come to possess official law schools. Their development, however, had come surprisingly late in the day, and one of the most striking features of higher education in antiquity was how very slow it was to provide organized courses of study for those wishing to enter the professions.

In higher education, as in the lower schools, the rhetoricians were the dominant force, and the formative Hellenistic interpretation of *enkuklios paideia* (the general culture or education appropriate to a freeman) to mean, above all, a *literary* education reigned supreme. So much so, indeed, and despite earnest worries about the profane content of the literature being studied, that those Christians who lived within the boundaries of the Empire chose not to set up their own special religious schools, but to attend (and eventually to teach at) the old pagan schools.[8] The educational ideal remained classical, and it was sustained with great fidelity right down to the fifteenth century at the great imperial "university of Constantinople," where no specifically religious subjects were taught, "the liberal arts supplying the foundation [of the education offered], and rhetoric, philosophy and law the crown."[9] In the *Banquet* of Xenophon (d. *ca.* 350 B.C.E.) we read of a certain Nicoratus who, wishing to become "an accomplished man," had learned the *Iliad* by heart. Fourteen centuries later, the Byzantine scholar Michael Psellus (d. *ca.* 1078), who did so much to revive the great school at Constantinople, was able to make the same boast, and he was proud to do so.[10]

But if the old secular classical education and the type of educational institution which had sustained it survived across the Middle Ages in the Byzantine East, the situation was very different in the West. Survival at one level or another was the pattern in those parts of coastal and southern Italy and Sicily (Rome, Ravenna, Naples, Salerno) that enjoyed protracted periods of Byzantine imperial rule.[11] But, in general, the old schools ceased to exist in the western half of the old Graeco-Roman world after the end of the fifth century, when the political structure which we know as the Roman Empire of the West had crumbled and its provinces had passed under the control of a congeries of Germanic invaders. Even in the African province where, under the reasonably enlightened rule of successive Vandal and Byzantine invaders, the classical educational tradition survived the breakup of the empire, the old educational tradition came to an end in 697 with the Muslim capture of Carthage.

Given this situation, it was extremely important for the future of Western intellectual life that St. Augustine of Hippo (354–430), the great North African theologian who was to be the architect of the type of Christian theology espoused by the Latin Catholic Church, had sympathized with the Platonic and Ciceronian endorsement of what came to be called an education in the liberal arts as an indispensable introduction to the more intensive study of philosophy. In his influential work *On Christian Doctrine,* he urged Christian scholars to retain what amounted to the established Roman education in the liberal arts as a necessary preparation for the more important and higher studies in Christian philosophy and theology. Given the turbulent political conditions of the early medieval period, it is even more important that educated monks like St. Jerome (d. 620) and Cassiodorus (d. *ca.* 575) should have succeeded in making some sort of study of the liberal arts an integral part of the monastic life.

That the monasteries should have become centers of learning and promoters of the liberal arts is by no means to be taken for granted. Things could easily have been otherwise and their mission could have been taken to exclude any such educational role. Education implies schools, schools imply libraries, libraries imply books and, at that time, the copying of books. If all of these were eventually to become intimately associated with the great monasteries of the early medieval West, they had little to do, in fact, with the religious aspirations that had originally given rise to monasticism and they could find little positive sustenance in the influential guiding *Rule* that St. Benedict of Nursia (d. 543) had originally drawn up for his monastery at Monte Cassino. There was nothing in that *Rule,* for example, about the copying of books; it was Cassiodorus, himself a product of the old, secular classical education and for most of his life one of Theodoric the Goth's Roman civil servants, who appears to have stimulated the process that was to make it an almost quintessential part of the monk's duty. "Oh, blessed the perseverance," he wrote (having retired from the world to the monastery he had founded on his estate at Vivarium), "laudable the industry which preaches to men with the hand, starts tongues with the fingers, gives an unspoken salvation to mortals; and against the iniquitous deceits of the Devil fights with pen and ink. For Satan receives as many wounds as the scribe copies words of the Lord."[12] Cassiodorus speaks here, of course, of copying the Bible. But in order to maintain the type of educational program he had bequeathed to them, the monks had to copy much else besides, and to their efforts we owe the preservation of the bulk of the classical Latin literature that has survived into the modern world.

The independence, economic self-sufficiency, and frequent rural isolation of the great landed monasteries fitted them admirably to be the principal bearers of learning during the turbulence of the early

Middle Ages, and the monastic schools retained their preeminence in educational matters until the beginning of the twelfth century. At that time, with the restoration of public order, the increase in population, the quickening of economic life and the revival in Western Europe of vital urban centers, the need for the monastic role in education and the congruence of such a role with the monastic vocation was called into question. The initiative in educational matters was already passing to the secular clergy (and even to laymen), to individual masters such as Peter Abelard (d. 1142), who pursued the subjects that interested them personally. In their quest for greater numbers of students, these men sought out the urban centers. There, they often held their classes at the cathedrals (some of which had long provided for instruction), or at other prominent churches in the more important cities.

As "the school followed the teacher,"[13] each of these urban schools tended to be focused on the particular interests of the dominant masters teaching there: law at Bologna, medicine at Salerno and Montpellier, theology at Laon, Rheims and Paris, and the science and philosophy of the Greeks and Arabs at the cathedral school of Toledo (since its inception in 1085 an important center of contact between Christian, Muslim and Jew). There the archbishop, indeed, had set up something approximating a translation factory, and Spain, along with Sicily, Syria (from the time of the first Crusade onwards) and Constantinople, became the source for Latin Christendom of a great influx of ancient Greek philosophical writing, along with more recent Jewish and Muslim work in the same fields. During the late twelfth and early thirteenth century, via translations made from the Greek itself, or from Arabic translations of the Greek, or, not infrequently, via both, the Latin world was gradually put into contact for the first time, not just with Aristotle's logic (long since absorbed) but with the whole body of his writings and with an extensive array of Arabic commentaries on those writings. Prominent among those works were those of the great Muslim philosophers Ibn Sina (d. 1031) and Ibn Rushd (d. 1198), the Persian and Spaniard known in the Latin world, respectively, as Avicenna and Averroës.

The impact of this great influx of knowledge was very dramatic. The fundamentally literary studies which (in ancient fashion) had dominated in the schools were pushed to one side, first by the growing interest in logic and then by the broader fascination with the whole body of Aristotle's writings—the first complete philosophic and scientific system medieval thinkers had encountered. The recovery of Aristotle coincided in time, and helped stimulate, the rise to prominence of the intellectual method and style that we call "scholasticism." And, along with a great increase in the number of students and (accordingly) in the number and size of the advanced schools, it also coincided in time with the emergence of the institution which for us has become almost coterminous in meaning with higher education—namely, the university.

2. Studia generalia and the rise of universities and colleges

Historians have not hesitated to equate the *madrasa* with the university, to speak of an "imperial" or "national" university at Beijing, or to allude to universities at Athens, Alexandria and Constantinople in the early Middle Ages.[14] With a carelessness no less anachronistic for all its generosity, they have applied the word to other schools that flourished in civilizations as yet untouched by the influence of Western educational models. Strictly speaking, however, such a usage is quite improper. Universities were a European invention and a medieval one at that, reflecting the rapid increase in the number of scholars crowding into the urban schools during the second half of the twelfth century and the concomitant need for organization and regulation.[15] The new institutional forms, which first rose spontaneously in Salerno, Bologna, Paris and Oxford, were later to be introduced deliberately by popes, emperors and kings. We refer to them simply as "universities" but contemporaries called them "universities of masters and scholars." The difference is a revealing one. For us, the word "university" denotes simply the institution of advanced learning which has come everywhere in the world to dominate our systems of higher education. But when medievals first spoke of them they were referring not so much to institutions as to people. They were referring, that is, not to the great schools or *studia generalia*—where at least one of the advanced professional disciplines (medicine, law, theology) was taught and to which students resorted from all over Europe—but to the guilds (*universitates*) of masters and students, which, from the last quarter of the twelfth century onwards began to appear *at* those great schools. Not until the fifteenth century, in fact, did it become common for the term *universitas* to be used as a synonym for the *studium,* school, or place of study.

The guilds involved were simply sworn societies or corporations of masters or students who had joined together for mutual protection, which eventually, like other guilds, elected rectors to lead them, and which were able to win for themselves the full corporate prerogatives of using a common seal and being able to act as a single fictive person at law. Modeled on the commercial and craft guilds, which had by then carved out for themselves a secure niche in medieval urban life and economic enterprise, they were a response to the need of the growing numbers of masters and students congregated in alien cities where they did not enjoy the rights of citizenship to protect their mutual interests against the pressures being put on them by townsmen and civic authorities. In addition, they came to serve also as a protection against pressures exerted by the local episcopal authorities, which frequently struggled, as, classically, at Paris, to retain over the educational activities of the new *studia* the degree of control they had long been accustomed to exercising over their own cathedral schools.

As the structure of the fledgling academic guilds or universities acquired more precise definition, they came customarily to be divided into "faculties," with the faculty of arts being regarded as preparatory to the "superior" professional faculties of medicine, law and theology. Their classes, at least during the twelfth and thirteenth centuries, were conducted in leased or borrowed buildings. As a result, they were unembarrassed by the extensive property holdings that are both the presupposition and burden of their modern descendants and could have been open to confiscation by hostile civic authorities. In their battles with those authorities, then, their trump card was the ability to declare a strike or cessation of studies, or even to move the whole operation to a more supportive city, thus emptying the offending town of its rent-paying student population, which, in some cases, must have constituted as much as one-tenth of the total populace.[16] Thus, in the early thirteenth century, cessations at Bologna, Paris and Oxford led, respectively, to the creation of universities at Padua, Angers and Cambridge. (Interestingly enough, though five centuries later, it was a roughly analogous secession from Williams College that led to the founding of its archrival Amherst.)[17] Of course, for maneuvers of this type to be effective, it was necessary for the masters or doctors themselves to control who could teach in the schools. This they did by regulating entry into their own ranks (recognized ceremonially at the commencement ceremony known as an "inception"), by imposing on the school what amounted to a closed-shop policy, and by establishing control over the granting of the *licentia docendi,* or licence to teach, the forerunner of all academic degrees.[18]

Such was the prestige of the two archetypical universities of Bologna and Paris that their degrees came to be accepted all over Latin Christendom, and popes and emperors, acting as appropriately ecumenical authorities, came later to confer this *jus ubique docendi* (the right to teach anywhere) on other universities which they themselves had chartered. That this should be so, of course, presupposed a preoccupation with academic standards and a measure of uniformity in those standards. Degrees were to be given only to the qualified; that a candidate was qualified was to be determined not simply by length of studies[19] but also by examination; and examinations to be both systematically effective and reasonably equitable presupposed coherent curriculum, organized teaching, and a regulated course of studies. "Curriculum, examinations, commencement, degrees, are all part of the same system; they are all inherited from the Middle Ages, and in some form they go back to the twelfth century."[20]

Given the marked degree of cultural interchange between Islam and Christendom in the Middle Ages and the intriguing parallelisms in their intellectual development,[21] it is not surprising that historians have been prompted to look to the Islamic world, the culture in which higher education and the institutions supporting it matured earlier, for the origins of the university. In particular, to the *madrasa*,[22] "the Muslim institution of learning par excellence," which had come into existence by the late eleventh century when Nizam al-Mulk (d. 1092), grand wazir of the Saljuk sultans, had created "a vast network of madrasas" right across the territory of the Eastern Caliphate.[23] *Universitas*, however, meant "corporation," a legal abstraction possessing juristic personality and capable of being the bearer at law of rights and responsibilities. Such a notion being alien to Islamic law, which "recognizes the physical person alone as endowed with legal personality," the university was, accordingly "utterly alien to the Islamic experience."[24] What was not alien, however, was the notion of the college endowed in perpetuity as a charitable trust. Such institutions had developed as early as the eighth century, when the smaller mosques (*masjid*) in many of the cities of Islam, themselves eleemosynary or charitable foundations under the law of *waqf*, had begun to be used as colleges for the study of the Islamic sciences, with Islamic law firmly ensconced as queen of the sciences. These colleges had provided salaries for their teachers and offered instruction to their students free of charge. In close proximity came frequently to be established, and especially so in the latter part of the tenth century, inns or *khans* providing free lodgings (and perhaps food) for students living away from home. And in the eleventh century appeared the *madrasa*, combining in one institution the functions of both *masjid* and *khan*, providing, therefore, for all the needs of the resident student, and embodying the combination of intellectual and residential functions that were later to be characteristic especially of the English universities, and of the colleges established from the seventeenth century onwards in the English North American colonies.

The *madrasas* enjoyed the status of charitable trusts under the law of *waqf*. Via the initial legal instrument, that law gave their original founders great freedom in establishing the purposes of the trust they as individuals were endowing and in charting their future course. In this they had so much in common with the first colleges to appear in the context of the fledgling universities of Europe that some have claimed that, if not the university, then at least the *college* was borrowed by Christendom from Islam.[25] Housing costs and shortages at Paris and Oxford had led early on to the imposition of rent controls on the student hostels and to the provision of special accommodations for the poorer students. It was the need to help the latter group that gave rise after 1180 to what came later to be known as the Collège des Dix-huits, the first of the seventy colleges that were to be connected with the University of Paris by the end of the fifteenth century.[26] At Oxford, similiarly, Balliol, University and Merton Colleges had been established by the mid-thirteenth century. University College and Balliol at their inception, and the Collège des Dix-huits and the other Parisian colleges throughout their histories, were all of them simply charitable trusts, closely akin, juridically speaking, to the Muslim *madrasa*.[27] But Merton College, right from the start, was something more than that; so, too, were all subsequent colleges at Oxford and Cambridge. And they were something more than eleemosynary institutions because "they took on [also] the essential attributes of the university, incorporation." That is to say, they were "*incorporated* charitable trusts ... artificial persons, protected by the law of the land." That law "ensured their constitutional rights as legal persons, and the perpetual application of their properties to the objects of their creation."[28]

Of course, although as self-governing corporations with elected heads the Oxbridge colleges were well positioned to resist absorption by the university itself, they were not endowed with the crucial university prerogative of being able to grant degrees, nor were they ever to be so authorized. During the later Middle Ages, however, first in Germany and then (even more markedly) in Scotland, colleges were established whose primary purpose was not "to provide for poor students" but rather "to supply the university with teachers," and college and university, accordingly, "were more or less completely fused into one." That fusion, moreover, was to be completed in Spain, where, in 1489, Pope Innocent VIII conceded the crucial university prerogative of granting degrees to the college that had been founded in 1477 at Sigüenza, whereupon the rector of the college became the rector of the university. "The new form of university thus evolved became the model upon which similar college-universities were afterwards erected at Alcalá and elsewhere in Spain."[29] So, too, in Ireland, at Trinity College, Dublin (1591), where the university "had no legal existence apart from the College; it was simply the degree-granting aspect of the College." As the legal decision in the case of *Yale University vs the City of New Haven* in 1899 correctly pointed out, it was customary in Dublin to refer to Trinity, not only as "Trinity College, Dublin," but also as "Dublin University," and even (most interestingly) as "The University of Trinity College, Dublin."[30]

If the emergence at the end of the Middle Ages of this "college-university" model was of crucial importance for the form later to be taken by our first institutions of higher education in Colonial America, the shape acquired by the modern American university as we now know it will not be fully comprehensible without a glance at the direction subsequently taken by the university movement in continental Europe during the early-modern and modern eras.[31]

During the fourteenth and fifteenth centuries the institution of the university spread outwards from Italy, France and England to Spain, Germany, Scandinavia, the eastern European countries and Scotland. In 1500, by Rashdall's count, there were approximately eighty of them in existence. The upheaval occasioned by the Reformation and the subsequent wars of religion ushered in a period of disruption, sponsoring the heavy-handed encroachment by governmental and ecclesiastical authority upon the traditional liberties of university life, impeding the free flow of teachers, students and ideas across what had once been but now no longer was an international community of learning. We now know, however, that this phase was followed in the seventeenth century, and, it seems, all over Europe, by "a period of astonishing growth..., [with] a staggering number of students... pouring into the universities."[32] Even the subsequent era of low enrollments and declining intellectual vitality (especially marked in England, France, Spain and Italy) which lasted from the latter part of the seventeenth to the early nineteenth century, and which led reformers in France and Germany to call for the abolition of universities,[33] was not one of unrelieved torpor in the academic world. The Dutch universities, for example, constituted something of an exception. In their curriculum and the scholarship they fostered, they responded to the burgeoning of the natural sciences. Leyden, indeed, developed what in the early eighteenth century was widely regarded as the best system of medical education in Europe. The achievements there of Herman Boerhaave, professor of medicine, generated responsive echoes in Scotland, where the universities at Aberdeen, Edinburgh, Glasgow and St. Andrews showed great vitality in medicine, the natural sciences and mathematics, as well as an openness to clinical instruction and even to such eminently practical and vocational studies as bookkeeping. By the latter part of the century, Edinburgh was enjoying an international reputation for the quality of its medical instruction and as the home of the Scottish "Common Sense" school of philosophy developed by such luminaries as Francis Hutcheson (at Glasgow), Adam Ferguson and Dugald Stewart. After the 1760s, indeed, "Edinburgh's literati and its university gave the city its well-known and remarkable international reputation as a center of learning... [and]... as the Athens of the North."[34]

In terms, however, of the subsequent development of the university as an institution, the most significant steps were being taken elsewhere, at Halle in Prussia and at Göttingen in Hanover, where the foundations were being laid for the new, reformed type of German university that was to find its archetype in 1810, when Wilhelm von Humboldt established the University of Berlin, and that was later to have so profound an impact upon the nature of higher education abroad.[35] Raised to university status in 1694 from its old position as a *Ritterakadamie* offering a rather dilettantish, courtly, "gentleman's" training to some of the nobility, and graced by the presence on its faculty of the distinguished jurist Christian Thomasius, Halle retained the accepted gentlemanly instruction in such activities as riding, fencing and music, while setting out also to modernize the traditional university curriculum. Adopting the vernacular rather than Latin as the language of instruction, it gave heightened attention to the study of law, modern foreign languages, the natural sciences, and even public administration.

Göttingen, founded in 1737 at the prompting of Gerlach Adolph von Münchhausen, the era's leading Hanoverian privy counsellor, was a much more carefully planned enterprise, designed to continue the push towards modernization of the curriculum along the lines initiated at Halle, but to so do in order to attract the sons both of the nobility and of the wealthy middle class and to offer them an education well designed to prepare them for service to the state. In this conscious "attempt to stabilize and legitimate the role of the more flexible part of the aristocracy with the aid of a small elite recruited from the middle class" it appears to have succeeded. It sponsored "the process of legitimization through university attendance" which helped create the notion of an "educated class" bridging the gulf between nobility and bourgeoisie.[36] As at Halle the old "courtly" subjects were retained and the vernacular was used as the language of instruction. Questions of religious orthodoxy were discreetly nudged to one side, and the study of the ancient languages was de-emphasized. A very strong legal faculty was established, and the faculty of philosophy, responsible for the teaching of languages, mathematics, science and history, was given unusual prominence. Finally, in his efforts to build up the visibility and academic prestige of the new university, Münchhausen set out to recruit distinguished scholars known through their publications. By so doing he began that emphasis on scholarship and research which, in a form so intensified as to redefine the very goal of the university, was to become characteristic of German higher education in the nineteenth century.

In the course of that great process of transformation, the foundation in 1810 of the University of Berlin was the turning point. It set the pace for other new universities like Bonn (founded 1818) which sought to compete with it. And it inspired efforts to reorganize and reform their ancient predecessors. The model of increasingly specialized research, already a success in the natural sciences, now became the dominant influence on scholarship in other fields. The commitment to creative scholarship and research came finally to be lodged at the very heart of the university enterprise, and the old, less specialized, education in the liberal arts regarded as the province of the advanced secondary education provided by the gymnasia. German researchers had concluded, it seems, "that the knowledge of their predecessors was superficial at best, and that bold acts of intelligence and will by the individual scholar would uncover the profound secrets of the human world and the universe beyond."[37] Their scholarly achievements and the nimbus of prestige that came to surround the German universities led university reformers in France, England and elsewhere to adapt to their own institutional and curricular contexts some measure of the German research ethos and of the attitudes and institutional infrastructure that went with it. But in no national system of higher education was the impact of the new, reformed German university felt more profoundly than in that of the United States.

This fact has loomed large in the histories of American higher education, and properly so. But, in retrospect at least, the transformation of the European universities by the research ethos is overshadowed in historical significance by three other developments markedly evident during the second half of the nineteenth century and continuing on into the twentieth.

The first is the planting of universities modeled directly on their European counterparts not simply, as heretofore, in such "settler colonies" as the Spanish imperial possessions in Latin America, or in Canada or Australia, but in places all over the globe from Africa to South-east Asia. Most striking of all was their successful planting and vigorous growth in India, China, Japan and countries of the Islamic world which had long harbored their own hallowed traditions of higher learning.[38]

By any standards this was an extraordinary development, and one with far-reaching consequences. But so, too, was the second development which, like the third, intersected with it. Namely, the progressive breakdown of the social and religious barriers which, in the post-Reformation era, at least, had in most countries conspired to limit university education to a socially privileged elite. And, not least of all, the denial to women of access to the university course of study. From the 1860s onward, that age-old barrier came down, successively, in Switzerland, France, the Scandinavian countries, Italy, Spain, Russia and Scotland. England and the German and Austrian empires were slower to respond to the pressure to admit women to university instruction and degrees. Respond, however, they eventually did, and by the early years of the twentieth century their universities were serving a broader-based clientele than ever before.

They were also serving a larger clientele. The third major development that became increasingly evident during the second half of the nineteenth century, continued (though with some marked fluctuations both regionally and across time)[39] into our own century, and has been the single most marked characteristic of higher education worldwide in the recent past, is the sheer growth in the overall numbers of students seeking university education. In the wake of the Second World War, as the democratization of higher education forged boldly ahead not only in Europe but right across the world, that well-established process of growth began, very dramatically, to quicken. Between 1945 and 1975 there was an eightfold increase in university enrollments in the German Federal Republic. In Great Britain, the percentage of the university-age group actually enrolled went up from 4.5 percent to approximately 20 percent. In Sweden, the comparable percentage increase between 1950 and 1973 was from less than 4 to more than 21 percent.[40] But even such massive increases, themselves enough to impose enormous strains on the national systems of higher education struggling to accommodate them, were dwarfed by the staggering jump in enrollment experienced by countries in the developing world. India, for example, saw its university population jump from a mere 225,000 in 1946 to 2.7 million as early as 1971.[41] Commentators on the quality of higher education are prone to arguing about many things, from the organization and financing of universities and colleges to academic standards, curricular matters and the plight of the liberal arts. All of these issues, however, must clearly be seen in the context of the massive enrollment growth that began to set in over a century ago. In the United States, that pattern established itself during the aftermath of the Civil War. And, when it did so, it helped transform what was already by then a well-established system of higher education with more than two centuries of history behind it.

3. The colonial college–university and the emergence of the modern American university

The institution of the university found its way to the New World during the course of the sixteenth century in the wake of the Spanish *conquistadors*. The English settlers in North America did not long delay in following the example they had set. In 1538 a first (if ephemeral) university in the New World may have been established in Santo Domingo. In Mexico and Peru, certainly, universities were founded in 1551 with all "the privileges, exemptions, and limitations of the University of Salamanca."[42] In 1636 the Massachusetts General Court provided by law for the establishment of the college we know as Harvard in the settlement of Newtowne, which we know as Cambridge.[43] At that college under its first president, Henry Dunster, a highly traditional course of studies was established. The language of instruction was English, but a firm grasp of Latin was required and the overall pattern was set by instruction in the classical liberal arts with more than a nod in the direction of religious instruction. The heart of the matter was grammatical and rhetorical instruction in the ancient Greek language and literature, with the addition of Hebrew and smatterings of Aramaic and Syriac.[44] With modest variations from place to place, Dunster's course of studies was to set the curricular pattern for subsequent colonial colleges.[45]

By the onset of the Revolution, no fewer than eight such additional colleges had been established in the English colonies of North America:

William and Mary (1693), Yale (1701), New Jersey at Princeton
(1746), King's, the future Columbia University (1754), Philadelphia,
the future University of Pennsylvania (1755), Rhode Island, the future
Brown University (1765), Queen's, the future Rutgers (1766), and
Dartmouth (1769). The years 1782 to 1802 saw chartered a further
nineteen colleges still in existence today—among others the University
of Georgia (1785), the University of North Carolina (1789), the University
of Vermont (1791), Williams (1793), Bowdoin (1794), Union
(1795), with Amherst coming along later, in 1825.[46] By the time war
broke out in 1862 the United States could boast of approximately 250
colleges (182 of which survive to the present), and it has been estimated
that "perhaps as many as seven hundred colleges tried and failed before
the Civil War."[47]

For a nation with a population of no more than 35,000,000 that
number of institutions is wholly extraordinary and the educational
commitment involved extremely impressive. But not, it must be conceded, to the pioneering presidents of the new-style American universities which emerged in the decades after the Civil War. Their
judgments are important if only because they have so often been un-
critically echoed.[48] To them, neither the age nor quality of the older
educational institutions nor the type of educational commitment they
characteristically embodied was at all worthy of commendation. To
Andrew D. White, the first president of Cornell, American higher
education prior to the advent of his own beloved university in 1865
had amounted to nothing more than "a regime of petty sectarian
colleges." In 1900, President Harper of the new University of Chicago
speculated that of every four colleges then extant, three could expect
to end up as academies (advanced level secondary schools) or merely
junior colleges. In 1903, President Jordan of Stanford confidently predicted that with time "the college will disappear, in fact, if not in
name. The best *will become* universities, the others will *return* to their
place as academies" (italics mine).[49]

Their words reflect not only an unwarranted degree of condescension towards their collegiate predecessors, but also a confusion
about the institutional origins and status of the American college that
has persisted down to the present among Europeans and Americans
alike.[50] We know that the model for Harvard was Emmanuel College,
Cambridge, and for William and Mary, Queen's College, Oxford, and
not any academy for advanced secondary instruction. But we also
know that the model represented by the Oxford and Cambridge colleges as self-governing, incorporated charitable trusts was not followed

faithfully in the New World. Because of the paucity of fully fledged masters or fellows, the governance of the colonial colleges came to reside, not in the hands of the resident faculty with the president functioning as *primus inter pares,* but in the hands of the founders and their successors institutionalized as boards of overseers, trustees or "visitors."[51] Further than that, in a departure from Oxbridge precedent less frequently noted, Harvard and its successor colleges were accorded, along the lines of the late-medieval college-university model established in Scotland, Spain and Ireland, the university prerogative of granting degrees. As the argument for Yale in the case of *Yale vs the City of New Haven* (1899) correctly pointed out, in committing "to found, erect and govern a college," the ministers who were to be the first trustees of Yale "formed themselves into a society at New Haven in 1700...and...founded the *University of Yale College*" (italics added). It also emphasized that

> In establishing the universities in the new world, the limitations of the people compelled the founder[s] to follow the example of Trinity College, Dublin, and Marischal College, Aberdeen, and not that of Oxford and Cambridge. Upon the *same corporation* was conferred the power of the university in granting degrees and of the college in government; and such community and the buildings required for its use were known as "The College."

And it pointed out further that the "College founded at Cambridge" (i.e. Harvard College) was recognized by the Massachusetts Constitution of 1779 as "The University of Cambridge."[52]

However revealing they may be in historical terms, one may properly doubt if legal considerations of this type would have cut much ice with the great *condottieri* of the university "revolution" of late nineteenth-century America. They *knew* what a real university should look like, and it was to look nothing, in effect, like the indigenous colleges of the antebellum era. Their chief model, instead, was the reformed German university, by now enjoying enormous prestige, with its distinguishing characteristics of marked specialization in its curriculum, elective freedom for its students, and, for its faculty of course, the priority of the commitment to research and to the training of future scholars. Thus Daniel Coit Gilman, the first president of Johns Hopkins University, which opened in 1876 and responded quintessentially to the German inspiration, could describe the guiding mission of the university as "the acquisition, conservation, refinement and distribution of knowledge."[53] The attempt by Clark University, founded in

1889 at Worcester, Massachusetts, to respond even further to the research ideal (Veysey describes it as "the first and only important all-graduate institution in the United States") was not a success. And that despite the vigorous leadership of its first president, the distinguished psychologist, G. Stanley Hall.[54] But the example set by Johns Hopkins in stressing the research imperative was profoundly influential. And that influence was felt not only at such new institutions as Catholic University (1889) or the University of Chicago (1892), but also at older institutions, both public and private, from the universities of Michigan and Wisconsin to Harvard, Columbia and Yale. While eschewing the extremes of Johns Hopkins and Clark and nudged on differentially by the spread at the undergraduate level of the elective system,[55] they moved in the 1880s and 1890s to add graduate programs (or to put existing programs on a more organized basis), and to commit themselves to the heightened specialization and departmentalism that went with that commitment.

If the German-inspired research ethos was a crucial factor shaping the modern American university as it emerged in the late nineteenth century, it intersected, however, with two other powerful drives. From that intersection, and from the array of differing interactions it spawned in the multiple institutional settings of collegiate and university life across the nation, have sprung most of the particular characteristics distinguishing American higher education on into our own day. And prominent among those characteristics are its unevenness in academic standards, its concern for student residential life, its responsiveness to community needs, its extraordinary variety, vitality and creativity.

The second of those drives, as much of native as of foreign provenance and even more evident at Cornell than the commitment to scholarship and research, was that which pointed in the direction of practical service to the community, with its related impulses of sympathy towards vocational studies and applied science. That drive received a powerful impetus in 1862 with the passage of the Land Grant College Act (the Morrill Act), which provided for the establishment or endowing (or both) in each state of a land-grant institution. That institution, without excluding other branches of knowledge, was to furnish institution in agriculture and "the mechanic arts." The legislation was flexible and a great variety of institutions benefited from land-grant funds. Prominent among them was Cornell, which "helped achieve respectability for the land-grant idea" by combining "the new spirit of scholarship" with the fostering and development of "the vocational subjects and the courses in applied science which were implicit in the land-grant idea."[56]

Moreover, Cornell's multiple innovations and its president's dismissive attitude to the contrary, that new university and many of the new foundations (both public and private) that were to follow came to reflect also a third and perhaps more unexpected drive—the impulse to preserve some of the features and commitments long since characteristic of the antebellum college-university. The provision of dormitories, support for co-curricular and extracurricular activities, a preoccupation with the development of the individual student—such traditionally collegiate concerns remained alive and well. "After an initial flirtation with the uncongenial German ideal of official unconcern for the student outside the classroom, the new universities returned to the distinctly American concern for the whole collegiate experience of their students."[57] At the same time, the old colleges were not themselves unresponsive to the new ideals, both curricular and scholarly, which the new university so powerfully represented. It is well to be reminded that in the last years of the nineteenth century colleges like Amherst and Wesleyan could boast of bigger libraries than the universities of Indiana, Michigan, Minnesota, Missouri and Wisconsin, and that the free elective system had made further headway at Amherst, Bowdoin and Oberlin than at Chicago, Michigan and New York University.[58]

The evolution of American higher education on into the twentieth century, then, has not proved to be unilinear in its direction. The push towards heightened specialization and departmentalism and the commitment to the ethos of scholarship and research has grown in intensity and has reached out to embrace the more selective among those old college-universities that did not choose in the nineteenth century to add graduate programs and transform themselves into universities of the new type. At the same time, even as the liberal-arts colleges came to represent, statistically speaking, a decreasingly significant segment of the whole spectrum of American higher education, the old collegiate values not only survived into the late-twentieth century but recovered much of their vitality and played a role in the shaping or reshaping of such enormous state university systems as those of California and New York. And the impulse towards community service found expression in the late nineteenth and early twentieth century in the creation of summer programs, night schools and the vast enterprise of the extension course movement boosted in 1906 with the proposal of the "Wisconsin Idea" that the entire state of Wisconsin should be viewed as the university's campus.[59] Since then, and especially since President Truman's Commission on Higher Education issued its report, *Higher Education for Democracy* (1947), that same impulse to service has made its presence felt in the creation of a burgeoning array of courses and programs for the non-traditional student, and, above all, in the establishment nationwide of a network of two-year comprehensive community colleges which now account for almost 40 percent of the total enrollment nationwide at institutions of higher education.[60]

Of course, the rapid expansion of the community college system, along with the earlier growth in the number of two-year junior colleges and the upgrading of normal (teacher-training) schools into four-year state colleges reflected the desire to open up to all segments of the nation's population the hope of access to higher education. Even more, it developed into a response to the massive challenge posed in the years after the Second World War, first by the effects of the GI Bill, then by enhanced educational expectations and, most of all, in the 1960s and early 1970s, by the impact of the postwar baby boom which led to an enormous increase in the numbers of those seeking access to postsecondary education. In the United States, as also in Europe and the world beyond the West, rather than any curricular issue in itself it is this massive shift in the demography of university and college attendance—the most dramatic phase in the growth pattern firmly established after the Civil War—that unquestionably bulks as the single most important factor determining the quality of our undergraduate education today.[61]

In this respect, I am struck by the pertinence of the claim Lawrence Stone has made in connection with the shifting demography of the Oxford student body across a period of over three centuries. "To argue," he says,

> that major changes in the size of the student body are the structural pivots around which the history of the university has to be built does not involve any assumption that quantity is more important than quality, that the life of the mind, which is what a university stands for, is subordinate to crude numerical size. On the other hand changes in the scale of university activities of the magnitude here described not only have obvious and far-reaching effects on the economics, the architecture and the teaching arrangements of the university, they also have profound repercussions on its intellectual life.[62]

4. College, university, and college-university: the matter of historical significance

For the growth and continuing elaboration across time of higher studies in "Islamic sciences"—those studies, that is, which pivoted on or supported the scrutiny and interpretation of the *shari*ʾ*a* or divinely revealed law—the line of development in Islam that led from *masjid* to *madrasa* was of great historical importance. It led to the provision, ultimately, not only of salaries for the teachers but also of free instruction, accommodations and (possibly) food for the students. By so doing it helped stabilize, support and routinize in Islam an elaborate and sophisticated tradition of higher learning, one that was crucial to the religio-cultural identity of a civilization that has been described as "a lay nomocratic theocracy."[63] It was a line of development financed almost entirely throughout the centuries which in Europe are termed medieval by private acts of charity of a certain type. These were not transitory acts of charity such as gifts to the poor, subject to discontinuation because of the donor's changing fortunes or wishes or because of his death. Instead, they were acts of charity under the law of *waqf,* establishing and endowing in perpetuity a charitable trust to serve the educational goals envisaged by the donor and to do so in accordance with the provisions he had stipulated in the original *waqf* instrument. Once that instrument was drawn up, that charitable trust was exposed to no intrusion or change in its terms either by the donor himself or by his descendants or by any trustees for whose appointment he had provided. And the only limit on the freedom of the donor in setting up the trust was that he could not insert into the *waqf* instrument any provision contrary to Islamic belief.

In this impressively sophisticated set of arrangements comparative historical insight suggests, however, the presence of a flaw. As we have seen, unlike the European universities and Oxbridge colleges which they predated, neither *masjid* nor *madrasa* were legally incorporated. As a result, they came to be exposed to two different dangers.

In the first place, as unincorporated charitable trusts they lacked the ability to respond to changing circumstances that came to be possessed by the Oxbridge colleges of the post-Merton era. Under the law of *waqf,* however unwisely restrictive the original trust agreement had been and however changed the circumstances confronting the institutions it had established, its trustees were not empowered to make any alterations in the letter of that original agreement. That is to say, they could not make any such changes even for the purpose of ensuring that the overarching purposes of the trust should continue to be fulfilled. The governing bodies of the incorporated English college, on the other hand, possessed precisely those powers. To the form of perpetuity, provided for by the charitable trust, incorporation added, in effect, an element of dynamism and adaptability. It also added, or so Makdisi argues, a more effective legal protection against government intervention and the type of misappropriation by powerful government officials that so often led, after the death of their founders, to the unlawful seizure of assets and properties belonging to *waqfs*. It is, he concludes, the crucial difference explaining the endurance and resilience of the Oxford and Cambridge colleges and the colleges modeled after them, while the unincorporated colleges of Islam and Paris failed to survive.[64]

In the second place, another drawback may have attached to the fact that the jurisconsults of the *madrasa* did not enjoy the benefit of incorporation into the type of guild-structure that found expression in the medieval university, jealous of its collective prerogatives and quick to take collective action when those prerogatives appeared to be threatened from the outside. That lack of incorporation may help account for the ultimate inability of the jurisconsults to protect and prolong, in the face of government intervention, "the free play of opinions, arrived at freely and freely debated to the point of consensus" once characteristic of Islamic higher learning.[65]

Of course, it would be easy enough to make too much of the degree of independence and freedom from outside interference in their intellectual endeavors which the existence of the university secured for scholars in Latin Christendom during the Middle Ages and for their successors in the universities of modern Europe and North America. In successive struggles with the burghers of Paris, the royal government and the local ecclesiastical authorities, the masters of the fledgling University of Paris were indeed able in the thirteenth century to vindicate their autonomy. Together with scholasticism, which provided a methodology geared to rendering compatible the contradictory and harmonious the dissonant, the universities certainly made it possible for medieval intellectuals to come remarkably close to achieving the impossible: namely, to domesticating within the alien confines of the Christian world-view the "naturalistic" and at many points incompatible philosophy of the pagan Aristotle. The ecclesiastical authorities might raise obstacles to this process—as they did at Paris in 1210, 1215, and again in 1231—but they could only delay it. By 1255 the faculty of arts curriculum at Paris included the whole corpus of Aristotle's writings.[66] By the next century, the Faculty of Theology at Paris was so confident of its independent standing as to denounce as heterodox a novel doctrinal view concerning the Beatific Vision that Pope John XXII had ventilated in a series of sermons preached at the papal court in 1331–32. And such was its standing that the hapless pope, a very distinguished canon lawyer but admittedly no theologian, accordingly withdrew his endorsement of the suspect doctrine.[67]

During ages of ideological turbulence, however, when the traditional rule of law came itself into question, legal incorporation and the well-established traditions of autonomy did not suffice to ensure the independence of higher learning. Thus, in France during the religious wars of the late sixteenth century, Henry IV was able simply to exert direct governmental control over the University of Paris.[68] Similarly, in our own century, and despite their influence, prestige and proud inheritance, the German universities were brought rapidly and abjectly to heel under the terms of the Nazi policy of *Gleichschaltung*.[69] Even in more benign times and settings, moreover, the torpor that settled in the eighteenth century over the ancient foundations and the short-sighted use of corporate autonomy to defend the quasi-aristocratic privileges and exclusions of the past positively invited governmental interference.

That interference manifested itself both via the sponsorship of adaptive reform and through the establishment of new-style universities subjected right from the start to more direct state supervision. The former was the case, for example, in England, where it took the intrusion of the royal commissions of the 1850s and subsequent parliamentary legislation to reform and reshape Oxford and Cambridge and to abolish religious restrictions on access to matriculation and to college and university office. The latter was the case, for example, in nineteenth-century Germany, where the individual professor was accorded a high degree of freedom in the discharge of his scholarly and instructional responsibilities, but where governmental funding of the universities brought with it close civil service supervision of administrative and even curricular matters and the emergence of comparatively weak "on campus" administrations. Even in America, where institutional continuity with the medieval past was a good deal more insistent, the transfer of the ultimate responsibility of corporate governance from the faculty body to boards of trustees or overseers (and that became the norm after the foundation of Yale in 1701),[70] brought with it, if not the intrusion of governmental power, at least the partial subordination of academic values and freedoms to the mores dominant in the larger and more practical world of business, industry and the professions. And it brought with it, too, at least the partial transformation of the faculty from proud collegiate bodies of resident fellows into something akin to mere employees. It was a state of affairs which led Francis Wayland, a reform-minded president of Brown University in the early to mid-nineteenth century, to ask: "How can colleges prosper directed by men[,] very good men to be sure [,] but who know about every other thing except about education. The man who first devised the present mode of governing colleges in this country has done us more injury than Benedict Arnold."[71]

Nonetheless, if it would be possible to exaggerate the long-term importance for higher learning in the West of the emergence of universities in the twelfth and thirteenth centuries, it would be hard to do so. Despite governmental encroachments in Europe on the degree of autonomy universities had originally possessed, they continued to secure for their faculties *some* measure of independence from non-academic pressures. Professors at the great reformed universities of nineteenth-century Germany, themselves governmental employees, certainly enjoyed no enhanced freedom of *political* expression, but they did enjoy *Lehrfreiheit,* the freedom to pursue scholarly research in their field, to publish their findings, and to incorporate those findings in their teaching. And in the late nineteenth and early twentieth century, the newly self-conscious and increasingly professionalized faculties of the new-style American universities, organizing themselves nationwide in the American Association of University Professors (1915), moved successfully, not simply to vindicate their own *Lehrfreiheit* but also to extend its reach to cover their extramural (and political) utterances.[72]

Moreover, the older inheritance from Europe of the institution of the college-university, with the status at law of an incorporated charitable trust, proved itself in the long haul to be a crucial factor in the development of a remarkably healthy, varied and vital private sector in American higher education. To the colonial and revolutionary eras, admittedly, the distinction we confidently (and anachronistically) draw between "private" and "public" institutions would have been as alien as the particular distinction we are also accustomed to draw today between "colleges" and "universities." Being incorporated under state law, the college-universities of the day were viewed as being in some sense public. Certainly, without state financial support it is questionable if such institutions as Harvard, William and Mary, Yale,

Columbia or Williams could have survived. During the first thirty years of its existence, for example, Williams received as much in state financing as it succeeded in raising itself from all other sources taken together. Later on, Mark Hopkins himself was to say of the $75,000 received from the Commonwealth of Massachusetts in 1868: "But for the unexpected gift by the state...I do not see how the College could have got on."[73]

But the quasi-public status that made them permissible recipients of state aid could also, under certain circumstances, make the old college-universities attractive targets for state intervention. And especially so if, as in the case of Dartmouth College in 1815, the president himself, locked in a struggle with his board of trustees for control of the college, invited state legislative action which would have had the effect of establishing a degree of state control over the institution. When, in order to vindicate their own control over the college, the Dartmouth trustees took their case to the courts, the Superior Court of the State of New Hampshire, deciding against them, ruled in 1817 that Dartmouth College was "a public corporation, that its trustees were public officers responsible to the people, and therefore subject to legislative control."[74] It seems safe to predict that, had the decision held, the subsequent history of American higher education would have been vastly different. But it did not hold. It was overturned by the United States Supreme Court in *Dartmouth College vs Woodward* (1819). It was a classic landmark case, and in the arguments made before the Court as also in the opinions rendered by the justices it made quite clear, as Makdisi has pointed out, "the dual legal character of the college-university: a privately endowed charitable trust, and a corporation, fused into one."[75]

Thus Daniel Webster, arguing for the trustees, quoted Lord Hardwicke to the effect that "the charter of the Crown cannot make a *charity* more or less public, but only more permanent than it would otherwise be," and himself went on to claim that "the granting of the corporation is but making the trust perpetual, and does not alter the nature of the charity. The very object sought in obtaining such charter [of incorporation], and in giving property to such a corporation, is to make and keep it private property, and to clothe it with all the security and inviolability of private property."[76] And thus Chief Justice Marshall, speaking for the majority of his fellow justices, stated:

> That education is an object of national concern, and a proper subject of legislation, all admit. That there may be an institution, founded by gov-

ernment, and placed entirely under its immediate control, the officers of which would be public officers, amenable exclusively to government, none will deny.

But, emphasizing that "these questions are of serious moment," he went on to ask: "[I]s Dartmouth College such an institution? Is education altogether in the hands of the government?" His answer was a carefully argued negative. "In most eleemosynary institutions," he said, "the object [for which they were established] would be difficult, perhaps unattainable, without the aid of a charter of incorporation." At the same time, "from the fact... that a charter of incorporation has been granted, nothing can be inferred which changes the character of the institutions, or transfers to the government any new power over it." It is not incorporation, then, that confers on a given institution the status of being a "civil," that is, a *public* institution. Instead, it is the fact that it is "an instrument of government, created for its purposes." Nor, concomitantly, can "the incorporating act change the character of a private eleemosynary institution" and change it into a public body subject, presumably, to the expropriation of its property. Dartmouth College, he concluded, was such

> an eleemosynary institution, incorporated for the purpose of perpetuating the application of the bounty of the donors, to the specified objects of that bounty; that its trustees or governors were originally named by the founder, and invested with the power of perpetuating themselves; that they are not public officers, nor is it a civil institution participating in the administration of government, but a charity-school or a seminary of education, incorporated for the preservation of its property, and the perpetual application of that property to the objects of its creation.[77]

The immediate and local effect of the decision in this great case was that the State of New Hampshire was unable to assert its control over Dartmouth College and to go ahead with its plan to give it a new form as "Dartmouth University." And its less immediate and less localized effect may have been to slow down the growth of interest in establishing state universities. But by making clear the freedom from legislative intrusion of the incorporated charitable trust, its long-term and most wide-ranging outcome was that of encouraging the creation of a host of new small colleges, not least of all by a broad array of religious denominations. In Rudolph's judgment: "The decision put the American college beyond the control of popular prejudice and passion.... [It] left the colleges free to work out their own future without orders from the state or political pressure from the people. It allowed all the incompetence, variety, and final achievement which are associated with competitive American enterprise."[78]

By so doing it also helped establish the preconditions for the distinctiveness of the American system of higher education when compared with the systems prevailing elsewhere in the world, and not least of all in Europe, from which, both earlier and later, it had derived and was to derive so very much. Europeans have long been puzzled by the unevenness in academic quality to be found in American colleges and universities and bemused by the degree of responsiveness to passing fads into which the competitive spirit periodically betrays them.[79] But in the wake of the enormous social and demographic pressures of the past thirty years, the extraordinary strengths of the private sector in American higher education, the sheer variety of colleges and universities, public as well as private, the extent to which they compete with one another, not only for prestige but also to respond to clear educational needs, above all, the unparalleled degree to which they enjoy freedom from centralized state control—all these characteristics deserve to become the focus of a much more positive appraisal. Nobody who sets out to assess in comparative fashion the degree to which the various national systems of higher education in Europe and America have succeeded in coping with the recent demographic challenges can fail to be impressed by the adaptability, flexibility and creativity that go along with the diversity and decentralized nature of the American system.[80] And it is hard to believe, however harsh the strictures of the critics, that those characteristics, deeply rooted in a singular history, will not serve the cause of undergraduate education well as it faces the distinctive challenges looming ahead at the turn of the century. Among those challenges, it is those of a curricular nature which have been most persistently the focus of attention in recent years. But to be understood, these, too, must be seen in their own larger and broader historical context.

CHAPTER II

INSTRUCTIONAL:
The Evolution of
the Tradition Itself

Writing about Greece was in part a way for the Victorians to write about themselves.... What actually constituted the most striking feature of Victorian Hellenism wherever it appeared was the tyranny of the nineteenth-century European experience over that of Greek antiquity.

Frank M. Turner (1981)

One of the prominent features of intellectual life in Victorian Britain was the revival of interest in classical Greece, the revitalization of Greek studies in the universities, and a revival of Platonic scholarship surpassing even that which had occurred in Italy during the Renaissance. Of the late Victorian and Edwardian classicists, however, Frank Turner concludes that "[t]hinking about Plato helped them think about themselves."[1] He analyzes in illuminating detail the way in which they superimposed their own religious, intellectual, social and political anxieties upon the alien contours of ancient Athenian life. And he charts the way in which, with the dawning of the "new liberalism" and collectivism of the Edwardians, their sympathies shifted across time from Socrates (seen as heroic individualist) to the Athenians who on grounds of civic solidarity had condemned him.[2] The stretch of intellectual history involved is a fascinating one, and it has the added merit of sensitizing us to the possibility that a similar process may now be at work in other realms of discourse—certainly in much of the modern literature concerning undergraduate education in America and the fate of liberal education in the "postmodern era." In that literature, the very terms "liberal education" and "liberal arts" are frequently used without any recognition of the changing meanings attributed to them across the centuries. "A particular understanding" of one or other terms is often seized upon, understood "as the normative definition" of that term, and casually projected onto the past.[3] Similarly, contemporary anxieties about curricular incoherence, creeping vocationalism, hyperspecialization, loss of cultural unity and an alleged failure to mediate the accumulated richness of the Western cultural heritage are often highlighted by the imposition on the past of a golden age of educational harmony, instructional integrity, curricular coherence, intellectual stability, and truly liberal educational values.[4]

The past involved is, of course, a *Western* past, but it is worth noting that the recalcitrant historical realities even of civilizations more culturally unified or monolithic than our own would present formidable obstacles to the plausibility of such a move. However stable, for example, the Chinese cultural tradition, we have well been reminded that "a thoroughgoing Confucian China is an unhistorical abstraction."[5] Similarly, we know that it was not until the period after 1790, when the Shogun reformed the central Hayeshi school in Edo (Tokyo) and ordered its head to banish "the heterodox doctrines of those who make a cult of novelty," that the doctrines of Sung Confucianism came so to dominate higher education in Tokugawa Japan as to end the interpretative disputes of the previous century and to make possible the formulation of "standard curricula independent of the personal bent of particular teachers."[6] Again, in Islam, it was only in the mid-ninth century, after the failure of the 'Abbâsid caliphs to impose Mu'tazilite rationalism as the norm of orthodoxy, that the "foreign sciences" of the ancient Greeks came to be banished from the Islamic schools and higher education in the Muslim world so exclusively focused on the study of Islamic law—grounded in the Qu'ran, the traditions (*hādith*) and the commentaries of the schools.[7]

Nonetheless, in China, Japan and the Muslim world alike, the intensive and highly sophisticated study of a collection of revered texts (enjoying sacred or quasi-religious status) did eventually become the focus of higher education, enjoying the sustained approbation of the powers that be, serving for centuries as the recognized gateway to higher civilian office, and fostering across time a remarkably high degree of intellectual concord and educational stability.[8] It would be hard to overemphasize the contrast evident in the conditions of educational life prevalent in what, with some misgivings,[9] but for shorthand purposes, we will call "the West." Had they not succumbed to alien conquest, it may be, the so-called scribal cultures of ancient Mesopotamia and Egypt, with their reverence for the past and their preoccupation with the conservation of knowledge,[10] might plausibly be expected to have developed educational patterns akin to those of East Asia. And the status accorded to the texts of Homer and Hesiod in archaic Greece suggests that there, too, a cognate line of development might once have been possible. That possibility, however, appears to have been deflected for the Greeks by the extraordinary intellectual and cultural flowering that occurred in Athens during the fifth century B.C.E. And even if that had not been the case—had not the tensions and disjunctions in educational theory and practice engendered thereby been as sharp and enduring as they eventually turned out to be[11]—a development of Western higher education along anything truly approximating East Asian lines was definitively foreclosed by the irruption of Christianity, its ultimate conquest of the Graeco-Roman world, and the uneasy nature of the accommodation it made with the literary and philosophical legacy of classical antiquity. As a result, the history of educational thinking and practice in the West has been a markedly tension-ridden and conflicted one.[12] Only if we overlook that cardinal fact are we likely to be tempted to play off the educational turmoil of the present against the supposed serenity of the past. Before trying, then, to make sense of our present educational discontents, we would do well to take a look, if only in sketchy and schematic fashion, at some of the past disagreements and disjunctions that continue, in one way or another, to shape and inform the present. We proceed, therefore, via a series of antinomies: Biblical revelation versus natural reason, philosophy versus rhetoric, liberal education versus liberalism, educational ideal versus pedagogic practice.

1. Jerusalem and Athens: Biblical revelation versus natural reason.

Our familiarity with the marriage of Athens and Jerusalem, and the very success of the accommodation reached between Biblical revelation and pagan literature and philosophy, has long since encouraged us to take it for granted and to overlook how very tense and qualified a partnership it has proved over the centuries to be. Even Matthew Arnold, who in *Culture and Anarchy* (1869) made much of the cultural distinctiveness of what he called "Hebraism" and "Hellenism" and of the need in modern culture for the one to complement the other, was also at pains to insist that "the aim and end of both Hebraism and Hellenism is...one and the same." Both, in effect, aim for "man's perfection or salvation;" both seek after "the love of God."[13] For so many of his fellow Victorians, moreover, believers as well as nonbelievers, his very insistence was redundant. From the *Introduction to the Study of Greek Classical Poets* (1830) by Henry Nelson Coleridge (nephew of the poet) to Mr. Gladstone's vast Homeric commentaries, Benjamin Jowett's influential translations of the Platonic dialogues (full of seductive echoes and harmonics of the language of the Authorized Version) and A.E. Taylor's "religious" interpretation of Platonic thought, the instinctive inclination was in one way or another to minimize the gulf between Christian beliefs and Hellenic values. Or, as Turner puts it, the tendency was "to understand the experience of ancient Greece" in such a way as to provide "a source of information on the natural, or secular, history of humankind that supplemented, confirmed, or replaced elements of sacred Judeo-Christian history."[14]

Such a disposition would have been inconceivable, of course, had not the early Christian communities of the Graeco-Roman world simply accepted as a given the Hellenistic program of higher education, an education pivoting largely on the study of the Greek (and, later, the Roman) literary classics. It would have been unlikely, too, had not the great Greek Fathers of the Church lent their authority to that acceptance by embracing in their theologies the legacy of Greek philosophy and by elaborating complex theories about the "preparation for the Gospel" in the writings especially of the pagan Platonists.[15] That the dominant Christian attitude towards the pagan literature of Greece and Rome in general (and the Greek philosophers in particular) should have been one of openness is no more to be taken for granted, however, than that monasteries should eventually have become centers of learning and promoters of the liberal arts. In both cases, it is only our familiarity with the outcome that suggests the necessity of the process. Cultivation of the pagan literature was not undertaken, in fact, without very deep misgivings. There was much in the classics to provoke and offend Christian sensibilities. St. Jerome (d. 420), fine classicist though he was, himself expressed such misgivings, even if he succeeded admirably in overcoming them; so, too, St. Benedict of Nursia (d. 543), founder of what was later to become the Benedictine Order; so, too, Pope Gregory the Great (d. 604). And yet these were the men who were in considerable measure responsible for the extraordinary fact that the Graeco-Roman pattern of instruction in the liberal arts became the very foundation of higher education in medieval Europe.[16] What were misgivings in them could easily deepen into constricting anxiety with later Christian educators less broadly humane in their vision.

If sensibilities were bruised by the worldliness and eroticism of so much of the classical literature, it was the purity of the faith itself, however, that appeared threatened by the insidious paganisms of a philosophic tradition that knew nothing of Yahweh, the personal God of Abraham, Isaac and Jacob, the Biblical God of power and might. Had not the New Testament itself warned against the seductions of that tradition? "See to it," St. Paul had written to the Colossians, "that no one makes a prey of you by philosophy and empty deceit, according to human tradition, according to the elemental spirits of the universe and not according to Christ" (Col. 2:8); and to the Corinthians: "The foolishness of God is wiser than men" (I Cor. 1:20). Whenever in subsequent centuries the purity of Biblical teaching seemed threatened by the incursions of the fashionable philosophies of the day, those warnings were to succeed in starting echoes, and never more dramatically than in the writings of the North African theologian Tertullian (d. ˙*ca.* 230), who, in one famous passage, having identified philosophy as "the material of the world's wisdom" and denounced Aristotle as "unhappy" for having equipped philosophy with the art of dialectic, exclaimed: "What... has Athens to do with Jerusalem? What concord is there between the Academy and the Church? What between heretics and Christians?... Away with all attempts to produce a mottled Christianity of Stoic, Platonic and dialectic composition! We want no curious disputation after possessing Christ Jesus, no inquisition after enjoying the Gospel! With our faith, we desire no further belief."[17]

Tertullian's fundamentalism, like that of Tatian (d. *ca.* 120) before him, represents something of an extreme, but misgivings about the philosophical pursuit of the sort he felt have frequently been expressed by Christian thinkers, not only by ecclesiastics or followers of the monastic life like Peter Damiani (d. 1072) and Bernard of Clairvaux (d. 1153), but also, paradoxically, by Christian laymen who were themselves philosophers. In this connection, Blaise Pascal (d. 1662) comes immediately to mind; so, too, for that matter, Søren Kierkegaard (d. 1855), who so profoundly influenced the development of modern existentialism. In the Islamic world, likewise, Muslim thinkers faced a very similar set of problems. They, too, had to reconcile with their religious beliefs a philosophical tradition which, while it represented the noblest intellectual tradition known to them, was at odds on some very critical points with the vision of God, of man, and of the universe conveyed to them in the Qu'ran. Among them, moreover, misgivings deepened eventually into rejection, and the study of the "foreign sciences" came to be extruded from the *madrasas*, or schools of higher learning. In the thinking of the great scientists and philosophers of the Islamic world—men such as Al-Ghazālī, Ibn Sina and Ibn Rushd—there came to be no real interpenetration of Qu'ranic revelation and Greek philosophical thought. Instead, the intellectual tilt was clearly to the Greeks, and many of these thinkers were to appear no less unorthodox to Muslim than to Christian eyes.

If the fundamentalist note which sounded so loudly in Islam remained a subdominant in the intellectual and educational life of Christendom, until the more recent past it was still powerful enough to generate repeated reverberations and harmonics. The tension and instability inserted thereby into intellectual life and educational thinking may have contributed, ironically enough, to the philosophical and scientific creativity of late medieval and early modern Europe.[18] But it was a source also of intellectual timidity, educational impoverishment and curricular turmoil. The repeated condemnations by ecclesiastical authorities down through the centuries of positions adopted by leading Christian thinkers are too familiar to warrant exemplification.[19] But the inhibiting effect of religious scruples upon the liberal arts curriculum at both school and university, if less dramatic, was no less damaging. The reception of Aristotle in the late twelfth- and thirteenth-century European universities was one of the great turning points in European intellectual history. But it was by no means easily achieved. If by the latter years of the thirteenth century the full corpus of Aristotle's writings had made its way into the curriculum of the faculty of arts at the University of Paris, it had done so in the teeth of a great deal of resistance on the part of the university's theologians and after being delayed by ecclesiastical condemnations in 1210, 1215 and 1231. Nor, later on, was the serene confidence of the Humanist curricular vision unshaken by anxieties of religious provenance. In the sixteenth and seventeenth centuries the humanism regnant in Protestant and Catholic schools alike was cabined and confined by the urgencies of Christian belief. Classical authors were studied only in highly selective fashion, and students at the Jesuit colleges had frequently to read those authors in carefully expurgated editions.[20] Similarly, the classicism dominant in the American colleges of the colonial era was one clearly shaped by the religious commitments of the day. At Yale under the presidency of Timothy Dwight (the elder, d. 1817) the request for "permission to use Homer as well as the New Testament in teaching Greek" was greeted with no little anxiety. At Williams the much-admired senior capstone course which Mark Hopkins taught throughout his presidency (1836–72), though "everywhere accepted as philosophy, ... was both in purpose and practice a mixture of religious orthodoxy and personal opinion." "It is pleasant," Hopkins noted in 1852, "to see young men study well, but that is nothing to seeing them inquiring earnestly and practically what God placed them in the world for, and giving themselves up to do his will."[21]

For the better part of fifteen centuries such considerations loomed large in Western educational circles as a source of persistent intellectual anxiety and intermittent curricular disagreement. And it must be acknowledged that they helped create the unreceptive historical screen onto which any romanticized picture of a golden age of educational serenity or curricular stability must necessarily be projected.

2. Plato and Isocrates: philosophy versus rhetoric

The ebbing in the West of formal religious belief over the course of the past century and the transformation of classical studies into a fairly confined scholarly concentration which attracts few students have both conspired to nudge from the forefront of our educational consciousness the age-old issue of the incompatibility between world-views of classical and Christian provenance. Its very disappearance, however, had an impact on educational thinking no less significant for being so often ignored or overlooked. With the ebbing of religious belief the stage was set for a change of no little importance. Nothing less than the *re*sacralization of the classical tradition and the attribution to the higher literary culture of the quasi-redemptive power which Christians (just as Jews before them) had naturally rejected, but which the Greeks themselves had attributed to it long ago in the Hellenistic era. In that era of cultural fusion they had come to invest *paideia*—or " 'culture' ... in the sense of a mind fully developed"—with a quasi-religious dignity.

> In the deep confusion caused by the sudden collapse of ancient beliefs, it was the one true unshakable value to which the mind of men could cling; and Hellenistic culture, thus erected into an absolute, eventually became for many the equivalent of a religion.[22]

The Renaissance of the fifteenth and sixteenth centuries in Europe brought with it some measure of conflicted sympathy with that point of view, and certainly a renewed sense of the dignity attaching to the ancient *paideia*. From that period onwards, it has been argued, under the tutelage of great humanist teachers like Vittorina da Feltre (d. 1446) or Guarino Guarini da Verona (d. 1460), with their far-reaching claims for the power of a classical education to mould moral character as well as to develop the mind, the West "became involved in the mystification of arts education."[23] So much so, indeed, that Levenson does not hesitate to compare the "gentlemanly" ideal of classical education prevalent in eighteenth- and early-nineteenth-century Oxford and Cambridge with the Confucian educational ideal of moral learning prevalent in Ming China.[24] In our own century, of course, it is to "the great books" in general that much of the moral and intellectual power once ascribed exclusively to the Greek and Latin classics has come finally to be attached. The Harvard Redbook of 1945 exerted an unparalleled influence on the great postwar debate about general education (or did so, at least, almost everywhere except at Harvard). And although it played its educational melodies in a somewhat different key from that favored by the traditionalist manifestoes lauding the virtues of a classical education, it is not without interest that it should have claimed "a close similarity between religious education and education in the great classic books" (themselves "the fullest revelation of the Western mind"), or that that form of education could "be looked upon as a secular continuation of the spirit of Protestantism."[25]

On this matter, as on others, the witness of Matthew Arnold is highly pertinent. Acutely conscious as he himself was of "the melancholy, long, withdrawing roar" of the ancient faith, he was conscious also of the degree to which his advocacy of "Hellenizing" the "Philistine" middle class was open to attack. He well knew that his project of enlarging their intellectual sympathies and sharpening their moral and aesthetic sensibilities by the cultivation of the humanistic studies which had flourished during the Renaissance but had been "checked" in England by the Puritan spirit could easily be depicted as a kind of "religion of culture."[26] If in that he proved to be correct, it was not least of all because of the presence in his own cultural and educational aspirations (as in those of his English and American sympathizers later on) of a tendency to mystify what actually goes on in the process of a liberal education, and even in some measure to "sacralize" the canonical "great books" upon the study of which that education was seen to pivot.

Some commentators have been content to dismiss as a return to "the genteel tradition" and as a redundant elitism any persistent veneration of classical studies or the nostalgia for the classical ethos embedded in the advocacy of a general education in the great books of the Western tradition.[27] Others, however, have gone much further and have indeed attached the "religious" label to the educational ideals and practice of those who have followed in Arnold's footsteps, advocating the civilizing pursuit of "the best that has been thought and known," whether via traditional classical studies, or, when the latter had been transformed into just another specialized branch of higher learning, via the broader study of modern literature. Speaking of the "generalists" of the turn of the century who were "spokesmen for the missionary view of literature they inherited from Arnold, Ruskin, and other Victorian apostles of culture" (men such as Charles Eliot Norton of Harvard, George Edward Woodberry of Columbia, William Lyon Phelps of Yale, or Bliss Perry and President Franklin Carter of Williams), Gerald Graff comments that they invested "the experience of literature with the redemptive influence their ancestors had attributed to the conversion experience."[28] Arguing more caustically and sweepingly and attributing the rise of English studies at the British universities from the late nineteenth century onwards to "the failure of religion," Terry Eagleton has pressed the claim that that "traditionally reliable, immensely powerful ideological form was in deep trouble," and that literature "was admirably well-fitted to carry through the ideological task which religion left off."[29] Such prophets of the New Criticism as F. R. Leavis and T. S. Eliot, purveyors of the notion of a Great Tradition in literature mediating to our own day the very ethos of Western civilization, he portrays as purveyors also of a form of religio-cultural mystification, as saddling a liberal education grounded in literature with a redemptive burden it could not reasonably be expected to sustain. The New Criticism, he insists, should at last be recognized for what it was, nothing less "at root [than] a full-blooded irrationalism, one closely associated with religious dogma."[30]

Not all, of course, would agree with this contemptuous dismissal. And, though the form they take bears the clear stamp of our own era, we should realize that disagreements of this sort in no way constitute a novelty. Just as such disagreements about the goals of liberal education postdate the loosening of the hold exerted by Christian beliefs upon the intellectual loyalties of the Western world, so, too, do they predate the original establishment of that hold. Even in the absence of the tensions we have seen to be engendered by the turbulent confluence of classical and Christian world-views and moral sensibilities, the long history of liberal education would have been an extremely conflicted one. And in a recent study Bruce Kimball has made a cogent and forceful case for believing that the most fundamental and persistent source of tension goes right back to the period of beginnings amid the intellectual turmoil of Athens in the fifth century B.C.E.

Kimball elaborates that case in *Orators and Philosophers*, a sustained attempt to navigate a way through the rocks and shoals of our modern arguments about liberal education. (He himself refers to that body of argumentation as a "morass".) He does so by turning, appropriately enough, to the history of ideas, tracing the career down through the centuries of such descriptive terms as "liberal education" or "liberal arts," and seeking "to evaluate the rationales associated with them."[31] The outcome is a very important book which deserves more attention than it has received, one that warrants close scrutiny, especially, by anyone interested in the fate of liberal education. Building on more specialized studies by such historians of the long tradition of Western education as Werner Jaeger, Henri Marrou, Paul Oskar Kristeller and Sheldon Rothblatt, he advances three basic claims. First, that despite the ease with which, when discussing liberal education, we characteristically reach for the example of ancient Athens, the formation of the "normative program" of studies in the liberal arts which an educated person could be assumed to have pursued is in fact to be attributed to late *Roman* antiquity, when something approaching curricular consensus was for the first time achieved. Second, and as its title signals, the central thesis of the book: that "the history of liberal education is the story of a debate between orators and philosophers" (p. 2), of the parallel and conflicting destinies of two rival educational ideals, each possessed of its own educational program and preferred curriculum. The one, essentially literary, traced its lineage back to Cicero (d. 43 B.C.E.) and Quintilian (d. 97 C.E.) in the Latin world, and, beyond that, back to Isocrates (d. 338 B.C.E.), the great Athenian contemporary of Plato. The other, essentially philosophical or scientific, traced its lineage back to Plato (d. 346 B.C.E.), Aristotle (d. 322 B.C.E.) and the great philosophers of Greek antiquity. Third, that amid the "alarms of struggle and flight" of our contemporary battle of the books the ancient tension between rhetoricians and philosophers lives on as a scarcely recognized factor, helping deepen thereby the night of confusion in which ignorant armies continue to clash. I will take up these three claims in turn.

First, the matter of historical origins. All would doubtless concede that, during the course of the so-called pedagogic century stretching from *ca.* 450 to *ca.* 350 B.C.E., the Greeks in general or the Athenians in particular "developed the idea of educating in a cultural ideal the free citizens with leisure to study."[32] In practice, however, and as Aristotle himself reminds us (*Politics*, 1337a, 11–39), this idea was quite variously interpreted, and, Marrou to the contrary, there seems no good reason to render the term *enkuklios paideia* (general culture or education of a gentleman) which came eventually to denote it, by the words "liberal arts." The latter term derives from the Latin *artes liberales* first found, it seems, in Cicero's *De inventione* (I, 35), though his usage suggests that it was already current at the time. And *tekhnai eleutherioi*, the most literal Greek equivalent to *artes liberales*, appears not to have anteceded the Latin term but to have been instead a later translation of it.[33] Although from the Hellenistic period onward the direction of educational development was reasonably clear, it fell to the Romans to develop the "normative program" of studies in the liberal arts. And it was some time before they finally established what we think of as the classical curriculum in the liberal arts, divided canonically into the *trivium*, focusing on matters linguistic—grammar, rhetoric and logic (or dialectic)—and the *quadrivium*, focusing on matters mathematical—music (theory), astronomy, arithmetic and geometry. That program appears to have crystallized no earlier than the fourth and fifth centuries of the Christian era (the terms *trivium* and *quadrivium* came later still), and it achieved the paradigmatic formulation that was to become a cliché during the medieval centuries in the strange tract of Martianus Capella, *On the Marriage of Philology and Mercury* (5th century) and in the *Institutes* (6th century) of Cassiodorus.[34]

Second, the matter of the orators and philosophers. At the root of the archaic Greek educational vision had been the determination to pursue virtue or excellence (*aretē*, understood in terms of the ethical code of a warrior aristocracy and inculcated via the memorization of the epic poetry of Homer in which that ethic was both celebrated and exemplified). With the decay of that aristocratic ethos and the emergence in the fifth century B.C.E. of democracy, not one but three groups, Kimball argues, "responded with programs of education to prepare the free citizens for their new role in governing society."[35] First, the Sophists—such teachers or "wise men" as Gorgias, Hippias and Protagoras—who, via their rhetorical instruction in the arts of speechmaking and political persuasion, claimed to be able to impart a type of political *aretē* or wisdom (*sophia*). Their eminently practical concentration on the arts of persuasion stimulated their fellow Athenians Plato and Isocrates to attack them on the grounds that they were helping undermine among the young the traditional moral values.

As a result, and second, Plato, holding high the Socratic ideal of a ceaseless questing after truth, transposed the Homeric *aretē* into a new key, "the pursuit of highest knowledge through dialectic, an endeavor that liberates the mind from the chains of its shadowy cave of ignorance" (Kimball, p. 17). In the absence of truth, to the discovery of which dialectic was the key, rhetoric was no more than "sophistry" (in our modern, pejorative use of that term). The educational ideal he proposed to the Athenians, therefore, was an essentially philosophic one, and that ideal was to be passed on to future generations by his pupil, Aristotle.

Equally critical of the Sophists, but critical also of Plato (who amply reciprocated the sentiment) was, third, his distinguished contemporary, Isocrates. Dubious about Plato's claims for pursuit of truth by the dialectical method, and claiming for the orator the title of "philosopher" (lover of wisdom), he attacked the Sophists, nonetheless, for their pragmatic preoccupation with successful rhetorical technique and their failure to link rhetorical training with ethical formation of character. In his school he pursued no profound questioning of the Homeric *aretē*. His goal, instead, was the eminently practical use of forming in the traditional heroic virtues an intellectual elite capable of providing the political leadership that Athens needed. As means to that end he advocated a predominantly literary education designed to produce eloquent orators and involving, not only the technical skills imparted by the Sophists but, further than that, an intense concern with moral content, with a subject matter capable of developing in the student moral virtue, powers of judgment, and the ability to make decisions in the conflicted arena of public life.[36]

When commentators on the modern educational scene evoke for their contemporary purposes the notion of a liberal arts education "in the original, classical sense of that term," they almost invariably link it with the Socratic quest and the essentially philosophical educational ideal espoused by Plato.[37] And yet, of the three educational programs we have just described, it was not Plato's philosophical approach but Isocrates' literary/rhetorical program which eventually carried the day in the ancient world and dominated educational thinking and practice for centuries thereafter. Unlike the rhetorical school which Isocrates ran and which was composed of fee-paying students, philosophical schools like Plato's *Academy* (itself dedicated to the Muses) took the form of religious brotherhoods or confraternities. To join them one had to embrace a demanding set of moral commitments, and joining involved a change of heart and the adoption of a new way of life via a process akin to our own understanding of religious conversion. It is not surprising, then, that philosophy remained in the ancient world "a minority culture for an intellectual élite prepared to make the necessary effort."[38] After the fall of the Greek city-states and by the dawn of the Hellenistic era, "Plato had been defeated: posterity had not adopted his educational ideals. The victor, generally speaking, was Isocrates," who "became the educator first of Greece and then of the whole ancient world." As a result, it was rhetoric that became "the specific object of Greek education and the highest Greek culture," practiced assiduously for long centuries at Byzantium until its capture in 1453 by the Turks and transposed successfully into a Latin key, first by the Roman schools and then by the schools of the medieval West. Cicero was the central figure in that transposition. For him the liberal arts, dominated by their linguistic and literary components, were nothing less than the *studia humanitatis*. But behind him stood Isocrates, whom Marrou can properly claim to have been "the original fountainhead of the whole great current of humanistic scholarship."[39]

Sweeping though it is, the claim appears to be justified. At least in its broad outlines, the rhetorical program of education which Isocrates had launched did indeed dominate the world of higher education from Hellenistic antiquity down to the early thirteenth century, and, again, from the late fifteenth century on well into the eighteenth. In its original Greek form, centered above all on Homer, Euripides, Menander and Demosthenes, it enjoyed, indeed, a continuous history right down to the end of the Middle Ages in the Roman Empire of the East, which endured for one and a half millennia until the final collapse of Byzantium. To that extraordinary fact we owe whatever it is that we know of the Homeric scholarship of antiquity, and it is to the teaching of émigré Byzantine scholars such as Manuel Chrysoloras that Italian humanists and teachers like Pietro Paolo Vergerio (d. 1444), Guarino Guarini da Verona (d. 1460) and Vittorino da Feltre (d. 1446), struggling with the lack of adequate grammars and dictionaries, were able to move on at last to a recovered and controlled mastery of the ancient Greek tongue.

In the Latin West the continuity was less marked. The knowledge of Greek was lost, the conditions of life, punctuated by barbarian invasions and worsened by the disintegration of central political authority, were at times conducive to no vital forms of higher education. But if medieval Byzantium enjoyed its own classical revivals (in the ninth, eleventh and fifteenth centuries), so, too, did the Latin West— during the Carolingian era in the eighth and ninth centuries, and again in the twelfth century. If the great Renaissance of the fifteenth and sixteenth centuries surpassed its predecessors, it is important to remember that it actually did have predecessors. Having achieved a mastery of the two ancient languages, what the great Renaissance humanists were able in fact to do was to complete "the process of assimilation of the ancients begun by the [Church] Fathers, set in motion again [in the seventh and eighth centuries] by the Anglo-Saxon scholars Bede and Alcium, and carried forward to great effect" in the twelfth and thirteenth centuries when so many of the Greek philosophical and scientific works were translated into Latin.[40] It is important to remember, too, that the scholastic era of the thirteenth and fourteenth centuries, distinguished as it was by the marginalization of the linguistic, literary and rhetorical components of the liberal arts and by the technical and highly professionalized nature of its preoccupation with philosophy, theology, medicine and law, stands out as in some ways an exception to the norm in the history of European higher education down to the modern period. That norm, instead, was the broadly humanistic and overwhelmingly literary range of studies in the liberal arts inherited from Hellenistic and Roman antiquity and constituting, except for the great scholastic era, the dominant tradition in higher education right down to the eighteenth century, when it began to face a challenge to its hegemony more serious than any encountered heretofore.

Given its crucial role in the shaping of European educational and intellectual life, it may be helpful to adduce a couple of characterizations of this educational tradition in the liberal arts and of the type of culture from which it derived and which, in turn, it helped prolong. The first, by Henri Marrou, is a straightforward historical judgment to the effect that despite

> all Plato's efforts, the higher Hellenistic culture remained faithful to the archaic tradition and based itself on poetry, not science. As a result of this, education was not so much concerned to develop the reasoning faculty as to hand on its literary heritage of great masterpieces. . . . As something essentially *classical*, Hellenistic civilization was the opposite of those revolutionary, innovating cultures that are propelled forward by a great creative drive. It rested essentially upon the peaceful possession of an already acquired capital.[41]

The second, by Kimball, represents an attempt "to abstract a general type, a frame of reference," a means, in effect, "to think generally about a certain approach to schooling that came to dominate the education called 'liberal' during Roman antiquity and that influenced the way the term 'liberal education' was subsequently employed." He calls this general type "the *artes liberales* ideal" because he regards it "as an ideal for those who are identified with it, especially the orators," and, chief among them, Cicero and Quintilian. And he sees this *artes liberales* ideal as possessing seven characteristics representing "points held in common by the great majority of Roman advocates for the liberal arts."[42]

Of those characteristics the first is the goal of forming and training the active, virtuous and generally capable citizen—for Cicero and Quintilian, that is, "the perfect orator capable of addressing any topic and assuming any position of leadership in the state." Second, and a necessary concomitant of the first (because, as Quintilian says, only "the good man" can become "the perfect orator"),[43] a commitment on the part of the teacher to stipulate moral norms for the shaping of character and the governance of conduct. Third, a willingness on the part of the student to respect such moral norms. Fourth, the dependence on a canon of classical texts for the furnishing of those shared commitments. Fifth, the identification of a cultural elite (originally those free men or gentlemen possessed of the requisite leisure for study) who stand out as more meritorious by virtue of having absorbed and manifested in their own lives the virtues, public and private, honored in the classical texts. Sixth, a certain pragmatic "dogmatism," in that those virtues were simply prescribed and not sought out through a process of philosophic inquiry. Seventh, a tendency to view the whole program of education in the liberal arts as being for the student a self-justifying process of self-development—an end, that is, in itself.

If it is to be conceded that this was the ideal that dominated liberal education in Roman antiquity and in subsequent centuries profoundly shaped the whole liberal arts tradition, it is time now to add (a point crucial to Kimball's whole thesis) that it never fully succeeded in shaking off its philosophical rival. "The conflict between Plato and Isocrates," Werner Jaeger has said, was nothing other than "the first battle in the centuries of war between philosophy and rhetoric."[44]

In antiquity, philosophers and rhetoricians represented "two hostile cultures." So far as the dominant educational tradition is concerned Marrou concedes that by the Hellenistic era Isocrates had defeated Plato. But he notes that the argument between rhetoric and philosophy nonetheless continued, and continued beyond Graeco-Roman times. "It is so fundamental," he says, "that I seem to see traces of it, either clear or implied, wherever the classical traditions persists or reappears—in semi-barbarous Gaul in the fifth century [C.E.] when Sidonius Appolinaris is balanced by Claudius Mamertinus, or in the twelfth-century Renaissance, when Abelard's philosophical culture is opposed by St. Bernard's literary humanism."[45] And to these examples we may add the onslaught launched by the humanists of the fifteenth- and sixteenth-century Renaissance against the scholasticism regnant in the universities of their day. For, despite the condescension of humanist propaganda, that scholasticism was "very much a going concern in the fourteenth and fifteenth centuries."[46] Or again, though in slightly different key, the seventeenth- and early eighteenth-century debate that raged in France as well as England between the Ancients, or advocates of a humane education grounded in the classics, and the Moderns, staunch proponents of the new science.[47] Or yet again, the lively exchange between "Darwin's bulldog," Thomas Henry Huxley, and Matthew Arnold, triggered in 1881 by the former's attack on Arnold's humanist educational ideal in his "Science and Culture," an address delivered at the opening of Sir Josiah Mason's Science College at Birmingham.[48]

The last example, an exchange that was to be played out in the New World as well as the Old, obviously speaks to Kimball's third claim—namely, that the ancient tension between orators and philosophers survived into the modern era, informing the great debate concerning the nature of liberal education which, punctuated by occasional intervals of quiescence, has gone on in England and America for a century and more, and contributing to that debate (the more so in that it is rarely recognized for what it is) an added measure of complexity. To that third claim we must now turn.

While arguing that the tension between rival rhetorical and philosophical ideals of liberal education has persisted down through the centuries from the time of Isocrates and Plato onwards, Kimball is not tempted to suppose that either ideal simply persisted without in any way evolving across time. Thus, he rightly concedes that in taking over what he terms the *artes liberales* ideal Christian educators did not endorse the Hellenistic view that an education in the liberal arts was an end in itself. Instead, they viewed it as a necessary preliminary to scriptural studies. The educational program was much the same but its goal was differently conceived. Again, he notes that when after two centuries of scholasticism the *artes liberales* ideal revived once more during the Renaissance, it entered upon a period of change. During the sixteenth century it was reshaped somewhat by coming into contact with Erasmus's argument that a humane education should reflect his "philosophy of Christ"—that is, should embody not only the values of the classical authors but also the moral values of the New Testament.[49] And the ideal was reshaped still further by its encounter with the "knightly" or "courtly" ideal set forth quintessentially in such works as Baldassare Castiglione's *Book of the Courtier* (1528) and Sir Thomas Elyot's *The Boke Named the Govenour* (1531). Thus reshaped, it became the accepted educational ideal for the gentleman in eighteenth-century England.[50] And this same education in the "genteel tradition" came to be valued in the colleges of colonial America as the appropriate formation for the "Christian gentleman."[51]

In the modern era as a whole, however, it was the rival philosophical ideal that was to undergo the more significant evolution—so significant, indeed, that Kimball abstracts from the transformed version as it has endured into the present century a general type parallel to his *artes liberales* ideal. That general type, which by way of contrast he calls the "liberal-free ideal," he sees as possessed, like its rival, of seven distinguishing characteristics.[52] First, and absolutely fundamental, a stress on the freedom of the individual, and "especially freedom from *a priori* strictures and standards." Second, a related emphasis on the power of the unfettered intellect and the priority of reason. Third, a skeptical distrust of intellectual certainty and the concomitant ascription of a fundamentally critical role to reason. Fourth, an endorsement of the "new virtue" of tolerance—understandable in the absence of certainty and in the context of an "epistemology of skepticism." Fifth, an anti-elitist conviction that men were originally and fundamentally equal. Sixth, a shift from the rival ideal's concern with the formation of the virtuous citizen to a preoccupation with the personal development of the individual. Seventh, the notion that the vindication of the individual's intellectual freedom in the open-ended search for truth is an end in itself.

Kimball abstracts this general type largely from the writings of those who contributed centrally to the scientific revolution of the seventeenth century and from the works of the Enlightenment *philosophes*. Although these thinkers shared with the humanists of the Renaissance a profound respect for the ancients, their intoxication with the heady possibilities of the new science led them to focus on a different aspect of the ancient legacy. For them, it was not Isocrates, Cicero or Quintilian who stood out as exemplary but, above all, Socrates "with his uncompromising, never-ending search for truth." Their liberal-free ideal Kimball sees as having gradually emerged in discussions of liberal education "between, say, the time of Descartes and Hobbes and that of Kant and Priestley."[53]

Powerful though it may have been in intellectual circles at large, in the eighteenth-century universities (so many of them in full decline)[54] the new ideal encountered considerable resistance. It made its way but slowly and in the teeth of entrenched educational commitments to a curriculum which combined, in varying degree, aspects of the old rhetorical ideal with remnants of the scholastic tradition. If the entry into the university curriculum of such "modern" subjects as the natural sciences and modern languages may be taken as evidence of the progress being made by the liberal-free ideal, then that progress was clearly very uneven. It was most marked in such centers of innovation as the universities of Halle, Göttigen and Erlangen in Germany, certainly present in the Dutch and Scottish universities, perhaps also in the (non-Anglican) Dissenting Academies of England. The latter were at least somewhat more open to the winds of change than were the demoralized dons of Georgian (and Anglican) Oxford and Cambridge.[55]

The judgment, however, is a comparative one, and the standard of openness being set was not very exacting. Throughout the better part of the eighteenth century, the ancient English universities were criticized, not so much for their failure to extend a welcome to the "modern" subjects (though that failure was real), as for the tenacity with which they remained loyal to the old peripatetic logic of the scholastic era and to the medieval pedagogic practices associated with it. Ironically enough, in effect, they were still being criticized for their inadequate embodiment of the Georgian ideal of a liberal education—the essentially rhetorical education in the Greek and Roman classics that had been deemed effective for the formation of moral character and viewed as the only education appropriate for a gentleman. Only with the successive Oxbridge reforms of the nineteenth century did change really set in. But, when it did, the changes involved proved to be both vitalizing and dramatic.

Reform began with the shift to a modern examination system initiated at Cambridge in the closing years of the eighteenth century but forcefully expressed in the Oxford Examination Statute of 1801. If the precise origins of the changes involved may be obscure, the cumulative impact across time is clear enough.[56] Linked with (and in turn stimulating) the development among undergraduates of a new work ethic, spirit of competition, and more disciplined approach to study, the new examinations helped reshape college teaching and place it at the service of a curriculum now "settled in favour of narrow preparation and early specialisation." The move, in effect, was in the direction of a "notion of liberal education as intellectual discipline." It was a move accelerated by the revival of the faculty psychology (under the influence especially of Kant), and it led to an emphasis, via the strengthening of an array of distinct faculties, on the overriding educational goal of training and disciplining the mind. "The sentiment 'It is the sole business of the University to train the powers of the mind' resounds through the famous reports on Oxford and Cambridge produced in the 1850s and is heard for decades afterwards."[57] And if the teachers of the classics, defending their entrenched position but downplaying the old stress on uniqueness of literary content, naturally argued that a classical education was peculiarly fitted to discipline the mind because it cultivated such a broad array of faculties, they increasingly found themselves pressed hard by the claims now being advanced for the competing efficacy of such modern subjects as mathematics, the natural sciences, and the modern languages.

When, after the mid-century, the proponents of the new ideas came progressively into more and more intimate contact with the German research ethos and the veritable "knowledge revolution" that was its outcome,[58] the stage was set for the revitalization of the old philosophical understanding of liberal education and its transformation into Kimball's liberal-free ideal. The stage was set, too, for the rise of that ideal to prominence, the concomitant understanding of a liberal education as "the exercise of the free intelligence or the critical intelligence, never satisfied, always restless, not comfortable in the presence of platitude," and the crystallization in the universities of "the intellectual characteristics now associated with academic work generally: the bold, inquisitive, speculative mind, challenging traditional beliefs and valuing most originality and discovery."[59]

It is not to be supposed, however, that the old rhetorical understanding of liberal education had been routed entirely. Had that been the case, the breadth and depth of current disagreement on matters educational, and in North America as well as Europe, would be inconceivable. As we have seen, the years which witnessed the rise to prominence in England of Kimball's liberal-free ideal were also the years that reverberated to Matthew Arnold's influential attempts to vindicate the continuing vitality, efficacy and power of the traditional rhetorical education in humane letters. "Culture," he argued, was not simply grounded in "the scientific passion, the sheer desire to see things as they are." It is "properly described not as having its origin in curiosity, but at having its origin in the love of perfection; it is *a study of perfection.* It moves by the force, not merely or primarily of the scientific passion for pure knowledge, but also of the moral and social passion for doing good."[60] Although in seventeenth-century England, he argued, Puritanism had checked the Renaissance of letters and a fate had befallen "Hellenism in some respects analogous to that which befell it at the commencement of our era," and although he made much of his uphill struggle against the Philistinism of his day, he was also convinced

> that the endeavour to reach, through culture, the firm intelligible law of things, ... that the detaching ourselves from our stock notions and habits, that a more free play of consciousness, an increased desire for sweetness and light, and all the bent which we call Hellenising, is the master-impulse even now of the life of our nation and humanity,—somewhat obscurely perhaps for this actual moment, but decisively and certainly for the immediate future; and that those who work for this are the sovereign educators.[61]

Against such views, his good friend, Thomas Henry Huxley, Darwin's great apologist[62] was moved to throw down the gauntlet on behalf of scientific education. Conceding that his views were "diametrically opposed to those of the great majority of educated Englishmen," for whom "culture is attainable only by a liberal education," and a liberal education synonymous with instruction in the literature of Greek and Roman antiquity, he argued passionately that "for the purpose of attaining real culture, an exclusively scientific education is at least as effectual as an exclusively literary education." "Indeed, we falsely pretend to be the inheritors" of Greek culture "unless we are penetrated as the best minds among them were, with an unhesitating faith that the free employment of reason, in accordance with scientific method, is the sole method of reaching truth."[63]

Although Huxley did not specifically identify Arnold ("our chief apostle of culture") with the opinions he was opposing,[64] the latter was stung into responding. He did so three years later in "Literature and Science," a lecture delivered at Harvard—though it may be, if Bliss Perry (then teaching at Williams) is right, that he did so in words "so inaudible that many ... students walked out."[65]

Referring to Huxley as "an excellent writer and the very prince of debaters," Arnold assured him (at a distance) that when he spoke about our need, if we are indeed "to know ourselves and the world," to know also "the best which has been thought and said," he was not simply talking about *belles lettres.* "In that best I would certainly include what in modern times has been thought and said by the great observers and knowers of nature." There was no disagreement among them on the need for any educated person to know "the *results* of the modern scientific study of nature." Where they parted company, instead, was on the sufficiency of "an exclusively scientific education" for "the generality of men." Knowledge was not enough. By our very nature as human beings we need to relate "what we have learnt and known to the sense which we have in us for conduct, to the sense which we have in us for beauty." The desire for good is present in us as an instinct or "fundamental desire," and "some kinds of knowledge cannot be made to directly serve the instinct in question." Scientific studies can give us only *knowledge,* and not knowledge "put for us in relation with our sense of conduct, our sense of beauty, and touched with emotion by so being put." For that we must rely on our acquaintance with the best that has been thought and said, an acquaintance mediated by an education in "humane letters." Although he did not yet know how they would do it, he was convinced that "poetry and eloquence" would "exercise the power of relating the modern results of natural science to man's instinct for conduct, his instinct for beauty." "The great majority of mankind ... would do well," he concluded, "to choose to be educated in humane letters rather than the natural sciences." For "letters will call out their being at more points, will make them live more."[66]

Huxley's and Arnold's disagreement turned out to be an influential one. It spanned the Atlantic, attracting a good deal of attention in America, and Kimball takes it, quite properly, to demonstrate "the reemergence of direct conflict between the philosophical and oratorical traditions of liberal education in the late nineteenth century."[67]

3. Kristeller and Frankel: liberal education versus liberalism

The world of higher education in late nineteenth-century America, the backdrop against which the Huxley-Arnold exchange was in part played out, was itself a world already in the grip of rapid and transformative change. From England the colonial college-universities had received a curriculum which reflected very much the rhetorical understanding of what constituted a liberal education—though it made ample provision for "Divinity Catecheticall," still honored the old scholastic commitment to logic, and contained a few remnants of the old quadrivium. At Harvard College a three-year course of study was in place by 1642 involving a fixed regimen of lectures, recitations, disputations and reading (with all subjects taught by President Dunster!). It covered, in the first year, Greek and Hebrew, logic, rhetoric, divinity, some history and botany; in the second, Greek and Aramaic, rhetoric, divinity, some ethics and politics; in the third, Greek and Syriac, rhetoric, divinity, some arithmetic and astronomy. A knowledge of Latin and some Greek was required for admission, and for graduation it was among other things expected that the student would be able to translate excerpts of the Old and the New Testament from the original languages into Latin.[68]

Harvard set in broad outline the pattern that most of the other colleges were to follow, not only during the colonial era but on well into the nineteenth century. When, at the other end of the Commonwealth, Williams College opened its doors a full century and a half later in 1793, its curriculum was broadly similar.[69]

There were a few exceptions to this pattern. In 1756 a curriculum had been introduced at the College of Philadelphia which included some English literature and devoted as much as a third of the student's time at college to subjects of scientific or practical bent.[70] During the first half of the nineteenth century a few institutions experimented with the introduction into the curriculum of more substantial amounts of instruction in such "modern" subjects as mathematics and the natural sciences, the modern languages and English literature. Most notable among such experiments was the curriculum that Thomas Jefferson introduced in 1824 at the new University of Virginia.[71] Other institutions made more timid gestures in a similar direction, especially to recognition of the importance of the natural sciences. The capstone seminar in moral philosophy taught by the president (and with which Mark Hopkins at Williams established his great reputation as a teacher) may seem an integral part of the old curriculum, but it had in fact been imported during the eighteenth century from the Scottish universities and the English Dissenting Academies.[72] And the famous Yale Report of 1828—which has been described as "a magnificent assertion of the humanist tradition," as stating "the case for the classic curriculum in America with such finality" that it was not to be challenged for another generation, and as putting "the weight of a great American college behind things as they were"[73]—itself revealed, in its stress on the effectiveness of a classical education in disciplining the mental faculties, a telling move in the direction of accommodating the old rhetorical understanding of a liberal education to Kimball's liberal-free ideal.[74]

But there is considerable scholarly disagreement about the degree to which the newer attitudes and more modern subjects had succeeded in reshaping the old collegiate curriculum in the half-century prior to the Civil War.[75] What is not contested is the dramatic nature of the changes that set in after that war and especially so during the last quarter of the century. The world of American higher education which took so great an interest in the clashing views of Arnold and Huxley was a vastly different one from that of the prewar years. The old collegiate culture, with its enduring allegiance to the ancient rhetorical understanding of what constituted a liberal education, had come under severe challenge from two very different directions. First, from the growing emphasis on the importance of the applied sciences and practical and vocational studies, fostered by the Morrill Land Grant Act of 1862 and exemplified so splendidly by the foundation of Cornell University in 1868.[76] Second, from the German university ideal, with its stress on the primacy of the research mission, vindicated so dramatically by the success of Johns Hopkins University (1876) and the extent of the influence it exerted on other American universities, old as well as new. Appropriately enough, Huxley had been invited to give the principal address when Johns Hopkins opened, and his views were understandably congenial to the growing body of academics who were committed to the essentially "liberal-free" ideal of higher education which they so powerfully embodied.[77]

Nevertheless, in the smaller college-universities still adhering, with various modifications and accommodations, to the rhetorical ideal, Arnold's views continued to find their own resonance. However unfashionable at the time, the ethos of those colleges was not destined entirely to be eclipsed; nor was it to be confined entirely to them. The Jesuit institutions of higher education continued faithful to the predominantly humanist vision of education embedded in the order's *Ratio studiorum* of 1586. And in the late nineteenth century, that humanist tradition continued to be defended by such prominent "generalist-professors" as Charles Eliot Norton of Harvard, Edward Woodberry of Amherst and Columbia, and Franklin Carter, who served as president of Williams from 1881 to 1901. In the first decades of the twentieth century it found new sympathizers and defenders in another generation of generalists—men such as William Lyon Phelps of Yale, John Erskine of Amherst and Columbia, and Bliss Perry of Williams, Princeton and Harvard—as well as in such influential "New

Humanists" as Irving Babbitt of Harvard, Norman Foerster of North Carolina and Iowa, and Stuart P. Sherman, a Williams product of Arnoldian sympathies who taught for seventeen years at the University of Illinois.[78]

Given the progressive intermingling of these competing approaches and attitudes,[79] it is hardly surprising that the understanding in twentieth-century America of what constitutes a liberal education has been one of formidable complexity. It has been characterized by considerable (though not necessarily mounting) confusion, and punctuated accordingly by periodic bursts of self-criticism and reforming zealotry—of which the current one, especially if compared with the great wave of self-examination stimulated by the Second World War, is not necessarily the most prominent instance.

The German university ideal, with its stress on the primacy of research had meshed uneasily with the whole Anglo-American approach to undergraduate education. Nonetheless, at the liberal arts colleges and the undergraduate colleges of the large universities alike, far-reaching attempts were made to accommodate that ideal. The multiplication of discrete academic departments, the proliferation of courses available for undergraduates to elect, and, during the long and influential presidency of Charles William Eliot at Harvard (1869–1909), the widespread adoption of the free-elective system, all represented such an attempt. So, too, did the creation of undergraduate majors permitting a high degree of concentration or specialization in a single discipline—a concept first mentioned, it seems, in the Johns Hopkins catalogue of 1877–78.[80] And so, again, the later adoption of honors programs designed for the more intellectually gifted undergraduates and pioneered most notably in the 1920s by Frank Aydelotte, then president of Swarthmore College.[81] So far as the conception of a liberal arts education is concerned, a version of Kimball's liberal-free ideal has clearly been in the ascendant. So much so, indeed, that in 1960 a nationwide study of the attitude of liberal arts faculty members found that they "equated liberal arts education to a major in the liberal arts" and viewed "as liberal any discipline which offers a student an opportunity to prove his intellectual ability by becoming competent in a narrow discipline."[82]

But that is only part of the story. Earlier in the century, the widespread adoption by colleges and universities either of distribution requirements (classically in the humanities, social sciences and natural sciences) or of some sort of core curriculum comprised of courses required of all students had reflected a concern to ensure that an undergraduate education would involve an appropriate measure of breadth as well as depth. It had reflected also the reaction of faculties to the excesses of the free elective system and their unwillingness wholly to abandon the notion that a liberal education should be one broadly based in the liberal arts. Given the fact that the major had clearly come to stay,[83] much of the attention of those concerned about the possibility that undergraduates were no longer being given a truly liberal education came to focus on the non-major part of the curriculum. And, since the Second World War, at least, it is largely over the fate of that particular piece of curricular territory that the defenders of liberal or general education (the terms are now sometimes used synonymously) have raised their defiant banners.[84]

The general education movement is often taken to be much older than it is. That that should be so is readily understandable. With its overall preoccupation with the mediation of the cultural heritage, and its reverential canonization of a selection of Greek and Roman classics (or, at least, of such classics in translation along with other "great books of the Western tradition"), it has represented among other things an attempt to recapture for the benefit of a broader, democratized clientele some of the values traditionally embedded in the rhetorical version of the old liberal arts ideal. Redolent though it is of a more distant and aristocratic past, and despite the recent rallying of some of the more conservative of educational critics to its standard, the movement is, in effect, a twentieth-century novelty. Thought its deepest roots reach back beyond 1914, its growth really got under way only in the wake of the First World War. The important benchmarks were the launching in 1919 of the "Contemporary Civilization" course at Columbia College, the creation in 1927 of Alexander Meiklejohn's Experimental College within the University of Wisconsin, and the general education core curriculum developed at the University of Chicago during the 1930s and 1940s under the presidency of Robert Maynard Hutchins. And it was only during and after the Second World War that the movement came finally of age.[85] Things could scarcely have been otherwise. Only in the context of a deepening global engagement on the part of the United States, and of the recovery of independence and vitality by ancient "non-Western" societies and cultures once deemed moribund, could the highly self-conscious preoccupation with the mediation of "the Western tradition" and the "revelation of the Western mind," which one finds, for example, in the influential Harvard Redbook of 1945, have become so salient a feature of the American educational consciousness. That preoccupation, indeed, may properly be taken to reflect the first uneasy stirrings of widespread cultural self-doubt.[86]

It is worthy of note, however, that while the Redbook speaks the language of heritage and affirms the abiding importance of the great classic books, it inclines more to the philosophical approach to liberal education than to the rhetorical. Nowhere do the names of Isocrates or Quintilian appear, and Cicero is mentioned but once. The canonical names, instead, are Socrates, Plato and Aristotle. Kimball seems entirely justified in his assessment that "[w]hat the report fundamentally respected and effected" was "commitment to the liberal-free pursuit of truth through its classical roots in the Socratic philosophical tradition, an accommodation of the *artes liberales* ideal congenial to a research-oriented university."[87] In this it may be said to share something of a common spirit with such earlier proponents of the general education movement as Hutchins and Meiklejohn, perhaps also with such recent contributors to discussion of the undergraduate course of studies as William J. Bennett and Lynne V. Cheney.[88] And much of the daunting complexity of twentieth-century debate about liberal education springs from the extraordinarily intricate and constantly shifting accommodations being made between the old rhetorical version of the liberal arts ideal and the more modern scientifico-philosophical liberal-free ideal.[89]

In those accommodations, it seems clear, the bulk of the ground has been conceded to the liberal-free ideal, with its stress on the centrality of the individual critical intellect in its free, skeptical, and unending pursuit of the truth. But unfashionable though it has come to be over the course of the past century, the old, rhetorical vision of liberal arts education in its purer form has not been lost sight of entirely. And, as recently as 1976, some of its classic virtues were evoked, appropriately enough, and with characteristic clarity and firmness, by the scholar to whom we owe so much for our understanding of its history: Paul Oskar Kristeller.

He did so in a paper "Liberal Education and Western Humanism" delivered at the Columbia University seminar "Liberalism and Liberal Education." Resisting the linkage suggested by the title of the series, he insisted that political liberalism and liberal education were not "related or interdependent," that liberal education neither produced nor was itself produced by political liberalism, and that "in a broad sense [it had] existed for many centuries before political liberalism was even heard of." It is to be identified, instead, with that humanistic education in the classics which had its roots in antiquity, had risen and fallen across the centuries, but in one form or another had flourished especially between the fifteenth and the early twentieth century. In its Renaissance form it had focused exclusively upon the humanities defined as grammar, rhetoric, poetry, history and moral philosophy, and it was predicated on the assumption that the best way "to teach and study them is to read and interpret the Greek and Latin classics in their original text." Advocating "the ideal of a general culture and of a continuing education in the service of this culture" and expressing sympathy with "the programs in the humanities and western civilization at Columbia College and elsewhere" which at least seek to teach the ancient classics (even if "in a hurry" and, regrettably, in English translation), he confessed that he himself remained "convinced of the intrinsic value of classical studies" pursued via study of the texts in Greek and Latin. They serve to foster precision and coherence in both thought and expression, and they convey a body of knowledge that in no way stifles "originality or creativity." "Ancient literature, historiography, and philosophy still provide us with valid standards of excellence," and "the student who develops critical judgment does not lose his freedom when he submits to what is true and valid." Indeed, without such ties "with our past and tradition" the present would be "thrown back on its own resources," and these Kristeller frankly judged to be "intellectually, culturally, and morally inadequate."[90]

In sharp contrast, Charles Frankel, in a paper presented earlier in the same series, clearly aligned himself, not with the rhetorical understanding of the liberal arts tradition but with something close to the liberal-free ideal. Arguing that "at least seven [different] important meanings" could be distinguished for the term "liberalism," he saw a certain affinity between liberal education and some of the features characteristic especially of what he called "philosophic liberalism" and "the liberal style and temperament." Among those characteristics, it would seem, are the "affirmative interest in the promotion of diversity and of the qualities of mind which encourage empathetic understanding and critical appreciation of the many-sided possibilities of human life," and "the belief in the supremacy of rational methods of inquiry" in which are the very presupposition of such a commitment to pluralism. In order to be open to diversity, the new, the different and the idiosyncratic, "without destroying itself, ... [liberalism] must also generate a capacity to judge, to sift and weigh evidence and, in the end, to resist the meretricious."[91] While a university cannot be political "in the sense that it cannot be bound to the uncriticized and unchallenged defense of a given economic system or of a given political system or social structure," it must be committed to certain "long-term aspirations" to which liberalism, in its broader meaning, is itself committed. And thus it is the purpose of a liberal education "to protect the liberal emphasis on critical method and a pluralistic, competitive society." To that end, a primary objective at a university cannot be "anything but the criticism of inherited ideas, institutions and cultures—and the pursuit of truth in this broad sense." To that end, also, we must exemplify "certain attitudes, certain principles. One of these principles is tolerance. Another is free speech. Another is the sovereignty of rational methods." And if, in education, "a principle is adopted as a basic guiding principle, it...becomes a goal in itself. Thus [he concluded] I view toleration as an end-value and not simply a means."[92]

It is not surprising, then, that twentieth-century discourse about liberal education should be widely viewed as being in something of a muddle. But despite the intricate accommodations and confusions by which it is characterized, it has clearly not lost sight of the ancient tension between the competing rhetorical and philosophical ideals. It is a tension which Jaeger and Marrou portray as having been central to the history of educational thinking in the Graeco-Roman world and as having generated periodic harmonics, at least, during the course of the medieval centuries. It is a tension which Kristeller views as being at the very heart of the frequently misunderstood clash between scholastics and humanists during the Renaissance era. It is a tension presence of which Rothblatt has detected in the debates about education at Oxford in the nineteenth century, and the longer history of which Kimball has mapped out in considerable detail, with great clarity and much persuasive force, arguing for its continuation right down to the present. In its absence, it would indeed be hard to make adequate sense of the point-counterpoint of the recurrent rounds of debate about liberal education in our own century. And failure to recognize its presence almost certainly dooms us to misinterpreting the current round which may be said to have begun with the publication in 1977 of the Carnegie Council's report *Missions of the College Curriculum,* which moved to the forefront of the public consciousness with the publication in 1984 of Bennett's characteristically forceful statement, *To Reclaim a Legacy,* and which now seems destined to continue on into the 1990s.

4. Reformer and practitioner: educational ideal versus pedagogical practice

Even as hasty a glance at the longer history of liberal education as the one above should serve to disabuse one of any idea that the present condition of undergraduate education in America can convincingly be criticized via an appeal, by way of contrast, to some purportedly stable ideal of liberal education shaping the undergraduate experience of the past. As we have seen, the history of liberal education—in the more distant as well as the more recent past—has been a history of competing ideals. It has been a tense and complex history of protracted rivalries between pagan and Christian, rhetorical and philosophical commitments, a history still further muddied by the affiliated cross-currents and eddies those rivalries helped generate. And it is clearly not a history that has unfolded along the axis of any unilinear development. In some periods, the classicists have dominated those of more fundamentalist religious temperament, and the rhetoricians those of philosophical bent. In others, the reverse has been true. And whatever the novelties of our currently "postmodern" educational situation, whatever the prominence in the West today of secular values or of the cast of mind associated with the liberal-free ideal, it would surely be rash to suppose that the bewildering alternations and shifts which have been so marked a feature of the past will have no place at all in the future.

It would also be rash to be so preoccupied with matters theoretical as to risk overlooking an endemic contrast of a very different type. Not the contrast evident between competing educational ideals, but that between theory and practice, between the eloquent evocation of some golden educational ideal and the fustian reality of what has actually been happening (and will doubtless continue to happen) in the challenging arena of the classroom itself. The contrast involved tends to be a matter of degree, straightforward enough, and not altogether surprising. Speaking of abstract natural ("metaphysic") rights, Edmund Burke said that like rays of light they tend to become refracted and bent from their original course when they descend from the theoretical empyrean and plunge into the dense atmosphere of day to day political life. Something similar can be said of educational ideals and curricular models.

Despite the enormous claims advanced, for example, on behalf of the value of a classical education, centuries of cultivation of the Greek and Latin languages had not necessarily eventuated by the present century in any flawless pedagogic practice capable of producing fluent and comprehending readers. No one who is the product of such an education would be tempted to claim that it had. Looking back at the flaws in his own classical education, Charles Francis Adams speculated in 1883 that over the previous thirty years less than a score of students could have graduated from Harvard College "who could read Horace and Tacitus and Juvenal, as numbers now read Goethe and Mommsen and Heine."[93] As "the chief requirement" for entry to college "the study of Greek," he concluded, was no more than "a superstition." Similarly, Bliss Perry found at Williams that "his first Latin lesson, in the preface to Livy," was in 1876 "exactly the same assignment" as his father had had in 1848 and his son was to have in 1916! He himself rather liked Horace but found that "in the college classroom [that author's] wit and wisdom seemed to evaporate and there was only the grammar and scansion left." Small wonder that he felt moved to confess to "a certain skepticism about the value of [all this grammatical] labor."[94]

It would be wise, looking back, to approach formulations of curricular intent with at least a comparable degree of skepticism. There seems, for example, little reason to suppose that the grand schemata of seven liberal arts set forth in late antiquity by such as Martianus Capella, Augustine or Cassiodorus were actually being put into effect at the time, or that they constituted much more, in fact, than theoretical plans which might prove valuable in the future. They did not reflect full agreement about the precise makeup of the seven liberal arts, and the practice of the day, as, indeed, that of the schools in the Hellenistic era, appears to have been tilted very heavily towards the linguistic subjects of the *trivium* at the expense of mathematics and the sciences.[95] In the Eastern Empire the full program of studies in the seven liberal arts was carried out for a while in the secular schools as "it never was in the West." But with the great Byzantine literary revival of the eleventh century, studies in language and literature came to dominate to such a degree that the quadrivial subjects were once again effectively marginalized.[96]

Sometimes, moreover, the gap between vaunted ideal and practical reality has been of such proportions as to serve as a salutary warning to anyone prone to compare to the disadvantage of the latter the noble educational programs of yesteryear and the tarnished realities of our own era. The former, after all, are now extremely difficult to study in their actual implementation, whereas the practical shortcomings and confusions of the latter are readily open for inspection and frequently the very spur or irritant leading to the comparison's being made in the first place. Given the argumentative confusions of the day, a comparison between past and present educational *ideals* is hard enough to do well. That between present *practice* and past *ideal* calls all the more for great restraint. Such an exercise may well have some value. But any implication, even by indirection, that in such comparisons one is moving on the same plane or comparing things of a similar kind should be greeted with robust skepticism.

Two recent studies of very different provenance and focused on disparate subject areas both speak powerfully to this very point. The first, by Gerald Graff and inspired no doubt by the current postmodern battle of the books between the literary theorists and the defenders of more traditionalist approaches to literary studies, dwells on the more recent past. It is "a history of academic literary studies in the United States, roughly from the Yale Report of 1828 ... to the waning of the New Criticism in the 1960s." Though it stops short of the current wave of controversy over literary theory which has generated so much alarm among the more conservative critics of higher education in America, it nonetheless provides a valuable measure of historical perspective on that controversy. Enough, in effect, to enable Graff to argue with a good deal of persuasive force that this recent round of controversy, far from making some sort of revolutionary break with the past, echoes older controversies "as far back as the beginning of the profession."[97] Rather than being characterized by any serene dominance of Arnoldian ideals, the history "of academic literary studies in America is a tale not of triumphant humanism, nationalism, or any single professional model, but of a series of conflicts ... classicists versus modern-language scholars; research investigators versus generalists; New Humanists versus New Critics; academic critics versus literary journalists and culture critics; critics and scholars versus theorists." Those conflicts "have tended to be masked by their very failure to find visible institutional expression,"[98] but they have in fact been endemic. History, he concedes, does not repeat itself. But it is nevertheless true that "the charges current traditionalists make against theorists [poststructuralists and others] are similar to those of a earlier generation against what is now taken to be literary history." Hence his conclusion:

> In an institution with a short memory, evidently, yesterday's revolutionary innovation is today's humanistic tradition. It is as if charges of antihumanism, cerebralism, elitism, and coming between literature and students are a kind of initiation rite through which professional modes

must pass before they become certified as traditionally humanistic. Though the terms by which the profession has defined treason against humanism never change, the activities that the terms refer to change in every generation.[99]

A salutary warning to those who, observing with alarm the current success among literary critics of deconstruction and other poststructuralist modes of analysis, are moved to vent in tiresomely apocalyptic vein.

The second study, by Anthony Grafton and Lisa Jardine, reaches back to a more distant past, to the great age, indeed, of humanist education in the fifteenth and sixteenth centuries. Focusing on the teaching at humanist schools and on humanist instruction in the faculties of arts at the Italian universities, the authors rely less on the statutes of the schools or on theoretical formulations of the ideal goals of a humanist education, than on a close and painstaking scrutiny of a body of documents produced as the characteristic outcome of pedagogic effort—textbooks, teachers' letters and diaries, the classroom notes and compositions of students. In the course of so doing they uncover an enormous gap between trumpeted theoretical ideal and actual classroom practice. And they do so not only for later humanist pedagogic practice when Ramist techniques (sometimes dismissed as a betrayal of true humanist ideals) came to be fashionable, but also for the earlier period. For that earlier period they take as their primary example Guarino Guarini da Verona (d. 1460), "the greatest teacher in a century of great teachers" and "a preeminent example of a humanist whose level of cultivation and scholarship was unmatched since antiquity."[100] In common with Perry's teachers at Williams in the 1870s (or, for that matter, some of my own teachers three-quarters of a century later at a Jesuit high school in England), Guarino believed in the classical *educatio* involving "the formation of character as well as the training of the mind," producing "as its ideal end product not the professional scholar but the active man of affairs." And intellectual historians have tended simply to assume that it achieved precisely that, by so doing taking over unwittingly "the *ideology* of Renaissance humanism...as part of a historical account of humanist achievement."[101]

The danger of so doing, however, becomes clear when an attempt is made to reconstruct from instructional and classroom materials what exactly it was that went on in Guarino's classes. Quite a lot, of course, for he was clearly a truly distinguished teacher. But like his successors in the nineteenth and twentieth centuries, he confronted the formidable task of helping students master a dead language. The fact that he (unlike so many of them) succeeded in producing students able "to pronounce and write in Latin on issues ancient and modern 'like a native'" was no small achievement. But it was only attained as a result of a degree of "relentless, saturating instruction in the finer points of classical Latin grammar, usage, history, culture, geography and rhetoric," that called for remorseless attention to textual detail and left no time either for extensive reading in the classics or for reflective consideration of their contents. Cicero was the most cherished of authors, but in the "scramble for detail" not much attention could be paid either to his "train of thought or [to his] line of argument." Moreover, given the nature of Guarino's lectures on philosophy, "Plato and Aristotle can have been little more than names" to most of his students.[102] "Ruthless drilling" did produce "routine competence," but Grafton and Jardine warn about "the *problematic* nature of any attempt to show a regular and causal link between routine competence and creative achievement, let alone civic qualities of leadership and integrity."[103]

From all of which there is a message to be drawn that is pertinent to any effort to make sense of the current debate about the quality of undergraduate education in America today. And not simply the primary message Grafton and Jardine are themselves concerned to extract. They contend that during the Renaissance

> Western Europe as a whole (and we include along with it the continent of North America, which learned the academic lesson so early and so well from its European forbears) became involved in the mystification of arts education—a connivance in overlooking the evident mismatch between ideal and practice which has clouded our intellectual judgment of the progress and importance of the liberal arts from the days of Guarino down to T.S. Eliot, Leavis and the twentieth-century guardians of European "civilisation."[104]

But it is also their conclusion—and it is one on which I wish now to focus attention—that in the name of an essentially rhetorical educational ideal making great but unsubstantiated claims for its power to mould moral character and form leaders of integrity, the perfectly sound scholastic mode of education then prevailing (and well adapted to the social needs of the day) was subjected to repeated condemnation and concomitant marginalization.[105] That the scholastic education had its flaws and shortcomings is not to be gainsaid. But it was a sound and going concern and deserved to have been measured, not against noble humanist ideals, with their propagandistic evocation of memories of a romanticized classical past, but against the more humdrum and less coherent realities of actual humanist pedagogic practice.

That is not the sort of mistake we should permit ourselves to repeat today. In educational matters, as any old hand at curricular debate can attest, the *best* is frequently made an enemy of the *good*. And, all too often, it is an ideal and theoretical "best" held up to expose the shabbiness and shortcomings of a known and practical "good." Today, as we struggle with the gritty and intractable realities of our own era, we are once again being bludgeoned by fashionable memories of an idealized and romanticized past. Let us be sure that it is not a past that never truly was. Let us be sure, too, that what is being measured against it is a present that really is. After the historical excursus of the past two chapters, then, it is to that present that we must now turn.

CHAPTER III

STATISTICAL:
The Present Context
of the Tradition

In thinking about education, many of us are autobiographical. We tend to make judgments about the future on the basis of our own experiences and the experiences of friends, which makes it difficult to anticipate changes in circumstances.

William G. Bowen and Julie Ann Sosa (1989)

In the course of his splenetic onslaught on the American professoriate, Charles J. Sykes pauses to exclude from the scope of his most sweeping charges faculty members teaching at "the outstanding liberal arts colleges."[1] For that charitable exclusion those of us teaching at such institutions should doubtless be most grateful. But much of the criticism leveled so indiscriminately of late against the enterprise of undergraduate education makes little or no distinction between the various types of institutions involved in that enterprise. Public and private, selective and non-selective, denominational and secular, research university and free-standing liberal arts college, comprehensive institution, state college, women's college, historically black college, junior and community college—their missions differ widely; so too, do the contexts, social, cultural, political, financial, in which they must go about their business. The distinctions to be made are multiple and they are not to be ignored. If we are to assess the present situation, to come to terms with the charges of the critics and accurately to assess their force, we would do well (without laying claim to any sort of statistical expertise) to attempt a rough inventory of the number and the type of institutions involved, the size, social composition and educational expectations of their differing student bodies, the numbers, makeup and characteristic preoccupations of the faculty members who teach those students, and the differing institutional missions they find themselves called upon to serve as they go about their educational duties. We would do well to take appropriate note also of the sweeping and historic changes—institutional, social and demographic—which have transformed the face of higher education, abroad as well as at home, during the years since the Second World War, and which, though moving now in different directions and at a slower pace, will continue to strain our resources and challenge our resolve on into the twenty-first century.

1. Institutions: universities, colleges, numbers and types

Neither counting nor classification is trouble free, but without entering into the methodological and definitional disputes of the statistician it is possible to give a reasonably accurate institutional profile of American higher education. We have seen that by the end of the colonial era nine "college-universities" had been established in what was to become the United States, and that by the onset of the Civil War some 250 colleges were in existence. By 1876 that number (including now universities of the new style) had risen to 311; by 1960 the comparable figure stood at 2,026.[2] A further increase of comparable dimensions has been crammed dramatically into the thirty years since then. Of the no less than 10,606 postsecondary institutions which the National Center for Education Statistics (U.S. Department of Education) identified in 1990, it designated some 3,535 as "institutions of higher education."[3] By eliminating (among others) private institutions run for profit, as well as those offering courses of instruction lasting less than two years, the Carnegie Foundation for the Advancement of Teaching whittles that number down to 3,389, a figure which comes close enough to the 3,406 "institutions of higher educations and branches" listed in the Department of Education's 1988 Digest of Educational Statistics to permit our rounding out of the overall number to 3,400.[4]

In comparison with other national systems the sheer *number* of institutions is itself wholly extraordinary; not even Japan or the Soviet Union comes close to matching it. Foreigners are quick to point out (and rightly so) that quantity should not necessarily be taken as a surrogate for quality. But they are frequently slower to recognize the somewhat bewildering range of institutional missions and characteristics that lurks behind that overall number. In an attempt to indicate that range the *Digest of Educational Statistics* is content to break the overall group of approximately 3,400 down into four-year and two-year institutions, distinguishing the former into "universities" and "other 4-year institutions," and dividing all subgroups into two classifications indicating institutional control, "public" and "private"—i.e. independent. Recognizing in earlier years, however, that a more finely tuned classification system was needed, the Carnegie Commission on Higher Education came up with the one that has come to be widely invoked in the literature on higher education.[5]

In general, the Carnegie Classification categorizes institutions by reference to two criteria: the level of the degrees they award (ranging from the associate degree to the doctorate) and the comprehensiveness of their educational mission. In its full complexity that classification postulates ten different categories: Research Universities I and II, Doctorate-Granting Universities I and II, Comprehensive Universities and Colleges I and II, Liberal Arts Colleges I and II, Two-Year Colleges and Institutions (community, junior and technical colleges), Professional Schools and Other Specialized Institutions. For our purposes, however, and following in this the lead given by Bowen and Sosa in their recent book, *Prospects for Faculty in the Arts and Sciences,*[6] I propose to consolidate the Research Universities II and Doctorate-Granting Universities I and II into a single category, and to group together similarly under one heading institutions belonging to the Comprehensive Universities and Colleges II and Liberal Arts Colleges II sectors. It thus becomes possible to reduce the number of categories from ten to seven, defined as follows:[7]

Research Universities I: These are institutions which place great emphasis on research and, in addition to offering the complete array of undergraduate baccalaureate programs, offer graduate education up to the doctoral level. They award at least 50 Ph.D. degrees each year, and each receives at least $33.5 million per year in federal support. Examples are such great universities from the public and private sectors as the University of California at Berkeley, Harvard, the University of North Carolina at Chapel Hill, Stanford, Yale.

Other Research and Doctorate-Granting Universities: Similarly committed to the full array of undergraduate baccalaureate programs and to graduate education up to the doctoral level, these institutions award each year either ten or more Ph.D.s in three or more disciplines or twenty or more in at least one discipline.

Examples of institutions falling into this category range from Temple University (in the Research II category) to Idaho State University (in the Doctorate-Granting II category).

Comprehensive Universities and Colleges I: These institutions, enrolling at least 2,500 students, award more than half of their undergraduate baccalaureate degrees in two or more of such pre-professional or occupational disciplines as agriculture, business administration, engineering, the health professions, law and library science. In addition, many offer graduate programs at the master's level. The University of Bridgeport, Wake Forest University and North Adams State College fall into this category.

Liberal Arts Colleges I: These are the highly selective colleges, with the bulk of their programs at the undergraduate level, and awarding more than half of their baccalaureate degrees in the liberals arts.[8] Examples are Amherst, Carleton, Holy Cross, Reed, Rhodes, Smith, Swarthmore, Williams.

Other Four-Year Institutions: These are less selective institutions than those falling into the category preceding, and include in their ranks the Comprehensive Universities and Colleges II (which award less than half of their degrees in the liberal arts but which enroll between 1,500 and 2,500 students) as well as other institutions similar in their mission but enrolling fewer than 1,500 students. Examples range from the University of Tampa to Albertus Magnus College.

Two-Year, Community, Junior, and Technical Colleges: With very few exceptions, these institutions award no baccalaureate degrees but offer "certificate or degree" programs up to the associate of arts level. Examples are Berkshire Community College, Blackfeet Community College, Southwest Mississippi Junior College.

Professional Schools and Other Specialized Institutions: A group of institutions which award degrees ranging from the baccalaureate to the doctoral level but more than 50 percent of them in a single specialized field. This category includes schools of art, music and design, business schools, engineering schools, medical schools, and teachers colleges, as well as an array of other specialized institutions. Examples are Iliff School of Theology, Saint

Louis College of Pharmacy, the American Graduate School of International Management.

Of the 3,389 institutions comprehended within this classification system, 1,548 are publicly controlled, and 1,841 private or independent. Broken down into the simplified version of the Carnegie Classification described above, 70 of them are Research Universities I (45 public, 25 private), 143 Other Research and Doctorate-Granting Universities (89 public, 54 private), 424 are Comprehensive Universities and Colleges I (284 public, 140 private), 142 fall into the Liberal Arts Colleges I category (all but two of them private), 601 are Other Four-Year Institutions (77 public, 524 private), 1,367 are Two-Year Community, Junior, and Technical Colleges (985 public, 382 private), and 642 (66 public, 576 private) are Professional Schools and Other Specialized Institutions.[9]

While some disagreement about judgment calls in borderline cases is to be expected and could scarcely be avoided, most commentators have been content to accept and to work with the set of judgments embedded in this Carnegie Classification System. I find it interesting, however, that Bowen and Sosa chose to combine the Comprehensive II and Liberal Arts II institutions into the unified category of Other Four-Year Institutions. That move apparently reflected some skepticism about the viability of the Liberal Arts II category, and persuasive grounds for such skepticism have since been provided by another economist of higher education, David W. Breneman. Applying both educational and economic criteria, he excludes 11 of the 140 private colleges listed by Carnegie in 1987 as falling into the Liberal Arts I category on the grounds that they offer professional and graduate programs and are really "small universities." And applying to the private Liberal Arts II colleges the admittedly "weak criterion" constituted by the award of at least 40 percent of their degrees in the liberal arts (as opposed to professional) fields, he is also led to exclude as really "professional colleges" no fewer than 317 of the institutions listed by Carnegie as belonging to that category. As a result, he proposes that the total universe of private liberal arts colleges be reduced from 540 to 212.[10]

Not all would agree with this exercise in reclassification, but Breneman rightly emphasizes that it serves to highlight a significant change of recent years in the nature of many of these institutions. Their survival threatened in a rapidly shifting marketplace, the bulk, it seems, of the institutions we are accustomed to think of as liberal arts colleges have in fact transformed themselves into "something else"—for want of a better term, into "small, professional college[s]."[11] Other changes occurring over the recent decades are much more obvious. The total of approximately 430 Liberal Arts II Colleges with which Breneman started in 1987 itself represented a drop from approximately 530 in 1970—some by disappearance but most by reclassification, and the majority of those by reclassification into the Comprehensive Universities and Colleges category.[12] Again, of the 2,837 institutions of higher education in existence in 1970, as many as 721 (or 25.4% of the total) were four-year liberal arts colleges, and only 1,063 (37.5% of the total) were Two-Year Community, Junior, or Technical Colleges. By 1976, however, when the overall number of liberal arts colleges had dropped to 583 and to 19 percent of the whole, the two-year institutions had risen in number to 1,146 (though dropping slightly to 37.3% of the total). And by 1987 the comparable figures were: Total: 3,389; liberal arts colleges: 572 (16.9% of the total);[13] two-year colleges: 1,367 (40.3% of the total). The change across the past half-century in the size and importance of the last category is even more striking than the drop in the number of bona fide liberal arts colleges. And it is all the more striking in view of the fact that the number of private two-year colleges actually decreased by about 50 percent during that period. That loss, however, was more than compensated for by a quadrupling in the number of public two-year institutions. In all categories, indeed, the rise to prominence of the publicly controlled sector is one of the most dramatic developments in the history of higher education since the Second World War. In 1949–50 that sector embraced only 641 institutions, or 35 percent of the total. In 1976 it had grown to some 1,466 institutions, 47.7 percent of the whole. By 1987, it included 1,548 institutions, or approximately 45.7 percent of the total.[14] Such changes in the number, distribution and control of institutions are striking enough. To grasp, however, the truly sweeping nature of the change involved, one has to look at the number and distribution of student enrollments.

2. Students: how many, where and who they are, what they study, and what has changed

According to the National Center for Education Statistics some 62 percent of our American high-school graduates "can be expected to enroll at some time in a degree-credit course at a college or university."[15] If we add to that group of part-time as well as full-time students of all ages those who are pursuing non-degree-credit programs, and if we extend the definition of college and university to include "professional schools, teachers colleges and two-year colleges" then the overall number of students in the country pursuing one or other level of further education was estimated in 1988 to come to some 12,849,000. Of these, no fewer than 10,045,000 were attending public institutions; only 2,804,000 were pursuing their studies at institutions in the independent sector. Thus although the private institutions constitute over 50 percent of the whole, they enroll fewer than 22 percent of the students.[16] That fact reflects the differential size characteristic of the public and private sectors. Almost 90 percent of the institutions enrolling more than 10,000 students are public, whereas 87 percent of those enrolling 1,000 students or fewer are private.[17] It also reflects the sheer importance of the two-year sector composed of community, junior, and technical colleges, the vast majority of them public, which enrolled an estimated 4,700,000 students in the fall of 1987, 37 percent of the total national enrollment.[18] In 1986 nearly three million of these students were part-timers (i.e. 65 percent of those enrolled that year in that sector), so that when two-year college enrollments are translated into Full-Time Equivalents (FTEs) they drop to fewer than three millions (28.5%). That is not so far ahead of the approximately 2,200,000 FTEs (24.9%) in the Comprehensive I sector, but still well ahead of the 1,400,000 FTEs at the Research I Universities and utterly dwarfing the less than half a million (or 2.3%) studying at the undergraduate colleges belonging to the Liberal Arts I sector.[19]

But consolidation into FTEs, however pertinent it may be to comparative judgments about enrollments, should not distract from the sheer dimensions of the part-time contingent which in 1987 exceeded five million students, more than 40 percent of the overall total. FTEs do not go to college, individual students do. And part-time status is directly relevant to the way in which those students *are* where they are, the way in which they both experience and shape college and university life, and it is to be linked with the fact that on-campus living, which we tend to take for granted as a characteristic part of the normal student experience, is almost certainly one in which less than one-fifth of our total student population today is privileged to participate.[20] Part-time status is pertinent also to who these students are; that is, it is intricately interrelated with matters of social class, race, age and gender. The fact that by far the heaviest concentration of part-timers is to be found in the two-year institutions tells one part of that story.[21] So, too, does the fact that when one looks beyond the traditional college-going years, one finds that almost three out of four part-time students are 25 years or older, and that the percentage of the over-24 student population enrolled on a part-time basis is more than twice as big as the percentage studying full-time.[22] Or, again, the fact that at our public institutions specifically, while women undergraduates now outnumber the men significantly, a far greater proportion of them are part-time students.[23] But it is not my purpose here to try to tell that complex story. Suffice it to note by way of summary that, as of 1986, 18 percent of American students belonged to one or another racial minority, and that in 1988 women made up approximately 54 percent of the overall total. In that latter year, students 25 years old or older accounted for over 40 percent of all college and university enrollments, and over 5,000,000 students (approximately 43 percent of the total) were pursuing their studies on a part-time basis.[24]

The bald recital of such statistics, whether they concern enrollments in general, or enrollments broken down by age, race, gender, full-time or part-time status, should not be permitted to conceal from us the dramatic and historic nature of the changes which have occurred over the past thirty years and of which they are themselves the outcome. The growth between 1960 and 1990 in the number of institutions of higher education from around 2,000 to approximately 3,400 is striking enough. But it is dwarfed by the staggering increase in enrollments from approximately 3,600,000 (already up by more than a million since the end of World War II) to in excess of 12,800,000, an almost fourfold increase and the most sizable and dramatic in the entire history of American higher education.[25] Just how dramatic, indeed, it is hard to grasp without the help of the sort of graphic representation reproduced on the facing page. And behind the scenes of this educational drama can be detected the working of three more fundamental demographic shifts. The first, and most basic, is the postwar baby boom. The second, reflecting the postwar opening up of access to higher education, is the entry into college of a larger proportion of high-school graduates than had earlier been the case. The third, a subset of the second, was a quickening of the rate of entry into college of population groups previously much less well represented—women, racial minorities, and students who had left behind them the "normal" college-going years (18–24).

Births in the United States rose sharply from the 2,900,000 of 1944–45 to the mid-1950s level of about 4,300,000 per year. And

Generalized View of Enrollments in Higher Education, 1640 to 2010

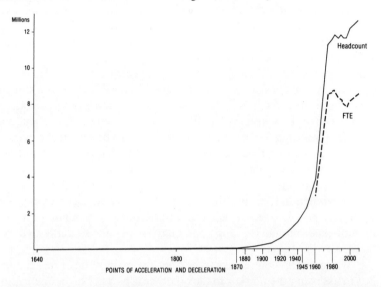

Sources: Carnegie Council estimates based on U.S. Bureau of the Census (1975) and U.S. National Center for Education Statistics, *Fall Enrollment*, appropriate years. Reproduced from *Three Thousand Futures: The Next Twenty Years for Higher Education*. Final Report of the Carnegie Council on Policy Studies in Higher Education (San Francisco and London, 1980), p. 33.

that level was sustained until 1960–61. Thereafter, the annual number of births dropped to a low point of about 3,100,000 in 1973–76 before climbing again to the fluctuating level in the upper three million range that has been sustained to the present. The baby-boom cohort reached the normal college-going age during the period stretching from the mid-1960s to the early 1980s.[26] That it should have had a marked impact on college enrollments is not, of course, surprising, just as it is predictable that there will be an analogous (if less transformative) impact during the last years of the present decade and the early years of the next century when the "echo" of that baby boom is experienced. That is to say, when the children of the baby-boomers begin themselves to arrive at the normal college-going age. That the impact in the 1960s and 1970s should have been quite so marked reflects, however, the national commitment to broaden access to higher education as well as the societal changes that led larger numbers of women, members of minority groups, and people older than twenty-four to take advantage of that widening access.

Thus whereas in 1960 women made up no more than 37 percent

of the overall student total, by 1988, as we have seen, they constituted 54 percent. During the same period, the percentage of students over twenty-two rose from 30 percent to 42 percent, that of minority students from 4 percent to around 18 percent, and that of part-time students from 30 percent to approximately 43 percent.[27] Given those figures, projections made in 1980 and suggesting that by the end of the century women would constitute more than half of the total student population, that the numbers of minority students would increase to 25 percent of the whole, students over twenty-two to 50 percent, and part-time students to 45 percent, are unlikely to be far off the mark.[28] What this means is that whereas in 1960 "the national student body ... was composed predominantly of young majority [i.e. white] males attending full-time," by the end of the century there will not only be "more women than men" (that, after all, is already the case), but also "as many people over 21 as 21 and under, nearly as many part-time as full-time attendees, and one-quarter of all students will be minorities."[29]

It should be unnecessary to belabor the magnitude of this change. But in assessing the mark it made on other aspects of higher education we would do well to remember that demography, however important, is not necessarily destiny.[30] While no country in the world has made a stronger commitment to the principle of open access to higher education than has the United States, nearly all the nations of the industrialized world have made significant moves in that direction. But the differential ways in which they made those moves did much to determine the overall effect of demographic stress and strain (which all, in some measure experienced) on their systems of higher education. By expanding the community college system, for example, and transforming teachers' colleges into comprehensive colleges and universities, by targeting financial aid in "portable" fashion on the individual student rather than channeling those funds to the educational institutions (helping assure thereby the maintenance of a strong private sector and of a broad spectrum of higher educational institutions with differentiated functions), and by choosing in highly pragmatic fashion neither to suppress the student movement of the late 1960s nor enthusiastically to embrace its goals, the United States made a series of distinctive choices in the area of national educational policy that gave particular direction to the impact of demographic forces on our colleges and universities. Confronted by analogous pressures other industrialized countries usually opted for different choices.

Only Norway and Yugoslavia chose to expand enrollments via their versions of community colleges. The United Kingdom more abandoned than converted its teachers' colleges. Most national governments chose to aid institutions as such rather than to concentrate financial support on students as our federal government decided to do. Other nations often either put down the student movement (Japan) or embraced it into academic governance through uniform laws (Germany and Holland) or some of both (France). Several nations, Italy and Sweden (the U68 reforms) in particular, responded to enrollment increases by opening their elite institutions to mass enrollments rather than by choosing the route of differentiation of functions.[31]

And because it is colleges and universities, in accordance with their differing aspirations and missions, "that establish the curricular options open to students,"[32] the nature of the policy choices made undoubtedly helped determine what the subjects were to be that the enlarged student bodies of the past quarter of a century had the opportunity to study or themselves chose to study.

Even to know with real precision what those choices have in fact been, one would have to have access to stable and reliable data concerning course enrollments in the whole vast array of subjects taught at our colleges and universities nationwide. Those global data do not exist. Individual institutions do collect such data, it is true, but they do so somewhat idiosyncratically, with varying degrees of completeness, and without any necessary cross-institutional compatibility in the disparate ways in which they go about collecting them. In the absence of reliable and reasonably complete enrollment data, then, patterns of majoring at the undergraduate level and numbers of degrees conferred by subject area or field of study at the graduate as well as the undergraduate level must serve as proxies for enrollments themselves. And while they tend to *under*state shares of enrollments in the various fields of study (for students do not limit their course-taking to their own departments or degree programs), such proxies do serve to give us a roughly accurate picture of the distribution of student interest across the educational spectrum, and perhaps a more accurate picture of enrollment trends across time both by fields of study and institutional sector.[33]

For patterns of intended undergraduate majoring we have the good fortune to have at our disposal the accumulated data collected annually since the fall of 1966 by the Cooperative Institutional Research Program and designed "to profile the characteristics, attitudes, values, educational achievements, and future goals" of freshmen entering college in the United States.[34] They reveal that of freshmen entering college in the fall of 1989 most planned to major in professional or pre-vocational fields: 9.2 percent, for example, planned to major in Education, 10.2 percent in Engineering, and no less than 24.5 percent in Business or Management. No more than 24.2 percent aspired to major in the Arts and Sciences as a whole: 8.7 percent in the Arts and Humanities, 9.6 percent in the Social Sciences, 3.7 percent in the Biological Sciences, and 2.2 percent in the Physical Sciences (including Mathematics).

The survey does not make use of the Carnegie Classifications, but, when the data are broken down by institutional sector, they reveal that interest in business appears to be strongest among freshmen entering the publicly controlled, predominantly black colleges (37.3%), the Catholic four-year colleges (29.4%), and the private two-year colleges (29.3%). It is least evident (20.3%) among those entering the private, non-sectarian four-year colleges and at the universities, whether public or private (21.2%). So far as Arts and Sciences in general are concerned, the strongest interest is to be found at those same private universities (36.7%) and private, non-sectarian colleges (36.4%), with a comparatively strong interest at the Catholic colleges (31.8%) and private, predominantly black colleges (28.3%). It is least strong, perhaps understandably, at the two-year colleges in general, whether public or private. For arts and humanities specifically, the private, non-sectarian colleges and private universities are the leading sectors, with 15.6 percent and 13.1 percent respectively, while the publicly controlled, predominantly black colleges (4.5%) and the publicly controlled two-year colleges (5.5%) form the rearguard.[35]

Given such dismal figures, especially those for the arts and humanities, and given the fact that freshmen might well be expected to change their minds later on about their major, it is tempting to assume some benign divergence in the actual patterns of majoring. But that turns out, in aggregate, not to be the case. We have good data, broken down by field of study, for the numbers of degrees conferred,[36] and the "aggregate freshman data" turn out to have been, over the years, "very good predictors of aggregate final choices and behaviors." That is to say, "the trends in *freshman aspirations* have been followed by similar trends in *bachelor's degrees*."[37] For anyone convinced, as I am, of the virtues of an education in the liberal arts, those trends have been extremely discouraging. The proportion of freshmen planning to major in the arts and sciences dropped significantly between 1966 and 1989—in the arts, humanities and social sciences alone from 32.5

percent to 18.3 percent, that is, from almost a third to less than a fifth. The natural sciences, furthermore, both physical and biological, also lost ground, though they did so less evenly, dropping from 11.5 percent in 1966 to 5.9 percent in 1989. The humanities, however, were the hardest hit. The figures for 1966 did not separate out history from political science, but with that inclusion held steady, the humanities share dropped from 24.3 percent in 1966 to 10 percent in 1985, before recovering in subsequent years to 11.8 percent in 1989. A similar pattern is evident in another significant loser over the past three decades—the field of education which dropped from a 10.6 percent share of all prospective majors in 1966 to 7.1 percent in 1985, recovering to 9.2 percent in 1989. And an inversely correlated pattern is evident in the big winner, business, which rose from a 14.3 percent share in 1966 to an all time high of 27.3 percent in 1987 before dropping back in 1989 to its current 24.5 percent level.[38]

When one turns from trends in the aspirations of freshmen to trends in the distribution of degrees actually conferred, the same broad pattern emerges, leading Bowen and Sosa to speak of a veritable "flight from the arts and sciences."[39] So far as degrees in general are concerned (Ph.D.s and M.A.s as well as B.A.s), there was a sharp drop in the arts and sciences from 40 percent of all degrees conferred in 1970–71 to 26.7 percent in 1980–81, followed by a more gradual decline to 24.9 percent in 1984–85. Similarly, degrees in education had dropped by 1984–85 from 24.7 percent of all degrees awarded in 1970–71 to a mere 13.2 percent. On the other hand, over the same period, the number of business degrees awarded, constituting in 1970–71 only about a third of the number of degrees awarded in the arts and sciences, had by 1984–85 almost achieved parity. And if one focuses on the B.A. alone, the decline in the number of degrees conferred in the arts and sciences is somewhat steeper, even, than the decline in general (from 47% of all degrees awarded in 1968 to approximately 26% in 1986), and most marked in the humanities where, for example, the percentage of B.A. degrees awarded in English dropped from 7.6 percent in 1967–68 to 2.6 percent in 1984–85.[40]

But the decline at all degree levels was bad enough. In the humanities alone the drop was from more than 10 percent of all degrees awarded in 1970–71 to 4.7 percent in 1984–85. And even the combined share of the humanities and social sciences in the overall number of degrees awarded shrank by over a half between 1970–71 and 1984–85. Since then, however, there have been some signs both in the humanities and social sciences that the steady decline in the shares of degrees being awarded is at long last bottoming out. But, with the exception of mathematics, it is not clear that that is yet the case with the natural sciences, which all lost ground between 1970 and 1990— though the physical sciences, after declining in degree-share at the start of the period, had stabilized at a lower level by the end of the 1970s, whereas the biological sciences, after experiencing a minor boom in the mid-1970s, were by 1985 dropping to a level below that enjoyed in 1970.

Such figures and trends seem so obvious in their impact and have been the occasion of so much gloomy commentary,[41] that it may well seem a little churlish to express any degree of agnosticism about what exactly they mean. When only 1.3 percent of our current crop of freshmen indicate an interest in majoring in English (0.8% in history, 0.2 in philosophy, 0.1 in religion!) sufficient ground for worry there seems, indeed, to be. But how much worry? Are we simply threatened as a nation with an unprecedented and catastrophic loss among the most educated segment of our population of any truly effective purchase on the richness of our own cultural heritage? Or do these data on majoring and degree-shares fail to speak to other developments which must be taken into account? Or, again, do they manage to mask affiliated trends that, if taken into account, would serve to cast their significance in a rather different light.

Without challenging the view that there are, indeed, substantial grounds for general concern, I am strongly inclined to answer the two last questions in the affirmative. And for three reasons. The first of these is admittedly speculative. It goes back to the point made earlier on that a student's commitment to a major or degree program does not preclude his or her taking courses in other subject areas. At many institutions, indeed, and in many programs, such a distribution of courses is in some measure required. That being so, and given the fact that the number of students attending college and university has almost doubled since 1966 (with that larger student population reflecting not only growth in the traditional college-age cohort but also the entry into higher education of a larger percentage of the population as a whole), then it is surely plausible to assume that more Americans are getting *some* college-level instruction in the arts and sciences than has ever been the case before in the nation's history. And not implausible to speculate that that fact may be playing a role in fostering the flowering in the "public humanities" in which Lynne Cheney and the National Endowment for the Humanities rightly take so much pride.

My second reason is happily less speculative. It is grounded in the recognition of the need to be very careful about the particular year one chooses (or is chosen for one) as point of departure for the establishment of trends. It is grounded also in the possibility of analyzing some of the demographic variables—more universal access to higher education, age, gender, racial and ethnic composition—that may be associated with the shifting curricular choices that students, in aggregate, make. Summaries of the data assembled via the Higher Education General Information Survey began appearing in the *Digest of Educational Statistics* in 1962. The data from the annual survey of freshman attitudes and aspirations began to appear in 1966. The National Research Council began publishing annual summaries of the results of the Survey of Earned Doctorates in 1967, and of the Survey of Doctorate recipients in 1977.[42] Perhaps the ease with which they have made the pertinent data available explains the pronounced tendency in the literature of commentary to fix upon the mid- or late-1960s as the point of comparison with the present and the point of departure for the charting of trends. So far as the "flight from the arts and sciences" is concerned, however, that choice of a point of departure can be very misleading. The fact is that, after a phase of continuous *increase* during the postwar years, the late-1960s marked the high point in the number of arts and sciences B.A.s conferred; a high point, also, in the percentage they constituted of all baccalaureate degrees awarded. If that cardinal fact is overlooked, the dimensions, gravity, and significance of the subsequent decline are, as a result, magnified. Moreover, a failure to analyze what was going on in the matter of student curricular choices during the 1950s and 1960s as well as during the 1970s and 1980s renders it well nigh impossible to determine which of the many possible variables at work one should appropriately turn to in one's search for explanations.

It would be easy enough to assume that the fundamental demographic factors at work during the 1960s *must* have had the effect of reducing the percentages of students entering degree programs in the arts and sciences. During that decade, after all, the baby boom of the postwar years produced as its fruit a 50 percent increase and more in the 18 to 24 years old cohort, traditionally the college-going group. And the bulk of that increased group who actually went on to college found their way into the rapidly growing sectors of higher education—the state colleges and the big comprehensive institutions—which had not by tradition focused heavily on the liberal arts.[43] Because of broadening access to higher education, moreover, the percentage of that 18–24-year-old cohort going on to college grew in the 1960s from

15.9 percent to 23.9 percent. And because those new students were coming from families without a tradition of college-going and were more likely to be preoccupied with targeted vocational preparation than with the goals embedded in an education in the liberal arts, it would be plausible to assume that their very entry into higher education *had* to have the effect of reducing still further the arts and sciences share of B.A.s

The pertinent data from the 1950s and much of the 1960s tell, however, a markedly different story. During most of the years of expanding enrollment (1952–69) there was a substantial *increase* in the percentage of B.A.s awarded in the arts and sciences. Decline set in only during the last years of the expansion (1969–74). And it was during the 1974–84 period, when the number of degrees being awarded had reached a reasonably stable plateau, that the most severe decline in the arts and sciences percentage was experienced. In this matter, at least, demography was certainly not destiny, and its influence was modulated by the educational priorities and curricular planning of the colleges and universities themselves. Many of them, it seems, some previously in parlous condition, seized the opportunity afforded by the burgeoning enrollments of the 1960s to upgrade themselves academically, qualifying their vocational orientation, introducing general education requirements, and strengthening their curricular offerings in the arts and sciences.[44] But with the leveling-off of enrollments in the 1970s, the concomitant growth of competition for students, the advent of a period of economic turbulence, and the growth among students of a heightened anxiety about their career prospects, the ability especially of the comprehensive and state colleges to impose on students their own academic priorities was accordingly diminished. Vocational and preprofessional programs of study boomed, and enrollments in the arts and sciences went into decline. Thus, for example, at Ball State University in Indiana, whereas the share of degrees conferred in the arts and sciences had risen between 1954 and 1970 from 2.5 to 29.9 percent, by 1986 that share had fallen back to 13.3 percent.[45] "[T]he overall increase in the AS [arts and sciences'] share during the 1960s," Turner and Bowen conclude,

> was associated with a fundamental change in the character of many state colleges and comprehensive institutions. It was at these rapidly growing schools, which had been heavily oriented toward professional and preprofessional programs in the immediate postwar years, that the sharpest

increases in AS shares occurred. Subsequently, the flight from the arts and sciences was most pronounced at these same institutions, even though it also occurred at many research universities.[46]

If demography *tout court* does not offer any truly powerful explanatory key to the "flight from the arts and sciences" at the undergraduate level, neither, it turns out, does the demographic composition of the student population in terms of age, race or ethnicity.[47] Nor, so far at least as the share of the arts and sciences as a whole in the number of B.A.s awarded is concerned, does the changing gender composition of that student population in itself. Until the mid-1980s, that is to say (at which time this particular "gender gap" began to close), while the share of the arts and sciences degrees awarded to men was higher than that awarded to women, the gap in question had remained stable across the years, with "the pattern of year to year changes" remaining "remarkably similar for men and women." At the level of the individual fields, however, that was by no means the case, and the most significant differences are evident in the humanities. For men, the humanities' share in the overall total of B.A.s conferred shows a gradual but more or less consistent decline from the late 1950s on to 1986. For women, on the other hand, that humanities' share *increased* very dramatically between 1954 and the late 1960s before showing an even more dramatic and steady decline in the 1970s and 1980s. Here, Turner and Bowen conclude,[48] although between 1954 and 1986 women increased their share in the total number of B.A.s conferred from 39 to 51 percent, the truly determining factor was not so much the changing male-female ratio in the undergraduate population, as the changes across the years in the *curricular choices* being made by women.

Those changing curricular choices dominated, in fact, what was going on in the humanities throughout the greater part of the period. Without the steady increase of interest on the part of women, the decline in the share of degrees awarded in the humanities would have set in long before the late-1960s. Again, "between 1970 and 1986, the declining participation of women accounted for more than three times the loss in share attributable to reduced interest in the humanities among men."[49] Similarly, the heightened entry of women into education programs during the early and mid-1950s, when the baby boom had generated so strong an interest in school teaching among women (though not among men) that degrees in education came by 1958 to constitute almost 50 percent of all the B.A. degrees awarded to women.

Decline set in almost immediately thereafter, so that in 1986 degrees in education accounted for only 13 percent of the total number of B.A.s awarded to women. A substantial number of those women who might earlier have entered degree programs in education moved in the late 1950s and across most of the 1960s, first into the humanities and then, to a lesser degree, into the social sciences. From the early 1970s onward, however, there was a shift in the direction of business-related studies. In 1970 only 2.8 percent of the B.A. degrees conferred upon women were in business; by 1986 that figure had risen to no less than 21.7 percent, and, though it did not account for all of it, that particular shift did account for a goodly proportion of the dramatic growth of enrollments in business programs over the past two decades that has so often been the focus of concern.[50] As a result, it is tempting to speculate that had the social and cultural norms that constrained women from entry into business-related careers eroded a decade or more earlier than they did, overall enrollments in the humanities might never have reached the heights achieved in the late sixties. And had that been the case, the subsequent decline would have been a much less precipitous one, and one less likely to have stimulated self-doubt on the part of those within the academy, or, on the part of those without, the exercises in gloomy and mordant commentary to which we have become, somewhat restively, accustomed.

But if an extension of the length of the period over which one chooses to study enrollment trends and an effort to identify gender-related differences in enrollment patterns at the level of particular fields of study serve both to complicate and enrich one's understanding of the significance to be attached to the shifts in student academic interests over the past three decades, so, too, does an analysis of the pertinent data broken down by institutional sector. And that is my third reason for caution about the drawing of unqualifiedly alarmist conclusions from those data. One of the things they reveal is an accelerating segmentation of higher education by institutional category. Computed as a percentage of all degrees conferred, the share of degrees awarded in the arts and sciences in 1984–85 ranged from a high of 65.1 percent at the Liberal Arts I Colleges, via 29.6 percent at the Research I Universities, to a low of 19.6 percent at the Comprehensive I Colleges and Universities. And these figures reflect the outcome of differential shifts across time. Between 1976–77 and 1984–85 in higher education at large, the arts and sciences share of all degrees conferred shrank from 31.2 percent to 24.8 percent. But, as suggested earlier, that decline was most severely felt at the Comprehensive I and Other Four-

Year Colleges. And it is clear that in those sectors significant decline has continued on through the 1980s. At the Research I Universities, on the other hand, the decline was comparatively modest and had eased by 1980–81. Similarly, at the Liberal Arts I Colleges, the 1980s witnessed no change, and the late 1970s very little.[51] Indeed, if we take Cornell University and Swarthmore College as examples of Research I and Liberal Arts I institutions at which there was no dramatic increase between 1954 and 1986 in the overall number of B.A. degrees awarded, we find that there were only the most modest changes across those years in the percentages of arts and sciences degrees conferred (from 49.3 to 47.1%, and from 76.1 to 82.1% respectively), and, at Cornell, no real change at all between 1970 and 1986.[52]

Further exercises in disaggregation along different lines would doubtless produce further refinements in our understanding of the complex phenomenon of shifting student interests over the recent past and generate one or two surprises. Here, and by way of conclusion, I will mention just one. So much attention has been focused of late on the "crisis in the humanities" that it has been all too easy to overlook the fact that the past two decades have also witnessed a significant decline of student interest in the basic sciences—biology, chemistry, geology, mathematics, and physics. And because of the great influx in recent years of foreign students into doctoral programs in the natural sciences, the inclusion in the statistics usually cited of graduate as well as undergraduate degrees conferred may be serving to mask a rather severe drop in the interest of *American* students in those fields.[53]

In 1985, then, concerned at the time about the mounting cost of scientific instrumentation and the "big-science" posture of the federal funding agencies, Carleton, Franklin and Marshall, Mount Holyoke, Oberlin, Reed, Swarthmore, and Williams convened a group of about fifty leading liberal arts colleges—all drawn from the Liberal Arts I category and all distinguished by the degree to which they were committed to maintaining high-quality instruction in the natural sciences.[54] Together, they initiated a piece of collective institutional research the results of which were in three respects very revealing. First, it demonstrated that the group of colleges in question had been disproportionately successful in attracting science students and graduating science majors. In 1985 some 29 percent of their freshman planned to major in the basic sciences; the comparable figure for the highly selective private universities was 15 percent, and, for other four-year colleges of high or very high selectivity, 13.3 percent. Similarly, in

1983 some 24 percent (in 1985, 25%) of the undergraduate degrees conferred by the fifty colleges were awarded in the basic sciences. In comparison, the twenty universities rated as best in the sciences by the National Academy of Sciences conferred in 1980 only 14 percent of their degrees in those fields.[55] The Oberlin study showed, in the second place, that the group of colleges involved in it had succeeded in sustaining their scientific successes in the teeth of the nationwide decline in student interest in the sciences. Between 1976 and 1984, the percentage of freshmen at all colleges and universities planning to major in the basic sciences dropped from about 10 to 6.6 percent. From 1976 to 1984 the comparable percentage at the fifty colleges declined from 31.8 percent only to 27.8 percent, and it edged up again in 1985 to 29.2 percent. Other selective colleges and universities saw much steeper declines. Even the twenty universities given a top rating by the National Academy of Sciences saw a 15 percent decline from 1976 to 1983 in the number of science majors being graduated—a period during which the comparable numbers at the fifty colleges declined by no more than 1.6 percent. In the third place, the study showed that the fifty colleges had a better track record than even the leading universities in sending on their graduates to doctoral work and to subsequent careers in basic science.[56] Finally, the study noted that the single most important reason for that fine track record was the opportunity these colleges offered to interested students at an early stage in their academic careers for "hands on" experience of collaborative scientific research with a faculty supervisor.[57]

This particular exercise in disaggregation serves to remind us that in the matter of shifting student interests and enrollment patterns there are likely to be significant variations even among the approximately two hundred selective institutions categorized in accordance with the Carnegie Classification as Research I Universities and Liberal Arts I Colleges. And its conclusion about the importance to the undergraduate experience of "hands on" collaborative research should serve also to bring us back to another important point. Embedded in the mythic lore, not only of Williams College but of American higher education at large, is the aphorism about his former teacher ascribed in 1871 to James A. Garfield, future President of the United States, to the effect that "the ideal college is Mark Hopkins on one end of a log and a student on the other."[58] Whether or not Garfield used precisely those words is unimportant. What is important is the reminder that neither institution nor student alone lies at the heart of the educational process, but rather the crucial encounter between teacher and student. It is time, then, to turn to the faculty end of the log.

3. Faculty: how many, where and who they are, how they spend their time, what has changed, and what the future holds

Given the crucial importance of the role that faculty members play in the educative process, it is much to be regretted that so few attempts have been made to collect at the national level a full array of pertinent quantitative data concerning them. For full-time faculty, overall counts and figures on average salaries have been available, along with data generated by periodic surveys of faculty opinion, but not a great deal more. As a result, much of the pertinent terrain has been left available very much as unfenced grazing land for peripatetic commentators prone to rampant anecdotalism. And, of late, the more apoplectically critical among them have made effective use of the license accorded to them thereby.

In 1987, happily, the National Center for Education Statistics of the U.S. Department of Education initiated for the first time since 1963 a National Survey of Postsecondary Faculty designed to collect data on faculty and faculty issues. Its stated plan was to collect such data at regular intervals, and to do so from three sources: faculty members themselves, department chairs, and institutional academic officers. The first cycle of the study was completed in 1988 and an overview of the data was published in 1990.[59] It was based on an institutional sampling selected from an overall "universe" of some 3,159 non-profit accredited institutions offering a two-year associate's or higher degree. The data presented from the survey are broken down on many issues by age, gender, race, part-time or full-time status, tenure status or academic rank. They are also broken down by institutional control (public or private), and institutional sector—with nine categories employed: public research, private research, public doctoral, private doctoral, public comprehensive, private comprehensive, liberal arts, public two-year, and other. While these categories lack the precision of the full range of Carnegie Classifications and are not fully aligned with them, they are close enough to permit useful comparison.[60]

Of the plethora of data garnered by this survey only a handful need be highlighted here. First, the basics: even if one excludes from the count the 100,000 and more temporary, adjunct, or visiting faculty, there were in 1987 around 670,000 faculty members at the more than 3,000 institutions covered by the survey. Of these, approximately 494,000 were full-time, 176,000 part-time. Of the full-time faculty approximately 28 percent taught at research universities, 26 percent at comprehensive institutions, 19 percent at public two-year colleges, and 8 percent at liberal arts colleges of one sort or another.[61] The distribution of part-time faculty was sharply different. No less than 46 percent of them were concentrated in the two-year colleges, with the next largest group (approximately 18%) at the comprehensive institutions, and only 11 and 8 percent, respectively, at the research universities and liberal arts colleges. A similar contrast is evident in the percentages (35 versus 19%) of full-time and part-time faculty teaching in the arts and sciences.[62]

Of the full-time faculty at both four-year and two-year institutions, some 60 percent were tenured, ranging from a high of 69 percent at the public research universities to a low of 48 percent at the private doctoral institutions, with the liberal arts colleges coming in towards the low end at 51 percent, and with above-average tenured cohorts in the arts and sciences. The mean age of the full-time group was forty-seven; at forty-four their part-time colleagues were slightly younger. Of the full-time faculty, only 2 percent were under thirty, 40 percent were between thirty and forty-four, and 55 percent between forty-five and sixty-four. On this dimension, no statistically significant differences were evident across either subject area or institutional sector. The same is almost as true among both part-time and full-time faculty for representation of the several racial or ethnic groupings across the several institutional sectors. Eighty-nine percent of the full-time and 90 percent of the part-time faculty were white. Asians constituted some 4 percent of the total; blacks, Hispanics and Native Americans 3, 2 and 1 percent respectively.[63] So far as gender is concerned, however, there is a fairly marked difference between full-time and part-time faculty. Whereas men constituted 73 percent of the full-time contingent, they totaled no more than 56 percent of the part-timers. Not surprisingly, then, in terms at least of their overall average of 27 percent, women were comparatively overrepresented at the public two-year institutions (38%), and underrepresented at the research universities (approximately 20%). At 29 percent, they possessed a comparatively strong presence in the liberal arts colleges.[64]

From the responses of faculty members to the 1988 survey, we learn that in the fall semester 1987 they reported themselves as working, on average, some 53 hours per week at all their professional activities, whether paid or unpaid. Eighty-seven percent of that average workload involved work at their academic institutions, while mean hours of unremunerated professional service constituted 6 percent, and mean hours of such remunerated outside work as consulting, 7 percent of the total. Faculty at the public and private research and at the public doctoral universities put in the longest hours (at 57, 56 and 54 hours per week); those at the two-year colleges (at 47 hours) the shortest. The amount of time devoted to outside professional work, whether paid or unpaid, differed little across the several institutional sectors, but mean hours of work at the institution itself did. Faculty teaching at the two-year colleges averaged, at 40 hours per week, less than those at any of the four-year institutions; those at the private and public research and at the public doctoral universities exceeded, at 52, 50 and 49 hours per week, the overall average of 46.[65]

Academic rank seemed to make no appreciable difference in the number of working hours devoted either to the institution itself or to outside professional activities, whether remunerated or not.[66] Field of study or program area, however, did make such a difference. Faculty in the fine arts, for example, while putting in the same number of hours as the overall mean and as the mean for unpaid professional services "outside," committed less time to the institution (44 hours) and more to paid outside activities (6 hours). In contrast, faculty in the humanities, who also aligned with the mean in relation both to overall workload and to amount of time devoted to outside unpaid professional services, devoted more time to the institution (48 hours) and less to outside remunerated activities (2 hours).[67]

Differences in the way in which faculty members allocated their working hours show up also by institutional sector. At all types of institution teaching activities naturally accounted for the bulk of that time, with the overall mean being 56 percent for teaching, student advising, grading, course preparation and so on, 16 percent for scholarly research (and, presumably, writing), 13 percent for administrative and governance activities of one sort or another, and 15 percent for such other activities as working with student organizations, community or public service, and outside counseling or free-lance work. But so far as the balance between teaching and research is concerned, whereas faculty at the two-year colleges devoted 71 percent of their time to teaching and only 3 percent to research, those at the private research universities (not surprisingly) devoted an average of only 40 percent to teaching but 30 percent to research. The comparable distribution of time for faculty members at the liberal arts colleges was

65 percent to teaching, 8 percent to research. At all types of institutions, moreover, academic rank made a difference in the differential amounts of time allocated to teaching, research, and administrative activities. Full professors devoted 51 percent of their time to teaching, 20 percent to research and 16 percent to administrative duties; assistant professors, on the other hand, spent 56 percent of their time teaching, 18 percent pursuing research and, understandably, only 10 percent on administrative matters. Similarly, differences show up when one controls for academic field or program area, with the extremes being set by faculty in agriculture and home economics (46% teaching; 28% research), and in the humanities (61% teaching; 17% research).[68]

For their efforts, full-time faculty respondents to the 1987 survey reported themselves to be receiving on average a total annual income from all sources in the neighborhood of $49,000. Apart from an obvious differentiation in earnings by academic rank, institutional sector and program area or field also accounted for substantial differences in mean annual incomes. The highest average income (about $75,000) was reported by faculty members teaching at private research universities; the lowest (about $33,000) by faculty at liberal arts colleges. Interestingly enough, faculty teaching at the public two-year colleges earned somewhat more than that (approximately $39,000).[69] When broken down by academic field or program area—and whatever the institutional sector involved—those in the health sciences emerge as the best remunerated ($75,000); those in the humanities the worst ($39,000). And that discrepancy reflects not only the differential in the income they received from their institutions but also a very marked differential in the income they received from outside consulting work ($9,431 per annum as opposed to $663). For full-time faculty, overall average income from such outside consulting work was $8,000. That average, however, conceals marked differences both in the amounts received in general and in the amounts received by faculty in different academic fields and at different types of institutions. In general, only 42 percent earned any income from consulting work and over half of that group earned less than $2,500. Nine percent earned $10,000 or more. Faculty members teaching in the health sciences were most likely to be in receipt of outside consulting income, and they earned most from that source; in contrast, faculty teaching in the humanities were least likely to make any money from consulting, and those who did so earned less on average than faculty in any other academic field. Similarly, if one breaks the data down by institutional sector faculty teaching at private research universities were most likely to be engaged in outside consulting work (61%) and to earn most from that source. In contrast, faculty teaching at two-year institutions were least likely (24%) to engage in such outside consulting work, though they earned somewhat more on average for their efforts than the 32 percent of faculty at liberal arts colleges who took on such assignments.[70]

In the case of faculty, it is harder to make reliable comparisons with the past or to chart the process of change across the past three decades that it was either with the institutions themselves or with the bodies of students who enrolled in them. The reason is the simple lack of data, or—where pertinent sets were indeed collected but assuming shifting definitions and using varying methodologies—lack of easily comparable data. In particular, given the ease with which commentators are prone to generalize on the subject it would have been helpful to have for the past survey data directly comparable with those reported in 1988 and enabling us to ascertain with some precision the degree to which there has been a change in the way in which faculty members characteristically divide their time between teaching and research. Such precisely comparable data we do not have. What we do have, however, are surveys and studies by scholars like Lipset, Ladd, Howard R. Bowen, Schuster, Fulton, Trow and Boyer, drawing in part on the faculty surveys conducted at intervals since 1969 (and most recently in 1989) by the Carnegie Commission on Higher Education and the American Council on Education.[71] And these surveys and studies do help fill the gap. The Carnegie surveys have all included questions pertaining to the topic. And the appropriately weighted data generated thereby (and we are assured that they "may be taken as reasonably representative of the entire population of teaching faculty at colleges and universities in the United States")[72] are extremely interesting. In common with the 1988 data they strongly suggest that the typical faculty member in the United States places a much higher priority on teaching and a lower priority on research and publication than is often alleged to be the case. Thus the data from the 1989 survey reveal that 70 percent of the professoriate reported their interests as lying primarily with teaching rather than research, that 56 percent had never published or edited a book, whether alone or in collaboration (although 6%, presumably composed of compulsive recidivists, had published six or more), than 59 percent had published *in toto* no more than five articles in an academic or professional journal, 26 percent none at all, and that 62 percent believed that teaching effectiveness should be the primary criteria for promotion of faculty.[73]

The data generated by that Carnegie survey in 1989 did attest to some movement in a research-oriented direction across the two decades since 1969, when 76 percent of the professoriate had considered themselves as primarily committed to teaching (as opposed to the 70% of 1979 and 1989) and 69 percent (as opposed to 56) had never published or edited a book.[74] Such changes, however, are dwarfed by other developments which, despite the incommensurability of some of the data, are easy enough to identify. The most obvious is the sheer growth in the overall size of the professoriate. In 1900 there were only 24,000 faculty members at American colleges and universities. By 1920 that number had risen to 45,000, by 1940 to 147,000, by 1972 to 603,000. As Ladd and Lipset point out, the biggest jump (of about 150,000) came between 1965 and 1970, "with the number of *new* positions created and filled exceeding the *entire number* of faculty slots that [had] existed in 1940."[75] After the early 1970s, however, as student enrollment levels stabilized, the demand for new faculty dried up and the growth rate accordingly slowed down.

With the dramatic process of expansion had come, however, an equally dramatic shift in the institutional location of the bulk of faculty members. In 1963, for example, one faculty member in six taught at a liberal arts college; by 1980, only one in twelve did so, and by 1988 the number had dropped to something closer to one in thirteen. On the other hand, whereas in 1963 only one faculty member in ten taught at a two-year college, by 1988 the figure was one in five, and their numbers, since then have grown still further.[76]

Although for the earlier years information about the age distribution of the faculty is not readily available, the enormous influx of new people clearly led to a significant drop in the average age of the professoriate, with the steady-state conditions of the 1970s and 1980s leading to a subsequent reversal of that change. It will be recalled that in 1987 some 2 percent of the full-time faculty were thirty years old, 40 percent between thirty and forty-four, and 55 percent between forty-five and sixty-four. It will be recalled, too, that the survey indicated no significant differences across subject area. Bowen and Sosa's calculation of the change in the age distribution of arts and sciences faculty should be reasonably representative of the age distribution of the faculty as a whole. Those calculations reveal that by 1977, with 42 percent under forty years old, "the age distribution of the arts and sciences faculty . . . was skewed dramatically to the younger age group (principally 30–34 and 35–39)." But by 1987 the percentage of those under forty had fallen precipitously from 42 to 22 percent, while the percentage over forty-nine had gone up by more than one third, from

27 to 39 percent. "This basic demographic message," the authors conclude, "is striking in its clarity."[77]

The roller-coaster conditions prevailing in the academic employment market across the years between 1960 and the present also had a marked impact on the economic status of the profession. Embedded in the figures reported in the 1988 survey for annual income is the effect of some demoralizing swings, as the excess demand for faculty generated by the surging enrollments of the 1960s (and prevailing until 1969) was replaced in subsequent years by a surplus in the number of candidates available for the rapidly dwindling number of openings. As a result, while "the rapid expansion of higher education in the 1960s was accompanied by the only significant, sustained improvement in the real income of faculty members since World War II," the subsequent slowdown led between 1970–71 and 1983–84 to a 19 percent decline in faculty salaries (in terms of real, non-inflated dollars), while, in contrast, "compensation in most other occupational categories more or less kept up with inflation." Over the period 1960–61 to 1983–84, most occupational groups "experienced increases in real [non-inflated] earnings of at least 20 per cent." In contrast, "average real faculty salaries in 1983–84 were no higher than they had been in 1960–61."[78]

Linked with these ups and downs in the economic well-being of the profession was the shifting relationship across these years of the number of enrollments in our colleges and universities and the size of the pool of Ph.D.s being generated by our graduate schools. During the 1960s the size of that pool grew dramatically as the graduate schools scrambled to keep up with the demand for new faculty. Between 1958 and 1972, indeed, there was a fourfold increase (8,800 to 33,000) in the overall number of Ph.D.s awarded by American universities. The rate of production then stabilized and has since fluctuated within the 30,000 to 33,000 range.[79] That overall stability, however, has not precluded some significant changes since 1972, changes which may well bode ill as we move forward across the next two decades. For those decades will witness, so far as college-age students are concerned, the ending of the demographic decline, the return to a pattern of growth in student enrollments, and a concomitant return to conditions of excess demand in the academic labor market. Of the changes in question, four may be singled out for emphasis.

First is the ninefold increase since 1958 in the number of foreign (or non-residents) earning Ph.D.s at American universities (from 600 in 1958 to 5,600 in 1987). That increase served to offset the steady decline since the early 1970s in the number of U.S. residents awarded doctorates. In 1962 U.S. residents accounted for 85.6 percent of the total number of doctorates awarded; by 1987 that figure had dropped to 72.3 percent. And in 1986 little more than a third of the nonresidents indicated that they planned to stay in the United States after they graduated.[80]

The second change in question is the significant decline of recent years, and in almost every field, in the percentage of doctorate holders employed in academia. Between 1985 and 1987, for example, the percentage of doctorate holders in the humanities who were working in business or industry went up from 8.7 to 9.8 percent, with the percentage among recent graduates reaching as high as 11.3 percent.[81]

Third, during the 1980s there has been something of a shift in the distribution across the several fields of study in the number of doctorates being awarded. In 1987, doctorates in the arts and sciences accounted for about half of the total number of doctorates awarded. But the trends since 1978 have been such as to produce a widening gap between "the number of doctorates in all fields and the number of doctorates in the arts and sciences," with the number of the latter awarded to U.S. residents manifesting a steady decline.[82]

Fourth, there has also been a decline since the late 1960s in the amount of federal support available to graduate students. Whereas in the mid-1950s only 7,500 graduate students were receiving federal support in the form of fellowships, traineeships or research assistantships, by 1969 that number had risen to 80,000. Between 1971 and 1975, however, federal funding for fellowships and traineeships was reduced by more than 50 percent. Universities had to scramble to try to replace at least part of that lost fellowship aid from their own institutional resources, and graduates were forced to take on larger loan burdens than their predecessors had had to risk. Moreover, in their attempt to finance their studies they may also have been led to depend more heavily than heretofore on teaching assistantships. And the excessive amount of teaching being undertaken by graduate students is presumably one of the reasons for the fact that the actual time taken by graduate students in all fields has gone up significantly in recent years. Data which the National Research Council collected and reported have even been read to suggest that the median time taken by graduate students in the humanities went up from 9.0 in 1972 to 12.4 in 1988—a startling increase of almost 40 percent. Further scrutiny of those data, however, reveals that they were being analyzed incorrectly, and that a 15–20 percent increase "in the median total time to degree in the humanities" is what has in fact occurred, so that "the time a typical humanities graduate student spends earning a doctorate" has been overstated "by as much as 2 years."[83]

The fact is, however, (and especially so, given the number who drop out of doctoral programs) that we can ill afford at the moment *any* lengthening in the time it takes a student to compete a Ph.D. All four of the changes outlined above are relevant to the nature, dimensions and gravity of the challenge that will confront our colleges and universities in the next few years as the demographic tide turns once more, and they are forced (to a degree not experienced since the 1960s) to compete with one another for the talented faculty they will need to replace those retiring or to fill the new positions that we will once more see being created. How brisk that competition will be and how inadequate the supply of new Ph.D.s is hard to predict. Projections in this area are hazardous and some extremely gloomy prognostications have been made.[84] But the general sense that the academy, after a debilitating glut of newly minted Ph.D.s is now heading into a period of faculty shortages is clearly not without foundation. And the fine study by Bowen and Sosa on which we have drawn so frequently in these pages represents the best and most systematic attempt to come up with carefully grounded and reliable projections of demand and supply for faculty in the arts and sciences.

Their conclusions are less than encouraging. While insisting on the fundamental point that projections are not predictions (indeed, that if they are taken seriously and the right policy changes made, they may turn out to be poor predictions),[85] Bowen and Sosa conclude that there will be "some significant increase in demand [for new faculty] relative to supply [of new Ph.D.s] as early as 1992–97—and then far more dramatic changes beginning in 1997–2002." Even their most optimistic model projects a "substantial" excess of demand to supply from 1997 to 2012. And the most surprising aspect of their findings is that the pinch is likely to be felt most severely, not in the natural sciences, but in the humanities and social sciences, with "the projected gaps between supply and demand [becoming] staggering" in the 1997–2012 period. "If," they conclude, "the assumptions used to derive these projections hold, there will be only seven candidates for every ten openings in the humanities and social sciences for roughly a ten-year period."[86]

Of late, there has been much loose talk among both academics and commentators on the academic scene about an impending "crisis in the humanities." Unless policy changes at both the national and institutional level succeed in engineering a rapid and substantial increase in the production rate of Ph.D.s, it now seems likely that that crisis is, indeed, destined to materialize and likely to do so in much more concrete and specific form than even the most assiduously conscientious attender of scholarly conferences and colloquia has even dared to imagine.

By now, even the most patient and long-suffering of readers will have been tempted to conclude that they have been told altogether more than they want to know about the numbers, types, characteristic commitments, concerns and challenges confronting the institutions, students and faculty that together make up the world of American higher education. About that barrage of numbers, proportions and percentages I have, however, no apologies to make. We have well been reminded[87] of the fact that "in thinking about education, many of us are autobiographical." That is to say, "we tend to make judgments about the future on the basis of our own experiences and the experiences of friends." Not only does that make it difficult for us "to anticipate changes in circumstances" and to plan properly for them, it also dims our awareness of the sheer scope and variety of the whole enterprise of higher education in America and the changes that have overtaken it even in our own lifetime.

That these changes have been massive, almost overwhelming, the array of data reported in this chapter leaves no room for doubt. The rapid increase over the past thirty years in the number of institutions of higher education and the sectors in which it has largely been concentrated have conspired to nudge the center of institutional gravity away, somewhat, from the leading research universities and liberal arts colleges and more in the direction of the comprehensive institutions and two-year colleges. The characteristic concerns of those leading institutions and the academic standards they set are now much less likely than they once were to set the tone for the whole enterprise. Similarly, the dramatic increase in the size of the student body, the opening up of access and the presence in far greater numbers on our campuses of women, members of racial minority groups, older students, part-time students, students who commute to their classes—all of these developments, which are destined to continue on into the future, have helped turn many of our colleges and universities in new directions and have left none of them totally unaffected. As we peer anxiously into the future, we simply cannot afford to forget for a moment that "roughly one-half of the students in the classroom of 2000 would not have been there if the composition of [the American student body as it was in] 1960 had been continued.[88] And there have been parallel, if less dramatic, changes in the overall numbers, age, gender, race and typical institutional context of the faculty members charged with the teaching of those students. Such transformations, crammed into the narrow compass of no more than three decades, must necessarily inform the perspective from which we make our judgments about the current undergraduate experience in America— its overall quality, the changes it reflects, the threat or promise it holds for the future.

CHAPTER IV

CRITICAL:
The Current Standing of the Tradition

Throughout this decade, we have repeatedly heard from foreign sources that our system of higher education is the best in the world in the quality of its scientific research, the inventiveness of its educational programs, its accessibility to all segments of society, and its flexibility in adapting to the differing needs of a vast student population. In international opinion surveys, our leading universities invariably dominate. We are the country of choice for students around the world seeking to pursue their education abroad. Business leaders and government officials from overseas extoll the quality of our academic science and admire its stimulative effects on the economy. At a time when America's ability to compete is being challenged in many spheres, these achievements should be a cause for celebration.

Derek Bok (1989)

[T]he foundations of the university have become extremely doubtful to the higher intelligence.

Allan Bloom (1987)

Almost single-handedly, the professors—working steadily and systematically—have destroyed the university as a center of learning and have desolated higher education, which no longer is higher or much of an education. The story of the collapse of American higher education is the story of the rise of the professoriate.

Charles J. Sykes (1988)

If the friction of constant repetition had not dulled the edge of surprise, I suspect that most of us would detect something quite odd about the recent spate of criticism directed against American higher education in general and the American undergraduate experience in particular.

In the chapters preceding I have been at pains to trace the liberal arts tradition as it developed across the centuries, to set it in its evolving institutional context, and to take appropriate note of the historic changes which of recent years have transformed the institutional matrix in which that tradition has been preserved and mediated. Although such things strike me as nothing less than an essential prerequisite for any reasonably nuanced understanding of our present situation, from the critics who have been so vociferous of late we hear next to nothing about them. One of the most striking features of their commentaries is the comparative lack of interest they show in the statistical data, even when such data are available in over rich abundance. Ernest Boyer, of course, is very much of an exception here.[1] But in these writings in general, prescription tends to preempt analysis, in place of evidence we get a species of disheveled anecdotalism, and a free-fire zone is created for eye-catching and sensationalist claims of the type favored by Charles Sykes, Page Smith, Roger Kimball, and Chester Finn. Striking also is the marked degree to which this critical onslaught is mounted in a contextual void—social, institutional and, above all, historical. While they differ a little among themselves in the degree to which they pay any attention at all to developments dating back beyond the recent past, in few of the books and articles involved can one discern any lively sense of the complexity and institutional variety of the American system of higher education or of the sheer magnitude of the transformations it has undergone during the past three decades and to which the statistical data adduced in the last chapter so consistently attest. In this respect, the silences of the critiques may well be their most significant feature. It is with the sounds of silence, then, that we will begin.

1. The silences of the critics

The single most important factor shaping the undergraduate experience in the United States today (and setting the indispensable context for an assessment of its strengths and weaknesses) is the enormous demographic upheaval of the past thirty years, the nature of the response it evoked, and the energy, imagination and adaptation going into that response. If one has the ambition to make a reasonably balanced appraisal of the nature and quality of undergraduate education today, the indispensable point of departure should be the straightforward recognition of three fundamental facts about the current situation of higher education in the world at large and the United States in particular.

First, that that situation, distinguished by unprecedented increases in the numbers of students crowding into colleges and universities all over the world, has (literally) no historical parallel. The issue goes beyond the marked fluctuations experienced in the demography of those of traditional college-going age; it concerns also the response to those fluctuations. Never before have societies attempted to make university and college education available to so large a percentage of their populations or to increase that percentage at so headlong a pace. India, for example, in the fifteen years after independence, saw a twelvefold increase in its student population. And if that generalization holds true, in varying degree, for almost every part of the contemporary world, it holds with particular force (and whatever our justifiable worries about equity of access) for the United States itself. Here the numbers of those going on to some form of higher education, which had tripled in the last great era of expansion after the Civil War, having already grown substantially during the 1950s, came close to quadrupling between 1960 and 1980, so that more than 60 percent of our high school graduates can now be expected at some point in their lives to enroll in a college or university course bearing credit towards a degree.

Second, that in terms of their religion, social class, age, gender, race and ethnicity, the diversity of students today has no historical parallel. In this respect, of course, there are variations and unevenness in the many systems of higher education around the globe. Never before, however, has the world of higher education betrayed so urgent an impulse to ensure equality of access for women and for those groups traditionally disadvantaged by race, religion, ethnicity, age and social class—barriers sustained in the past by custom, prejudice, snobbery, stupidity and age-old ingrained privilege. Again, if that generalization holds true, in varying degree, for practically every part of the contemporary world, it also holds with particular force (and however understandable the severity of our self-criticism on this very score) for the United States itself. Members of minority groups and students from low-income families are to be found in significant numbers at every level in our complex system of higher education, not only in community colleges or in the state college system, but also in the great state universities and the highly selective colleges and universities of the private sector. The 1990 national census revealed that almost one in four Americans now traces his or her roots to a minority group, a dramatic increase from one in five as recently as 1980. So that the prediction made in 1980 that "[r]oughly one half of the students in the classroom of 2000 would not have been there if the composition of [the student body in] 1960 had been continued" may have erred by being too conservative.[2]

Third, that in responding to these seismic demographic shocks, the U.S. higher educational system—with its decentralization, its extraordinary combination of public and private, its great variety of institutional forms, its pluralism of standards and educational aspiration and its tradition of responsiveness to shifting social needs—has proved to be remarkably effective. And especially so when its performance is measured against that of such other well-established systems abroad as the French, the German or the Italian.[3] Unlike so many of the European systems, it has made more than a mere beginning on the process of shifting its commitment from training professional elites to the more taxing endeavor of mass education. It could hardly have done so without the willingness to respond to local needs, the ability to adapt to varied challenges and the disposition to encourage innovation, qualities that go along with the distinctly un-European dispersion of initiative and power among a congeries of autonomous or quasi-autonomous universities and colleges—institutions engaged of necessity in the effort to compete for capable students and faculty. That among the corollaries of so rapid a response to the demographic shifts of the past thirty years have been an enhanced difficulty in maintaining equivalence of standards, the growth in some sectors of confusion over institutional mission, an obsessive preoccupation with "marketing," a marked lurch in the direction of heightened vocationalism, an upsurge in the demanding particularisms of gender and race, and a certain amount of curricular disarray, nobody, I assume, would be disposed to contest. New populations of students, teachers and scholars tend understandably to surface new issues, raise new questions, introduce new perspectives, feel their way towards new configurations of knowledge, and to do so often with a degree of angry and peremptory confusion. As a result, even apart from the intense "postmodern" debates about language, interpretation, and the nature and grounding of knowledge currently roiling the waters in the humanities and social sciences (and making consensus on matters curricular so very hard to achieve), demographic shifts of the dimensions we have experienced would themselves have imposed enormous strains upon traditional attitudes towards liberal education and upon curricular formations to which we have long since become habituated, and would have generated powerful currents tugging even the most conservative of institutions in the reluctant direction of change.

Such developments notwithstanding, the United States is now "the country of choice for students around the world seeking to pursue their education abroad,"[4] and, if we can believe surveys conducted overseas, it is now home to "two-thirds to three quarters of the best universities in the world."[5] This being so, the sharp contrast between foreign acclaim and domestic discontent is very striking indeed. So, too, is the unremitting harshness of tone that distinguishes the writing of the critics, as well as the lack of measure (and occasional silliness) evident in much of the academic response. To understand why that should be so, one has to recognize that some of the worst things said about our universities have been said by university people themselves, and that the present outcropping of discontent, however gleefully it has been mined by outside commentators, is in no small degree of ultimately academic provenance. And its geology is quite complex. Laid down across a considerable stretch of time, at varying depths and in distinct strata, it has since, by some great upheaval of the spirit, been thrust up to the surface of our educational consciousness where it now looms so very large—buckled, folded, jumbled, eroded, surrounded by a litter of accumulated intellectual debris which sometimes betrays moments of truly incongruous juxtaposition. If we were fully to come to terms with this formidable apparition, to grasp what it portended, we would have first to sort out the surface rubble, identifying its disparate provenance, distinguishing at least some of the strata from which it derived and the varying moments at which those strata had originally been deposited. Neither the understanding itself nor the assimilation of its results would be particularly rewarding. We will content ourselves, instead, with singling out for attention just a few aspects of this complex whole.

2. The geology of alienation

At the deepest level in this veritable geology of alienation lies a stratum about the origins of which one can only speculate, but which must surely have been deposited quite early on in the history of American higher education. The pressure generated by the late nineteenth-century infusion into American academic life of the German research ideal seems to have thrust it to the surface, and it received its quintessential expression in the early years of the present century at the hands of such educational critics as Thorstein Veblen and Abraham

Flexner. Both were products of the new Johns Hopkins University in its heroic age. Both disposed of a degree of vituperative elegance which such latter-day successors as Robert Maynard Hutchins, Robert Nisbet, Allan Bloom and Page Smith, if, indeed, they so aspired, have rarely been able to emulate.[6] It is not that such critics are all necessarily in agreement in their substantive views. Hutchins, for example, was essentially in sympathy with the educational ideal which Cardinal Newman had espoused in *The Idea of a University* (1873); so, too, in some measure, is Allan Bloom. Veblen, on the other hand, and, with him, Flexner, saw the undergraduate college which was the very focus of Newman's attention as no more than an "appendage," belonging "in the educational schema as senior member of the secondary school system" and bearing "no peculiarly close relation to the university as a seat of learning."[7] Research, which to Newman did not belong in a university at all, they saw as its central mission. Veblen's ideal, indeed, appears to have been something akin to the Institute for Advanced Study at Princeton, the institution of which Flexner, appropriately enough, was the first Director.

What links together these academic critics of the academy, then, is not so much the arguments they make as the tone of those arguments (sarcastic, contemptuous, vituperative) and the disposition that lies behind them. At its least offensive, that disposition partakes of the angularity and contrasuggestibility that also leads some of our most gifted students to do their best learning in the teeth of (rather than because of) the curricular arrangements we all labor so frustratingly to shape. In a more self-deluding vein it has helped sustain the note of sardonic condescension towards academic administration that Veblen sounded over seventy years ago when he derided the university presidents of his day as "Captains of Erudition" and took his stand on the surprisingly innocent "assumption that an autonomous faculty, free of any bureaucracy, would return to a primal state of disinterested, generous and collective pursuit of idle curiosity."[8] Finally, in its most unappealing registers, the disposition in question sounds a note of contempt for the masses of more pedestrian colleagues laboring in the academic vineyard, and evokes that mood of dyspeptic edginess which led academics themselves, in the aftermath of the turmoil of the late 1960s, to produce a depressing string of books with such arresting titles as *Academia in Anarchy* (1970), *Academics in Retreat* (1971), *Academy in Turmoil* (1970), *Back to the Middle Ages* (1969), *Bankruptcy of Academic Policy* (1972), *Confrontation and Counterattack* (1971), *Death of the American University* (1973), *Degradation of the*

Academic Dogma (1971), *Destruction of a College President* (1971), *Embattled University* (1970), *Exploding University* (1970), *Fall of the American University* (1972)—and so on. The trail could well be pursued right down through the alphabet. Such titles, as Clark Kerr observed in 1975, tend to "leave in the mind associated ideas like Academic-Anarchy; College-Chaos; Dogma-Degradation."[9]

Beyond recognizing its presence as the subterranean source of contemporary stridencies, there is not a great deal to be said about this particular stratum in the geology of educational discontent. Academics themselves, even when they disagree with it, seem to find its presence vaguely comforting, as if it affirms a healthy measure of distance from the inflated pretensions of their own less guarded moments. But all would do well to recognize the fact that critics outside the academy, taking its hyperbolic negativities at face value, have found in it welcome fuel for the barrage of intemperate accusations they have been directing against the world of higher education with such tiresome and damaging insistence. Noting that "[i]t is commonplace today to come across articles by tenured professors referring to higher education as 'ignoble,' 'decadent,' a 'desert' or words to that effect," Derek Bok has properly warned that "[i]f faculty members speak so harshly and repeatedly accuse their colleagues of everything from sabotaging affirmative action to destroying intellectual standards, the public is bound to wonder whether something is not badly amiss."[10]

Of the jumble of charges most commonly encountered, I propose to select three for closer scrutiny. While they do not lack interconnections, they are in fact distinct, trace their origins to different eras, and differ in their implications.

The first charge concerns the dominance of the research imperative and its alleged concomitant, the withdrawal of faculty from a concern with liberal education and the shortchanging of teaching frequently assumed to go with it. While that imperative was firmly established by "the enormous expansion of research as a major source of support and of eminence for faculty members at both public and private universities"[11] which took place during and after the Second World War, its origins lie much deeper in the past, in the years around the turn of the century when some of those who had embraced the new scientific research ideal began to experience a certain seepage of doubt about the fruit it was beginning to bear.

The second charge concerns the fragmentation of knowledge, the triumph of academic specialization and the plight of general education.

It was worry about the destructive impact of the free-elective system and the dangers of premature specialization that helped launch the general education movement in the decade after the First World War and to push it to its apogee in the years after the Second. In the 1960s it began to crumble, and by the mid–1970s it could be labeled as "an idea in distress."[12] Since then, with the growing sense that students were in full flight from the humanities, it has been the focus of almost continuous debate.

The third type of accusation is of more recent vintage. A preoccupation with the mediation of the Western cultural tradition had informed the general education movement right from the launching of the first coherent core-course program at Columbia in 1919. Doubts about the intensity of that preoccupation manifested themselves as early as 1945, but it was only in the 1970s and 1980s, in the wake of decolonization abroad and the civil rights movement at home, the long anguish of the Vietnam War and the campus upheavals of the 1960s, that those doubts really proliferated. Then it was that the rise to prominence of feminist concerns, the diversification by race and gender of our student bodies and faculties, and the pressures increasingly exerted on the majority consciousness by minority cultural claims and "Third World" concerns began to give rise to increasingly anguished charges that our universities and colleges were capitulating to special interests, permitting the politicization and balkanization of the curriculum, and abandoning in the humanities their crucial mission of mediating to successive generations of students the grandeur and richness of the Western cultural heritage. And those concerns have picked up an additional charge of passionate indignation as they have been drawn into the magnetic field exerted by a totally different debate of epistemological import—that stimulated by the renewed flirtation with cognitive and cultural relativism evident in so many of the intellectual movements of the past three decades, whether in anthropology, critical legal studies, literary theory, or history. These three sets of charges warrant more extended examination and we will take them up in turn.

3. Teaching and research

At their harshest, the charges focusing on the issue of teaching and research are clear enough and they are twofold. First, that despite (or because of) the great emphasis the university community places upon research and the mounting surge of publication resulting therefrom, much of what is produced is trivial, dull, pedestrian, or esoteric (or, God forbid, some mind-numbing combination of all four). As Sykes puts it (and with characteristic delicacy): "It is not necessary to insist that *no* worthwhile or valuable research is being done at the universities to recognize that much of what passes for knowledge creation makes only the most piddling contribution to the pool of human wisdom. Much of it is merely humbug."[13] Second, that teaching is undervalued in the world of higher education; that the American professoriate is in "full flight from teaching"; that "the academic culture," indeed, "is not merely indifferent to teaching, *it is actively hostile to it.*"[14]

While the two charges are usually run together on the grounds that academics are shunning teaching in order to mount their overpriced and oversold research effort, they are, in fact, both separable and distinct. The first is something of a standard theme in the writings of the more disgruntled of in-house commentators on the academic scene, with a lineage in the United States easily traceable back to the era when the German university research *ethos* first rooted itself firmly in American soil. From William James's denunciation of "the Ph.D. Octopus" at the start of the century to Irving Babbitt's sardonic commentary and Whicker's "Doctors of Dullness" in the 1920s, or Jacques Barzun's critique in the 1950s, all the way down to the diatribe published last year by Page Smith,[15] the line of descent is direct enough, and commentators like Lynne Cheney or Charles Sykes, speaking from vantage points outside the academy, have had no difficulty at all in adducing academic authorities of some stature to document their own highly critical accounts of university research.

In his book, *Killing the Spirit* (another cheery title!), Page Smith, at one time provost of the University of California at Santa Cruz, having devoted (under the heading of "publish or perish") a couple of dozen pages to research, concludes with some satisfaction (and with tongue, one has to hope, firmly in cheek) that he has "demonstrated conclusively that the vast majority of what passes for research/publication in the major American universities of American is mediocre, expensive and unnecessary, does not push back the frontiers of knowledge in any appreciable degree, and serves only to get professors promotions."[16] Of course, he has done nothing of the sort, nor is it at all clear how anyone in principle could—especially when the method used is, as in these critiques, selectively illustrative and adamantly anecdotal. However amusing at times (and it is), it throws little if any light on the overall quality of the vast amount of scholarship the academy produces. That pretentious rubbish finds its way into print, scholars are in a better position than most to attest. They, after all, are the ones who have to read it. That in this area, as in others, bad coinage sometimes drives out good, they would also be the last to deny. But if there is a better way to winnow out the wheat from the chaff than the patient process of peer review, publication and subsequent scholarly scrutiny, sometimes across long periods of time, no one has been quick to come up with it. Certainly, anyone tempted, as is Sykes, to generalize the Senator Proxmire-Golden-Fleece-Award-approach to the evaluation of research would do well to ponder how often in the course of intellectual history forms of investigation dismissed by contemporaries as uselessly esoteric have in fact borne within them the seeds of future creativity. I myself think immediately of the ignorance with which Renaissance humanists derided the disputations in natural philosophy being conducted in the universities of the day by their scholastic contemporaries. The reflective hindsight afforded by modern studies in the history of philosophy and science strongly suggests that those humanists simply did not *understand* what was at stake intellectually in those debates and missed, accordingly, the original consequences attaching to some of the arguments being generated.[17]

Fortunately, if we prescind from attempts to judge the overall significance of academic research and the quality of the results it generates, and if we focus instead on the second charge—that the academy in general overemphasizes research and accordingly undervalues teaching—then we are on more solid ground capable of supporting a less agnostic appraisal. And some of that ground is statistical. Pointing out recently that the "number of books and articles published annually on Shakespeare grew by 80 percent between 1968 and 1988," Lynne Cheney simply assumed a direct causal connection between what she called this recent "surge in publications" and "the increased emphasis on research." But before one accepts that assumption one has to take into account the enormous increase during those years in the number of potential authors. I do not have the specific numbers for those teaching in English departments, but between 1965 and 1988, after all, the overall number of faculty members at American universities and colleges more or less doubled.[18]

Moreover, at a less crude level of analysis, we have at our disposal for the period from the late 1960s to 1989 quite rich sets of survey data concerning the disciplinary and institutional loyalty of faculty, their attitudes towards teaching and research, time devoted to these and related activities, research productivity as measured by the publication of articles, monographs and books, and so on. Although these data have been studied and added to by such scholars as Oliver Fulton, Martin Trow, Howard Bowen, Everett Carll Ladd and Seymour Martin Lipset, they have largely been ignored by those alleging the occurrence in the academy of a flight from teaching. And yet they have a great deal to tell us about the subject—some of it quite startling, some a little puzzling, but all of it tending to reshape the issue along more complex lines, rendering it less rewarding material for those energized by the joys of polemic.

Among the various sets of data available the most helpful are those generated by the Carnegie surveys of faculty attitudes and behavior conducted at intervals since 1969 and most recently in 1989. These data are particularly valuable because of the stability of the questioning across time and because they can be broken down in more than one way—by age, academic rank, and, most revealingly, by institutional sector from research university to two-year college. And they have been subjected to careful professional scrutiny. In analyzing the 1969 data, Trow and Fulton were at pains to emphasize the degree to which they reflected not only the sheer diversity of institutional missions and conditions in American higher education but also the differing "research contexts" prevailing in the various disciplines. They warned, therefore, that "there is a real danger that any generalization may be the spurious result of adding together a series of quite different, sometimes contradictory relationships derived from a great variety of contexts."[19] That caveat having been posted, they extract from the data a series of conclusions which would not have startled earlier researchers on the topic, but might well surprise many academics themselves, and should certainly reassure those outside the academy whose views about faculty attitudes toward teaching have been framed by the sensationalist charges levied by such commentators as Sykes and Smith.

In the first place, taking into account both the degree of interest in research faculty members themselves express and their actual research performance as measured by numbers of publications, there is an enormous difference between the attitudes and achievements of faculty at the leading research universities and those teaching at the two-year colleges. That, of course, one would expect. What is perhaps more surprising is that "some research activity, and publication, can be found almost everywhere."[20] Most surprising of all, however, even when one notes the diversity of attitudes in the various institutional sectors, is the fact that 77 percent of faculty overall indicated in 1969 that their primary interest lay in teaching and 50 percent of those at the high quality universities did likewise. "Even at the largest state universities . . . ," Trow and Fulton observe, "where for years the doctrine of 'publish or perish,' large semiautonomous research 'empires,' excessive student numbers, and poor faculty-student ratios have been criticized, only a very small minority of faculty are uninterested in teaching, while half the total faculty claims to be more interested in teaching than research." Hence they conclude that "judged by the staff's self-conceptions, the American academic system as a whole is *primarily* a teaching system. Any notion that teaching generally takes second place to research is certainly not borne out." Or again, if one leaves aside "all questions of the amount of research actually done, and the extent to which American universities facilitate and reward it, the *normative* climate in the United States, as reflected in academics' personal preferences, is far more favorable to teaching than most observers would have predicted."[21]

But if, in the second place, one takes a further step and works into the picture actual research productivity as measured by publication activity, what, then, does one find? The answer is broadly congruent with what faculty members themselves reported about the primary focus of their interests. Fifty-three percent overall were either inactive in research or viewed themselves as active but had in fact published nothing in the previous two years. When that figure is broken down by institutional sector, the percentages range from 86 percent of those teaching at the two-year colleges to (perhaps more surprisingly) 21 percent of faculty at the leading research universities.[22]

In the third place, if, contrary to what is so often alleged, research is not the primary interest (or even much of a subordinate activity for a clear majority of American faculty), where in the higher educational system is research activity primarily located? Or, better, since our great research universities are clearly the primary location, how is research activity distributed across the various institutional sectors of the system? Here Trow and Fulton found something that is really quite interesting. While some research activity occurs at every sort of institution, there *is* something of a division between so-called research and teaching institutions. But it lies, not between the universities with a substantial commitment to graduate education and the four- and two-year undergraduate colleges, but between the universities and top tier of four-year colleges, on the one hand, and the less highly selective four- and two-year colleges on the other. On this, they note, as on other matters, a "fault-line" runs between the "high quality" four-year colleges and the rest. Below that level "research seems to be a spare-time activity, whereas above this point it is recognized and fostered by the institution." And the "high quality" four-year colleges "show levels of research activity by their regular staff that in sheer rate of publication are close to those of the lesser universities, and markedly higher than those of the great majority of four- and two-year colleges."[23]

Given the fact that these leading undergraduate colleges are celebrated (and justifiably so) for the intensity of their commitment to undergraduate education, this particular finding naturally led Trow and Fulton to a final set of questions pertaining to the relationship of research to teaching and other professional commitments in those universities and colleges where most of the research was being done. And here (still analyzing the 1969 Carnegie date) they found that while those faculty who published most frequently did more graduate teaching than the non-publishers, they were "not much more likely to discourage undergraduates from seeing them outside office hours; and scarcely less likely to see undergraduates informally." At the leading research universities, indeed, there was "surprisingly little difference between researchers and non-researchers in their level of teaching activity" overall, and, so far as governance and administration were concerned, the most active researchers were "much more likely [than their less active colleagues] to be involved in the administrative processes of their department and their institution."[24] The data being used, of course, speak to the *quality* of that teaching or administrative work no more than they do to the quality of the research being accomplished. But they do suggest that one should not simply assume that some sort of zero-sum game is necessarily involved. The common view that a heavy commitment to research is necessarily bought at the cost of reduced attention to teaching and other institutional service is clearly not warranted. In aggregate, at least, it does not appear to be true of highly productive scholars at our leading research universities. Such people seem to do more of everything, and the crucial variable may well be, not differing interests, but differential levels of energy.

Trow and Fulton noted that their basic conclusions concerning the comparatively favorable climate to teaching prevailing in American higher education were consistent with independent findings reported earlier on by others in the 1960s.[25] And they are consistent also with the data generated by the 1989 Carnegie survey. These more recent data, it is true, reveal something of a shift over the previous twenty years in a research-oriented direction. Whereas in 1969 some 77 percent of the professoriate had considered themselves to be committed primarily to teaching, only 70 percent reported that commitment in 1989. And whereas in 1969 some 69 percent had never published or edited a book, in 1989 the comparable figure was 56 percent.[26] But the general picture is not dissimilar to that painted earlier on by Trow and Fulton, and it is congruent also with that sketched in 1979 by Everett Carll Ladd on the basis both of the Carnegie data and of independent surveys which he and Seymour Martin Lipset had conducted in 1977 and 1979. With only 7 percent of the American professoriate indicating that their interests lay heavily in research, and with less than one-fourth publishing extensively (i.e. 20 or more articles and/or 3 or more monographs), he concluded that "[m]ost college and university professors in the United States do not think of themselves as research people. Their interests lie primarily in teaching. They spend most of their time in teaching and related activities. And a clear majority of faculty have published little or nothing."[27]

All of this seems clear enough. It has to be taken into account, and it offers cold comfort to those intent upon claiming that the atmosphere in the academy is "hostile to teaching," that academics characteristically "shun" teaching for research, that they are, in effect, in "full flight from teaching."

So far as self-reported attitudes are concerned, moreover, the most recent data do little to support the sense, now commonplace, that because of their training and research commitments the allegiance of faculty members is to their academic disciplines rather than to teaching or to their colleges and universities.[28] Only 2 percent of faculty overall were willing to admit that their academic discipline was fairly *un*important to them; 98 percent proclaimed it to be "very" or "fairly" important, and, in that respect, faculty at the two-year colleges, where little research is done, felt exactly the same way as those at the research universities.[29] At the same time, 85 percent of faculty overall also declared that their college or university was "very" or "fairly" important to them. That figure does reflect a range running from 91 percent at the liberal arts and two-year colleges to 80 percent at the research universities. But it is still an impressive and reassuring one. And whereas disciplinary allegiance has remained stable, institutional loyalty appears to be growing. In the 1984 Carnegie survey only 29 percent of the respondents reported that their college or university was "very important" to them. By 1989 that figure had risen to 40 percent.[30]

Not all the data, however, are as reassuring. As Ernest Boyer has pointed out, whereas in 1969 some 21 percent of those surveyed "strongly agreed" that it was difficult in their department to attain tenure if one did not publish, by 1989 that figure had risen to 42 percent. Sixteen percent, moreover, strongly agreed that the pressure to publish was having the effect at their college or university of reducing the quality of teaching. That figure ranged from 24 percent at the research universities to 8 percent at the liberal arts and two-year colleges.[31] There is some room for argument about the degree to which that pressure is self-imposed, imposed by the institutional structure of extrinsic incentives and rewards, or, for that matter, imposed by the expectations that society at large has for our universities and colleges.[32] But it seems clear that the institutional incentive and reward structure (in aggregate, at least) is strongly tilted in the direction of research. And therein lies ground for concern. After brooding about the survey data, which he conceded did not provide "any firm information" on the matter, and after talking to hundreds of faculty members and administrators nationwide, Ladd concluded in 1979 "that most faculty don't like research and don't do it very well, if at all." In effect, he added, "an ascendant model in academe, positing what faculty *should be doing,* is seriously out of touch with what they *actually do* and *want to do.*"[33] Most faculty, after all, indicate that their interests lie primarily in teaching; and over 60 percent believe that teaching effectiveness rather than research and publication should be the primary criterion for the promotion of faculty. That 92 percent of the faculty at the two-year colleges should feel that way should come as no surprise; that they should be joined in that sentiment by 41 percent of those at the doctorate-granting universities and 21 percent even of those at our research universities is somewhat more startling. The research-oriented incentive and reward structure dominant (though not universal) in the academy appears at least to be poorly aligned with what most faculty are doing, want to do, and believe it to be their mission to do. And that being so, it is hard to resist Boyer's conclusion that "the research mission, . . . appropriate for *some* institutions [has] created a shadow over the entire higher learning enterprise," and that "far too many colleges and universities are being driven not by self-defined objectives but by the external imperatives of prestige."[34] On this matter there are clearly plausible reasons for criticism and persuasive grounds for a call to reformative change. To this point we will return in the following chapter. But it is a far cry from alarmist and punitive talk about a flight from teaching or even a hostility to it, the existence of which the available evidence simply does not support.

4. The plight of the humanities and the matter of general education

In connection with the current state of general education and, in particular, the condition of the humanities at our colleges and universities, the charges commonly made are both quantitative and qualitative. That is to say, they concern the decline in the number of undergraduates choosing to major in humanities subjects as well as what our universities and colleges are doing (or not doing) to respond to that discouraging trend. And the latter naturally connects, in the second place, with the degree to which general education has, indeed, become "an idea in distress."

So far as the first, or quantitative issue is concerned, decline in the percentages of undergraduates concentrating in the humanities there certainly has been, and few academics would be disposed to take that decline at all lightly. But the terms on which it has usually been understood have been framed by the citation of statistics by Bennett and Cheney that cover the last two decades only, and by the suggestions that they and others have made to the effect that our universities and colleges must bear the brunt of the blame for that decline because of their failure "to reestablish a sense of educational purpose, to give form and substance to undergraduate curricula, and to restore the humanities to a central place."[35] The "high cost [i.e. high *price*] of higher education," encouraging college students to pursue vocational courses of study, academic specialization, incoherent curricula, failure "to bring the humanities to life," the obscure, tendentiously ideological and politicized manner in which the subject matter is approached— such are the explanations of the "flight from the humanities" that these and other critics have offered. "It may well be the case," Roger Kimball speculates in *Tenured Radicals*, "that the much publicized decline in humanities enrollments recently is due at least in part to students' refusal to devote their college education to a program of study that has nothing to offer them but ideological posturing, pop culture, and hermeneutic word games."[36]

Such explanations, however, rarely depart from the realm of the speculative and themselves smack of a certain amount of ideological posturing. As we saw in the last chapter, to which for a more extended discussion I must refer the reader,[37] the whole statistical question is a complex one, calling for a more carefully nuanced and certainly less casual treatment than it has usually received. In particular, if we are not to exaggerate the significance and extent of the decline in humanities enrollments we must pay due attention, in determining the trend line, to our chronological point of departure. And we must also be cognizant of the marked differences in what has been going on in the very varied institutional sectors into which American higher education is divided. Roger Kimball, for example, has a good deal of fun at the expense of the authors of *Speaking for the Humanities* (the American Council of Learned Societies' pamphlet responding to the Bennett and Cheney reports) for their piecemeal and rather fumbling attempt to question or qualify the evidence indicating a decline in humanities enrollments. *"Speaking for the Humanities,"* he says,

> responds in essence, with the time-honored two-step known as backing and filling. It goes something like this: Yes, there has been a nationwide decline in humanities enrollments, but it was not due to the way the humanities were being taught; no, there wasn't such a big decline in enrollments after all, and even if there were, people such as Secretary Bennett and Lynne Cheney don't understand its real significance; O.K., there was a precipitous decline in humanities enrollments, but... [etc.].[38]

But, Kimball to the contrary, their puzzlement is understandable. It was not, after all, the type of institution with which they were affiliated—the "high-price," research-oriented university where what Kimball parodies as "ideological posturing, pop culture, and hermeneutic word games" are most deeply entrenched—that accounted, statistically speaking, for the decline in question. At *their* sort of institution, as they (rather woundedly) claimed, the humanities were alive and well and, of late, attracting increasing enrollments. Instead, and as we have seen,[39] among the baccalaureate-granting institutions it was the (lower-priced) comprehensive colleges and universities and such other four-year institutions as the state colleges that have seen the sharpest and most continuous declines in arts and sciences enrollments since the early 1970s. These are institutional sectors which by tradition had not focused very much of their attention on the liberal arts but which had nonetheless seen during the 1960s the sharpest *increase* in arts and sciences enrollments. What seems to have happened, Bowen and Sosa suggest, is that under the pressure of shrinking applicant pools from the early 1970s onward, "and, in some cases, even threats to institutional well-being," there was a decline at those institutions in their commitment to the arts and sciences in general. And, having suggested that, they are led, accordingly, to raise "the question of whether we are witnessing a movement in American higher education toward greater specialization by sector," with greater polarization "between sectors that have a strong professional/vocational orientation and sectors that give a greater emphasis to traditional fields within the arts and sciences," the humanities, of course, not excluded.[40]

While such a development would bring with it its own set of worries and concerns, it would be a far cry from talk linking a decline in humanities' enrollments with such phenomena as high tuition charges, curricular incoherence, and the politicization of teaching. And a far cry, too, from the dominant preoccupation of the critics, who appear to reserve the full force of their disapproval for the nation's leading research universities—the institutions, precisely, that enjoy such a good press abroad.[41] Foreign reputations notwithstanding, such institutions stand accused of having permitted themselves in their undergraduate course of studies to drift away from the tried and true modalities of general education. They are seen to have reneged, no less by choice than indirection, on their fundamental obligation to familiarize generations of students with their own cultural heritage by acquainting them with "the best that has been thought and said." And, with that charge, we arrive at the qualitative question.

That academic specialization, the balkanization of disciplines, the fragmentation of knowledge, the inability (or unwillingness) to honor and nurture the generalizing spirit should be the focus of concern in so many of the recent reports and critiques should not be cause for surprise. That well-justified concern has long been commonplace in educational circles. Even before the German research ideal had begun to exert its full influence on the English and American universities, Cardinal Newman had argued that "the end of a Liberal Education is not mere knowledge" and that intense application to a particular specialized field did not conduce to the end of truly enlarging the mind.[42] And once that research ideal had been installed in the leading American universities, old as well as new, it was not long before the first notes were heard of what was quickly to become a steady drumbeat of complaint about its damaging impact upon undergraduate education. From the literary "generalists" of the late nineteenth century to the "New Humanists" of the early twentieth, from the contemporaneous opposition to the free-elective system to the advocacy between the two world wars and after the second of the type of general education advocated so passionately by Robert Maynard Hutchins and Mortimer Adler, the line of descent to the current chorus of concern is easy enough to trace.[43]

That oppositional lineage is by no means an ignoble one. We should not permit ourselves to forget that before the First World War some prominent institutions were managing with even fewer curricular requirements than is usually the case today, and that at institutions like Harvard, where President Eliot's advocacy of the free elective system had eventually met with sweeping success, the degree of confusion and disarray in the undergraduate course of study was truly formidable and called urgently for rectification.[44] And a nagging and, in many ways, understandable concern about curricular incoherence has continued to plague higher education ever since and to generate the periodic, passionate, intensely serious, and invariably long drawn-out debates about the undergraduate course of study with which no academic can be totally unfamiliar. Precisely because of that it seems almost redundant to recall that, just as there is no general agreement today about such things, neither was there any general agreement at the start of the century about the best means for rectifying the excesses of the free elective system. Instead, the means urged (and employed) were multiple. The establishment of subject majors and minors was one part of the story; so, too, a little later on, the creation of honors programs for juniors and seniors. The pattern of concentration and distribution (with the student required to concentrate in a major field of study and for purposes of educational breadth to take a stipulated number of courses from each of several groups distinguished from one another by disparate intellectual methods) was by far the most widespread response. The general educational or core-curricular approach (with stipulated courses required of all students), and especially the "great books" version of that approach, was a somewhat later arrival on the educational scene. It rose to prominence in the interwar years, flourished for a while after the Second World War, but failed to establish a firm foothold in the bulk of American colleges and universities. That approach made its strongest appeal by way of reaction, it may be, at places like Chicago and Stanford where the free elective system had been "indulged with complete and enthusiastic abandon."[45] But there were colleges of comparatively conservative curricular bent whose traditionalism had served in the late nineteenth century as a bulwark against the inroads of the free elective fashion, and where the core-curricular approach made no impact at all.[46]

This being so, one could hardly expect the recent commentaries on the American undergraduate experience to speak with a common voice when they turn from the depiction of curricular disarray (real or imagined) to the prescription of remedies for that condition. And they do not, in fact, do so. Two of them, indeed, the American Association of Colleges' *Integrity in the College Curriculum* and Ernest Boyer's *College: The Undergraduate Experience in America,* place their emphasis not on "structure" or "coverage" but on the "how" of teaching and learning. Thus Boyer, while proposing an unusual sort of core pivoting on "common themes" cutting across the various disciplines, expresses his confident sense that "the goals of general education, when properly defined, can be accomplished through the major."[47] And the authors of *Integrity in the College Curriculum* boldly "propose that faculties focus on the 'how' and allow their sense of what is essential and appropriate to a common culture to shape the selection of the 'what'."[48]

But that is precisely what those critics of more conservative bent who have attracted the most public attention are simply not prepared to do. For them, it is content, above all, that matters. "[M]erely being exposed to a variety of subjects and points of view is not enough. Learning to think critically and skeptically is not enough." What is crucial is that students be called upon to "master an explicit body of knowledge" and to "confront a series of important original texts."[49] And the determination of that content and the choice of those texts is hardly something to be left to the vagaries of faculty selection or to the demonstrably uncertain sense among academics of what it takes to enable us to "become participants in a common culture, shareholders in our civilization." That content, indeed, is seen as so obvious that it does not call for extended justification. At its heart lies the mediation of the Western cultural heritage, a task to be achieved above all through the required exposure of all students to the great works of the Western cultural tradition. Those works are not to be "approached exclusively as documents of time and place." For they have been recognized as classics precisely because of the profundity with which they address "perennial matters of human experience" and the power with which they mediate the culture's "lasting vision, its highest shared ideals and aspirations, and its heritage."[50]

The virtues attaching to this approach are considerable, not only because of the stature of the works usually proposed for study or the degree to which they do indeed serve to acquaint students with a sense of shared heritage (and, therefore, with the inherited furnishings of their own minds), but also because it serves perhaps more effectively than any other approach to establish among all students on a campus a rudimentary foundation on which to build a community of shared discourse. About the enthusiastic advocacy of such a position, then, there is nothing at all odd, and it has served on countless campuses to sharpen the endless and (in my experience) deeply thoughtful and conscientious debates about the undergraduate course of study. What is odd, however, is the *nature* of the current advocacy: its lack of historical self-consciousness, its serene assumption of self-evidence, its impatient dismissal of alternative approaches, however widely followed, and the edge of passionate dismay that has sometimes led its proponents to impute unworthy motives to those who disagree with them.

By lack of historical self-consciousness I mean two things. First, the ironic failure of the proponents, in the very process of emphasizing the importance of a knowledge of the Western cultural tradition, to recognize how conflicted in its intellectual commitments and educational ideals that tradition has been. In that very conflictedness, indeed, may be found the wellsprings of that cultural singularity which the proponents of the great books approach rightly think students should be helped to recognize and understand.[51] But of this one hears nothing. Nor is there anything to suggest that those proponents recognize the persistently destabilizing impact across the centuries of the fundamental tension between some of the positions characteristic of the Greek philosophical tradition, and other commitments, both intellectual and moral, that are ultimately of Biblical provenance.[52] Nor do they appear to realize that by their own emphasis on the required study of the "great works of the Western tradition," on the duty of the university or college to convey "the accumulated wisdom of our civilization," and on the duty of the scholar to "preserve the record of human accomplishment and make it accessible in many ways,"[53] they have themselves tilted toward the rhetorical vision of liberal education. And to say that means that they have also inclined away from the philosophical-scientific vision which (as we have seen)[54] has been less concerned with the preservation and mediation of the cultural heritage than with discovery, critical originality, and the advancement of knowledge through the overthrow of received assumptions.

Almost fifty years ago, in his own advocacy of the approach to general education with which these critics sympathize, Robert Maynard Hutchins was moved to contend that "Education implies teaching. Teaching implies knowledge. Knowledge is truth. The truth is everywhere the same. Hence education should be everywhere the same." Despite the quasi-syllogistic form in which he and his rather irascible colleague Mortimer Adler liked to cast their arguments, and despite the appeals to the authority of Aristotle and Aquinas with which he garnished them, his extraordinary claim failed to convince many of his contemporaries to accept his educational vision. As Harry Gideonse, his colleague on the faculty at Chicago pointed out, "it may be true that no consistent philosophy or metaphysics 'lies beneath the American university of today.'" But to insist that the work of higher education should be informed by "a unifying philosophy, without specific indication of the type of unity or of philosophy, is to miss the essential problem underlying the modern dilemma."[55] Nor, despite periodic attempts at revival, has Hutchins's vision fared all that much better in subsequent years. For most, the drawbacks to the approach he favored appear to have outweighed its indisputable strengths. And the classic reasons for their dissent, though they long predate the present discontents, remain pertinent today. Among them are the following: That the "great books" version of the core curricular approach sponsors amateurishness in teaching (faculty rarely do their best teaching when required to handle subjects they may know little or nothing about); that it dampens enthusiasm for learning (students learn best when they are free to pursue their own curricular interests); that it encourages superficiality by treating profound and classic texts as "quick reads," as the "best sellers of ancient times"; that far from deepening the student's sense of the past, it fosters a superficial and misleading "presentism" by approaching ancient texts as if they were "contemporary documents," which they clearly are not.[56]

Of such long-standing concerns we do not hear much from the most fashionable of current critics,[57] whose lack of historical self-consciousness extends not only to the more distant European past, but also, and perhaps more surprisingly, to the more recent history of educational debate in America. They focus tightly on the present, urging their curricular agenda with a degree of confidence that comes close to suggesting an unreflecting conviction of self-evidence, and betraying a disagreeable tendency to explain its otherwise inexplicable failure to carry the day by invoking the specters of intellectual confusion, laziness and self-interest on the part of faculty, compounded by spinelessness and failure of leadership on the part of administrators. And fueling this tendency, at least in such conservative critics as Allan Bloom and Roger Kimball, is a sense of profound alienation from our contemporary academic culture, and a surge of passionate dismay at the direction in which some of the most powerful intellectual currents

of our postmodern era now appear to be sweeping our universities
and colleges.

5. Core, canon, grounding, and dissent

The fabric of this passionate conservative critique is tightly and com-
plexly woven. It is not at all easy to tease apart the strands that make
it up and my own attempt to do so will almost certainly strike some
as an oversimplification. There is a sense, in this case, in which the
whole is at once both less and more than the sum of its parts. And
the several strands that compose that whole, while they may currently
enjoy a sort of elective affinity one with another, should be recognized
as essentially distinct—distinct in their origins, distinct in their implications, and, in all probability, distinct in their respective destinies.

While a multitude of strands, then, have gone into the weaving
of this bitter fabric of dismay, what more than anything else seems to
hold them together is a continuing sense of revulsion, viscerally felt,
for the "radical vision" and "emancipationist ideology" prevalent
among the student insurgents during the campus upheavals of the late
1960s. Those students, according to Bloom, were peddlers of a species
of "values with fallen arches." They were people who substituted the
"claims of passionate commitment" for the disinterested quest for
understanding; sweeping aside in a veritable paroxysm of indignation
("of all experiences of the soul ... the most inimical to reason and
hence to the university") the pallid pretensions of academic intellec-
tualism.[58] According to Bennett, it was the "collective loss of nerve
and faith on the part of both faculty and academic administrators"
when confronted with this leftist upheaval of the student spirit that
proved to be so "destructive of the curriculum."[59] And he appears to
have assumed that campus conditions of the 1980s could properly be
assimilated to those prevailing during those earlier years of turmoil.[60]
In few instances, indeed, is more strikingly evident the way in which
so much "of our critical and cultural argument operates on a principle
of guilt-by-association" than it is in the neoconservative evocation of
the 1960s.[61] For some historians, certainly, those of robustly objectivist
convictions who felt threatened by the drift toward cognitive and
cultural relativism evident in contemporary historical studies, Peter
Novick has suggested that "the sixties" became

> a term of art which encompassed student insurgency and faculty members
> who had cravenly or opportunistically condoned it; Black Studies, Wom-

en's Studies, and affirmative action programs; "ideological" scholarship" (of the left), and any scholarship not pursued "for its own sake." For many hyperobjectivists, bitter memories of the sixties, and often exaggerated estimates of its residue, were lumped together with various relativistic "postmodern" currents into an undifferentiated and monstrous Other which had to be combated if liberal rationalism was to survive.[62]

Given the degree of anachronism which that point of view involves, its sympathizers appear to have condemned themselves to a "losing battle with ghosts and chimeras."[63] Nonetheless, under the looming shadow of that "monstrous Other" fears have continued to proliferate, and none more luxuriantly than those focused on the growth of a preoccupation with "multiculturalism," the unraveling of the general education approach pivoting on required core courses in Western Civilization or on the study of the canon of great books of the Western tradition (or on some combination of the two), and the flowering of programs in Third World studies, Women's Studies or minority studies of one sort or another. Thus for Bennett the study of Western civilization which should properly be "the heart and soul" of the American college curriculum has been shunted to one side.[64] For Lynne Cheney that fact reflects the growing politicization in our era of studies in the humanities.[65] And for Roger Kimball the voice dominant "in the humanities departments of many of our best colleges and universities" is one that with "remarkable unity of purpose" seeks to subvert "the tradition of high culture embodied in the classics of Western art and thought."[66]

From this point of view what we are currently witnessing in our universities and colleges—perhaps most strikingly at our high-prestige institutions—is a debilitating balkanization of studies in the humanities and social sciences, a ragged retreat into a congeries of competing (and often aggressively ideological) particularisms, an abandonment of the high ground of disinterested universalism which it had once been the great distinction of the academy to occupy. And that conclusion provides a ready linkage with another principal strand in this gloomy pattern, a set of fears that resonate more broadly throughout the intellectual world, starting echoes of older inconclusive confrontations, calling for a clarifying alignment in opposition of the forces of light, and evoking the age-old specter of the Final Days, in this case a great and cataclysmic struggle for survival on the war-torn battle ground of cognition.

The fears in question appear to be stimulated by the open enthusiasm with which literary theorists of poststructuralist bent in some of our leading departments of English and Comparative Literature have reached out to embrace one or other form of cognitive or cultural relativism.[67] Similarly, though the focus tends to be on those in literature, those fears have been stimulated also by the "postmodern" drift of anthropologists, philosophers, cultural historians, law-school faculty sympathetic with critical legal studies in a similar direction. Such fears resonate in the critiques of Bennett, Cheney, Kimball and D'Souza, all of whom to one degree or another invoke the specter of an undifferentiated "intellectual relativism," an "anti-foundationalist creed" that supplants "reason by rhetoric, truth by persuasion," denying the very possibility of "objective" and "genuinely universal" truths, seeing "all meaning" as "subjective and relative to one's own perspective," subordinating our studies, accordingly, "to contemporary prejudices," infusing the whole intellectual and educational effort with a debilitating measure of skepticism, "reducing all truth to the level of opinion," ceding, in effect, the hard-won ground secured by Plato from the Sophists of his day, and, as a result, denying ultimately the very "legitimacy of any distinction between truth and error."[68]

But it is left to Allan Bloom to confront this set of fears most directly. He does so in the course of his passionately quirky dissent from much that is commonplace in our contemporary intellectual life, articulating what he regards as the crucial points at issue with a candor no less brutal for being quite so eloquent. Relativism—cognitive, cultural, moral—is something, he suggests, that our students have absorbed from the very first day they set foot in school. "[O]penness . . . is the great insight of our times," and it is relativism "that makes it the only plausible stance in the face of the various claims to truth and various ways of life and kinds of human beings" in which our world abounds. "[T]hat values or culture are relative" is the "philosophical premise," at once both "dogmatic" and "unproven" that "we now bring to our study of them." On the one hand, "cultural relativism" has succeeded "in destroying the West's universal or intellectually imperialistic claims, leaving it to be just another culture." On the other, "value relativism" and "the radical subjectivity of all belief about good and evil" have left us in a situation where no value is "rationally or objectively preferable to any other." To Friedrich Nietzsche, the nineteenth-century John the Baptist to this point of view, its ascendancy was an "unparalleled catastrophe" involving nothing less than a free fall "into the abyss of nihilism, the decomposition of culture and the loss of human aspiration." To contemporary Americans, however, easy-going and unquestioning consumers of the form of "pop relativism" currently fashionable, that nihilism is no more than "a mood of moodiness, a vague disquiet. It is nihilism without the abyss." And it is a mood well adapted to the ingestion of the ripe fruit of the Nietzschean intuition—most commonly by our departments of English and Comparative Literature and with remarkably little curiosity about philosophical origin or foundation. Harvested by the German philosopher Martin Heidegger, packaged by "the post-Sartrean generation of Parisian Heideggerians" (notably, he says, Roland Barthes, Michel Foucault and Jacques Derrida), and marketed under the brand name of Deconstruction, it has been eagerly appropriated by many American literary theorists and critics as a brilliant and supple textual strategy capable of producing new and exciting readings of old and hackneyed texts.[69] But there is more to it than that. Proclaiming the priority of language to meaning, the inability of our words to escape the orbit of language itself and to establish referential contact with an extra-linguistic reality, the possession by texts, therefore, of "an *irreducible* plurality" of meanings,[70] Deconstruction, as Bloom intuits it, renders "the interpreter's creative activity ... more important than the text," so that "the one thing most necessary for us, the knowledge of what these texts have to tell us, is turned over to the subjective, creative selves of these interpreters, who say that there is both no text and no reality to which the texts refer." It represents, in effect (he says), "the last, predictable, stage in the suppression of reason and the denial of the possibility of truth in the name of philosophy."[71] Or, as one of the earlier American critics of Deconstruction put it, it seems clear that in its most extreme forms, at least, what is being urged by these thinkers, so eagerly oversold by their American admirers, is "a mode of reading which undermines ... the possibility of understanding language as a medium of decidable meanings," and, even in its less extreme versions, one that in its thoroughgoing relativism or "perspectivism" "eventuates in a radical skepticism about our ability to achieve a correct interpretation."[72]

Caught up in this whole formidable tangle of concerns and fears are some truly substantive issues that clearly warrant a serious and painstaking exercise in appraisal. But it is not one that can readily be mounted without a prior effect at clarification. That task is destined to be a difficult one. The more so, given the willingness of some spokespeople for the cultural left to match the hyperbolic confusion of their conservative critics and, by the heated imprecision of their own confessions of ideological faith, to lend a patina of credibility to the sweeping charges of intellectual malfeasance and moral confusion levied against them.[73] The effort, however, has to be made. And as an opening move we should separate from the campus events of the late 1960s and the contemporaneous flowering of the counterculture, such developments as the rise of minority and feminist studies, the decline of the Western Civilization and core-curricular approach to general education, and the rise to prominence in our intellectual discourse of various forms of perspectivism and relativism. That move is a crucial one because the tendency to portray all these disparate phenomena as a tarnished residue of the 1960s serves not only to heighten the degree of passionate confusion surrounding the discussion that swirls about them, but also to trivialize them and to diminish their historical significance.

When attempting to assess the validity of charges about the alleged "politicization" of our studies or the damaging impact of "multiculturalism" (a word with more than one meaning), it is important, for example, to take due note of the fact that the roots of the women's movement are deeply engaged in nineteenth-century soil and that the growth in our universities of programs in women's studies actually occurred during the 1970s and 1980s when the tumult and upheaval of the late 1960s had begun to recede into history. We should similarly recognize the fact that the establishment of programs of study in the range of areas that later came to be lumped together as the "Third World" took place in the 1950s and early 1960s, and that the impulse which led in the 1960s and 1970s to the establishment of programs in Afro-American studies was generated by the change in relations between the races that had begun in the years after the Second World War and had peaked in the mid-1960s with the historic achievements of the civil rights movement.[74] And, as for the Western Civilization/core-curricular approach to general education, seeds of doubt about its viability had begun to germinate even before the 1950s, when that approach was to enjoy its heyday. It is often forgotten that the compulsory core courses advocated in 1945 in the Harvard Redbook, the committee report "that thereafter became the scripture in the general education movement," never came to be offered at Harvard College itself. Instead, they came to be replaced at first by two to four optional courses and, later, by many more. To serve as the core course in the social sciences the Redbook had provided for a history course in Western civilization. But the faculty did not approve it. And one of the reasons for rejecting it was their objection to the notion that "Western history" was "the 'high history' of mankind." "In rejecting the course," Allardyce has said, "Harvard faculty members, in principle, rejected the historical pre-eminence of Western man." And he goes on to say that

> this breakup of an educational creed coincided with the breakup of the world that inspired it. Much of the deep structure of general education lay in a psychology developed during a half-century of U.S. involvement in the "crusade for democracy" in Europe. In logic that mixed patriotism and pedagogy, educators equated core courses with common values, the need for unity in the republic with the need for unity in the curriculum, and the Western military alliance with Western civilization. With the passing of the Cold War, however, there passed also the illusions that sustained general education as a civil religion.[75]

Even if that claim is somewhat exaggerated, and on more than one point (and it is), it still has the merit of reminding us that the Western Civilization course was "a war baby" in "both its remote and immediate origins," as "a continuation [at Columbia College immediately after World War I] of the 'war issue courses offered during hostilities" and as a reflection at Harvard after World War II of "the need to provide a 'common learning' for all Americans as a foundation of national unity."[76] It has the merit also of underlining the fact that the "politicization of the curriculum," no less worrisome in the past, it may be, than it is today, has been with us for a long time. Certainly, so far as history is concerned, while the ideological polarization characteristic of Europe was absent in America, the eager embrace by historians of a propagandistic role during World War I and "the overall development of American historical writing in the interwar years" served to give "cold comfort to those who had pinned their hopes on a convergent, objective historiography." Like their predecessors all the way back to "the early days of the profession," historians engaged in the writing of textbooks were forced to "adjust" their texts in response to the lobbying of "local, regional, ethnic, or patriotic pressure groups"—veterans of the Grand Army of the Republic, Minnesotans determined to vindicate the discovery of America by their ancestral Norsemen, Irish and German groups reacting "against the Anglophile version of the American Revolution promoted [patriotically] by historians during the [Great] war" and so on.[77] And it was the growing recognition of the impact of a degree of "politicization" and of the shaping presence in our historiography of ideological commitments of one sort or another that led so many in the interwar years to sympathize with the relativistic challenge that Carl Becker and Charles Beard (both of them, in their turn, presidents of the American Historical Association) handed down to what Theodore Clarke Smith of

Williams College attempted passionately in 1934 to vindicate. Namely, what he referred to as the "noble dream" of an historiography inspired throughout by "the ideal of the effort for objective truth."[78]

Relativism, of course, whether cognitive, cultural or moral, was no more a novelty in the 1930s than it is today in the 1990s. Its foundations are so deeply embedded in the Western philosophical tradition as to make it an integral part of the Western cultural heritage. As is evident from Plato's attack in the *Theaetetus* on the relativism of Protagoras, it had put in an appearance at the very dawn of European philosophy. But it began to make a truly strong impact only during the course of the nineteenth century. It did so in the wake of Kant's overriding emphasis on the role of the mind in shaping the way in which we experience the world and of Herder's sharp reaction "against the Enlightenment idea of a single universal human nature and of an inevitable development of all societies through the same series of fixed stages ending in an ideal state."[79] Thus later thinkers were led, while abandoning Kant's own objectivism, to radicalize his idea that "the mind provides basic concepts with which experience is organized and interpreted." At the same time, they were led to link that idea with the notion of cultural differences and historical development in such a way as to suggest that, in interpreting our ongoing experience of the world, we are destined to have to negotiate our way among alternative and differing conceptual schemata, none more natural or valid than the other.[80]

During the course of the twentieth century that notion, entailing one or other form of cognitive or cultural relativism, has become so widespread as almost to constitute a characteristic feature of our modern intellectual landscape. Certainly, it has made a profound impact on historical studies as well as upon anthropology and the other social sciences. And what seems to have been of decisive importance in thrusting the issue of historical relativism into the center of debate during the interwar years was (properly or improperly understood) the revolution which had occurred during the late-nineteenth and early twentieth century in mathematical and physical thinking. Among other things, that great upheaval undercut the "conception of science as highly organized common sense, continuous with everyday experience," one that provided "unambiguous truth; knowledge that was definite, and independent of the values or intentions of the investigator." Upon that conception of science "the traditional understanding of historical objectivity" had been based, and with its collapse the way was opened up for the entry onto the historiographic stage of the relativistic challenge with Becker, Beard and their associates handed down to the profession. They did so, by and large, with moderation and good humor, but, in the great uproar that ensued, they were harshly attacked as promoters of skepticism and a debilitating irrationalism. Indeed, as Novick points out, "the responses they received" from their objectivist colleagues "were often uttered in the voice of the Church denouncing and excommunicating heretics."[81]

That fact suggests gloomy comparisons with the tone of our current debate concerning higher education at large. But it should also help us to put the current "postmodern" vogue of relativistic views into a less misleading perspective than that provided by the suggestion or assumption that it is the outcome of some great fall from intellectual or educational grace encouraged by the leftist insurgency and countercultural confusion of the late 1960s. Nor should its strong resonance for those involved in feminist or black studies be taken to reflect much more than an elective affinity. Given the degree to which the earlier historiography, so often universalist and objectivist in its claim to present the results of a disinterested enquiry into the past, had somehow contrived to reserve for women and members of racial minorities a condition of quasi-invisibility, it would be odd, indeed, if such an affinity did not exist. After a postwar interlude of quiescence and retreat it is from developments of a different nature that the more recent recrudescence of relativistic views stems. And among those developments the most important is a philosophic turbulence comparable in severity with that which sapped the foundations of mathematics and physics at the turn of the century. But the upheaval this time does not concern our understanding of the natural world but rather the very "concept and understanding of language" itself. And it has evoked nothing less than the specter of the "dissociation of language from reality" and the "subversion" of our common sense notion of a "correspondence between the word and the empirical world."[82] Although there are some novelties in the current and specifically "postmodern" evocation of relativistic or perspectival views, what is more striking is the intensity with which it has focused our attention, not on anything new, but on what has emerged over the course of a century and more as the central intellectual dilemma of modernity. "Postmodern" is a markedly flexible and accommodating word. But in this respect at least there is clearly something to be said for those who have argued for an understanding of postmodernism "not as a break with romantic and modernist assumptions, but as a logical culmination of these earlier movements,"[83] as a direct continuation, indeed, of the modernist past from which it has so proudly proclaimed its secession.

To say that, it must be insisted, is not to dismiss as unimportant the current vogue of relativisms of one sort or another. It is, rather, to situate that vogue in a different and somewhat broader intellectual context and to see it as a manifestation of one of the central philosophical dilemmas of the whole modern era. And it is an issue that will not lend itself to resolution by some sort of quick rhetorical fix or by a triumph of the cognitive will of the type for which some of the critics seem to yearn. If the matter is to be effectively engaged we will have to resist the temptation to adapt the stance of philosophical Canutes bidding the tides of history to stand still. (Emulators of King Canute tend to emerge from the experience with their feet wet.) What is called for, instead, is a careful discrimination among the various species of relativism—some of which are clearly self-refuting, some less obviously so—and a sustained and probing exercise in philosophical reflection of the type mounted so impressively of recent years by such fine practitioners of the art as Charles Taylor and Alasdair MacIntyre.[84] And that type of philosophical reflection simply does not lend itself to marketing in eye-catching packages for instant mass consumption.

The brief exercise in historical contextualization and statistical exploration to which this chapter has been devoted is a regrettably sketchy one and it should not be mistaken for some sort of substantive effort to respond to the full range of charges our recent critics have levied against higher education in America. Its goal is other than that, and it will have achieved it if, as in the case of the alleged flights from teaching and from the humanities, it has succeeded in "downsizing" somewhat the dimensions of the problems being canvassed while in some degree refocusing the precise issue to which those of us in higher education would be well advised to devote our attention. It will also have met its goal if, as in the case of general education and the fate of the Western Civilization or great books approaches to general education, it has conveyed a reasonably clear sense of the degree to which such approaches, rather than being some comparatively timeless deliverance of an age-old Western past, are themselves of comparatively recent and specifically American vintage, and represent a by no means universal response to a very particular and time-specific set of educational challenges. Or again, it will have fulfilled its purpose if, as in the case of the rise to prominence in contemporary intellectual life of various forms of relativism, it has succeeded (by clarifying the intellectual lineage and underlining the importance of the issues involved) in detrivializing those issues and locating them where they properly belong—not amid the longueurs of our current educational malaise here in the United States, but somewhere closer to the conflicted heart of modern intellectual life worldwide.

This exercise in contextualization would not, however, be complete if, amid the distracting and discordant clamor of crisis talk,[85] and even as the corruption, collapse, and demise of American higher education are being so mystifyingly and obsessively proclaimed, one did not raise a puzzled voice to insist on a few simple and commonsensical facts. First, that more faculty are teaching at our colleges and universities than ever before, most of them (if my personal experience is not wholly misleading) with great dedication and care. Second, that more students than ever before are learning, some of them at levels of intellectual sophistication not often achieved by undergraduates in the past, and many for whom, not so long ago, a college education would have been wholly out of reach. Third, that colleges and universities continue to labor (with a degree of conscientiousness and commitment that the more punitive among their critics somehow contrive to ignore) to ensure that the whole great enterprise of teaching, learning and discovery to which our campuses are devoted will continue with undiminished vigor on into the future. That they are likely to do so in ways that will differ somewhat from the admired patterns of the past and the contested pathways of the present is only to be expected. But that they will do so is not to be doubted. The attempt to discern the future shape of the liberal arts tradition and the role, especially, of the liberal arts college in its mediation is not, then, to be abandoned as redundant. What can confidently be dismissed, instead, and as more than a trifle premature, is the tiresome (if plangently profitable) vogue of writing obituaries for the life of the mind as it has traditionally been pursued at our universities and colleges.

CHAPTER V

AGAINST NOSTALGIA:
The Future Shaping of the Tradition

... [I]n the last resort classical humanism was based on tradition, something imparted by one's teachers and handed on unquestioningly. This, incidentally, had a further advantage: it meant that all the minds of one generation, and indeed of a whole historical period, had a fundamental homogeneity which made communication and genuine communion easier. This is something we can all appreciate today, when we are floundering in a cultural anarchy. In a classical culture all men have in common a wealth of things they can all admire and emulate: the same rules; the same metaphors, images, words—the same language. Is there anyone acquainted with modern culture who can think of all of this without feeling a certain nostalgia?

Henri Marrou (1956)

Nostalgia, from νόστος (return home) and ἄλγος (pain):
A form of melancholia caused by prolonged absence from one's home or country; severe homesickness.

The Oxford English Dictionary

Without attempting to resolve the issues being raised, we reflected in the last chapter on the criticisms of higher education that have surfaced with such insistence of recent years, on their historical roots and on the contextual factors that have so often imparted to them their current force.

We are called upon now to come to a judgment about what all of this portends for the future of the tradition and for the role of the liberal arts college in mediating it. And one thing immediately seems clear: that given the burden of the past (the distant as well as the more recent) the likelihood of any spontaneous coincidence of views emerging on the matter is remote, and the viability of any publicly engineered consensus questionable. On this matter, as on others, we must expect people of perfectly good will to continue to differ. At the very outset, accordingly, we are called upon to recognize that fact with whatever grace we can muster, and cheerfully to proceed as best we can to make the case we ourselves find convincing. From this point on, then, perhaps I may be permitted to speak with a more personal voice. And as I myself ponder the future shaping of the tradition, several further things stand out to me as clear. The first involves the potent mixture of nostalgia and resentment that characterizes the harsher vein of recent criticism of American higher education. The second concerns the enormous institutional variety of that educational system and what it implies for the shaping of the tradition. The third speaks to the matter of multiculturalism—or, better, what may be referred to as the issue of cultural inclusion in the curriculum. The fourth involves the historical lineage of the current debates on the undergraduate course of study and the degree to which they mirror the great intellectual disagreements of our era. These four points I propose to take up in turn.

1. Nostalgia, cultural inclusion, rhetoric, and teaching

About the vein of resentment that runs through so much of the recent criticism of higher education in general and of the professoriate in particular I have nothing to say. It is by no means a feature of all the critiques[1] and any observations I might be tempted to make about it would be purely speculative. But about the kindlier, less troubling and more broadly distributed vein of nostalgia that often accompanies it a brief comment is in order. Nostalgia is doubtless one of the most distinctively human of emotions. But today, as the future presses in upon us so imperatively, I see little to recommend any extended indulgence in nostalgia for a spiritual homeland in which Americans have never dwelt or for a past that never was. Or at least, if in this we follow Henri Marrou,[2] for a past that was already under siege as long ago as the Hellenistic era when the liberal arts tradition was first crystallized. It is not through the evocation of such a past that we can expect today to find a pathway to the future. That the great educational achievements of days gone by warrant our admiration and attachment is not, of course, in question. In this as in other matters we would do well to pay heed to Edmund Burke's observation that "people will not look forward to posterity who never look back to their ancestors."[3] Few authors have succeeded so well in evoking the mysterious measure in which institutions contrive to embody human meanings and intentions and project them boldly forward across the hostility of time. But Burke was also deeply conscious of the degree to which individual societies are shaped by the dense particularities of their own histories. That is no less true of educational communities than it is of others, and no reasonably conscientious effort to canvass the past of those communities discloses even fugitive glimpses of that high plateau of pedagogic distinction, educational rectitude and curricular cohesion against which we might measure the dimensions of that great fall from grace which the recent critics seem so ready to attribute to the present.

Some years ago, in the course of writing a book on the Western church on the eve of the Reformation, I was forced to come to terms with the extent to which the allegations of widespread corruption and decay so prevalent in the works of the chroniclers and publicists of the day, far from being sober descriptions by reasonably dispassionate observers of the contemporary scene, were often crudely propagandistic or nationalistic in purpose. And many that were not were shaped, nonetheless, by an unreflective commitment to the view that the world was necessarily destined, as it grew older and left behind it the pristine ideals of its youth, to become more and more corrupt. So powerful, indeed, was the hold of this latter view on some contemporary commentators that they saw nothing problematic about using to describe what they saw as the decline of religious life in the fifteenth century whole passages lifted (as we now realize) from *twelfth-* and *thirteenth-*century writers describing the conditions prevailing in the Church of their own day.[4] That experience taught me a lesson that conduces to a certain wariness about the ease with which contemporary commentators deplore the curricular and pedagogic practices of our own day as if they must necessarily reflect some declension from the high standards of the past. We should not allow ourselves to forget, for example, that as far back as the beginning of the present century, it had become common to remark upon the drawbacks of the then ascendant mode of instruction by lecture. At that time, indeed, a Harvard committee concluded that "there was too much teaching [at Harvard College] and not enough studying." Students, it was felt, were spending altogether too much time in the classroom. Moreover, as Rudolph alleges, "too many of those classroom hours, everywhere not just at Harvard, were a calculated insult to students." But it is well to remember, too, that the lecture system was itself (and was seen to be) "vastly preferable" to the older recitation mode of instruction, with its overwhelming emphasis on rote memorization.[5] Commenting on the period during which that latter method had reigned supreme at Harvard, Samuel Eliot Morison notes that "almost every graduate of the period 1825–60 has left on record his detestation of the system of instruction at Harvard. . . . [President] Quincy himself described the ideal college course as a 'thorough drilling'; and that is just what the Harvard course was."[6] Moreover, during the same antebellum and pre-elective era, the rigidities of the classical curriculum prevailing at so many of the colleges of the day—dry, narrow, rigid, increasingly out of touch with student sensibilities, helped generate, by way of reaction, the student-sponsored co-curriculum of "literary societies and their libraries, the clubs, journals and organizations which compensated for the neglect of science, English literature, history, music and art in the curriculum." In effect, it helped generate, in one historian's happy description, a sort of " 'bootlegged' education."[7]

Things changed, of course, after the Civil War, and during the years since then the undergraduate course of study has been in more or less constant flux, with individual institutions making first their own particular accommodations between the old classical curriculum and the free elective system, and later their own particular selections from the various, more novel curricular patterns of election and requirement, majoring and minoring, specialization and distribution, core curriculum and guided election, great books programs, special freshman programs, honors programs and the like. These particular programs, rooted in institutional history and tradition, have naturally tended to constrain the possibilities and shape the direction of curricular change on into the present. And that enlarges the extent to which, in a higher educational system as complex and pluralistic as the American, even the appropriate form of *dissatisfaction* with the status quo is likely to vary from one type of institution to another.

That fact serves to underline the second general point that stands out for me as totally clear. Namely, that the sheer size of the American system of higher education and the marked degree of institutional variety that distinguishes it preclude the feasibility of any fully unified response to the educational challenges of the future and suggest the undesirability of any such unified response even if it were feasible. Not only are the problems confronting our colleges and universities too various, so, too, are the characteristic strengths they can bring to bear in responding to those problems as also the resources at their disposal as they struggle to advance that process of accommodation. That is palpably the case in the matter of the uneasy balance between teaching and research, and only a little less so in the matter of curricular formation.

So far as teaching is concerned, I begin with the assumption that what is at issue today is not some sort of decline in quality—though that is what the critics, unembarrassed by any systematic canvass of the available evidence, seem simply to assume. Instead, the question confronting us is that of how best to go about encouraging and effecting the improvements in quality that can always be made.[8] And here I would judge the central impediment to be, not any lack of interest on the part of the professoriate in their teaching responsibilities, for the evidence examined in the last chapter leaves little room for such a conclusion. Instead, it is the degree to which the incentive and reward structure in the profession is focused on research productivity, fails to encourage attention to teaching, and, as a result, fails also to respond to what most faculty are called upon to do most of the time, to what they apparently want to do, and to what they, in fact, actually do.[9]

Here, we would do well to pay attention to the conclusions Ernest Boyer draws in his recent report *Scholarship Reconsidered* and to the set of recommendations advanced in that work. He argues that "far too many colleges and universities are being driven not by self-defined objectives but by the external imperatives of prestige," that institutional prestige has been far too generally linked with the sort of research that we properly expect the faculty at our great research centers to do, and that the unhappy outcome has been a progressive homogenization of the extraordinarily varied range of colleges and universities that make up the American system of higher education, and a regrettable diminution in the distinctiveness of institutional mission in which they should rightfully take pride.[10] Without questioning the intimacy of the connection between good teaching and research, he concludes that that latter term has come to be far too restrictively defined, suggests its replacement by the more capacious term "scholarship," and argues for a broader and more nuanced understanding of the scholarship in which we properly expect faculty members to engage, one that "brings legitimacy to the full scope of academic work."[11]

If scholarship does indeed mean "engaging in original research" of the type classically pursued at our research universities, "the work of the scholar also means stepping back from one's investigation, looking for connections, building bridges between theory and practice, and communicating one's knowledge effectively to students." So far as scholarship is concerned, then, Boyer proposes that "the work of the professoriate...be thought of as having four separate yet overlapping functions:...the scholarship of *discovery;* the scholarship of *integration;* the scholarship of *application;* and the scholarship of *teaching.*"[12] While all can well be pursued at any type of college or university, the different institutional sectors will necessarily provide, in accordance with their characteristic educational missions, a more appropriate and congenial setting for one rather than another. And the incentives and rewards in the several sectors should be so structured as to take into account all forms of scholarship that serve their mission, instead of focusing so obsessively on the scholarship of discovery.

That form of scholarship, which clearly deserves to be honored and supported, "comes closest to what is meant when academics speak of 'research'." It is the sort of original investigative work in which the American research university has come to excel during the past half-century and more. Its marked success in this area warrants, indeed, a measure of national pride. But it should not lead us to assume that that sort of original basic research is the only sort of worthwhile scholarship, or that it can appropriately be demanded of all faculty members at all sorts of institutions. Among other things, it can be extremely costly, and neither the funding nor the other support systems needed to sustain it are universally available. Boyer proceeds, accordingly, to describe the other three types of scholarship and to match them with the institutional sectors whose missions they seem to complement or advance.

Thus, although along with original research it is the sort of scholarship that we should expect to find also at the doctorate-granting universities, he sees the liberal arts colleges as providing "an especially supportive climate for the scholarship of integration," by which he means "serious disciplined work" that makes "connections across the disciplines, placing the specialties in a larger context," seeking "to interpret, draw together, and bring new insight to bear on original research." Similarly, while liberal arts colleges have long taken great pride in it, he sees the community colleges as appropriately paying great attention to what he calls "the scholarship of teaching," recognizing that "teaching can be well regarded only as professors are widely read and intellectually engaged." Finally, "the scholarship of application," service activities on behalf of the larger community but tied directly to a faculty member's specific area of academic specialization (and involving the professional application of specialized knowledge to problems of real consequence) is something we might expect to find pursued at (and rewarded by) institutions in more than one sector of higher education, doctorate-granting universities, community colleges, comprehensive colleges and universities alike. Though it is true that the last-mentioned sector, which Boyer thinks stands most to gain by an attempt to define scholarship more broadly, certainly includes institutions which could well define their scholarly mission as being one of integration. And so on. The overall point is to resist the homogenization of higher education, to promote "diversity with dignity." "While the full range of scholarship can flourish on a single campus," he says, "every college and university should find its own special niche. Why should one model dominate the [entire] system."[13]

Why, indeed? While the institutional scholarly alignments Boyer suggests may conceivably be a little too pat, the general loosening up of the definition for which he argues has a great deal to recommend it. If generally adopted and recognized in the structure of institutional incentives and rewards, it would work to reduce the amount of third-rate "original" research being produced, would serve to bridge the gap that tends to open up, in some institutional settings, between teaching and research, and would complement the efforts so many colleges and universities are already making to improve the quality of teaching on their campuses. And if "diversity with dignity" is an appropriate slogan when it comes to the type of scholarship to be pursued at our very diverse institutions of higher education, it may be suggested that "diversity without disapprobation" might serve as an equally appropriate slogan when it comes to the nature of the curricular arrangements we are willing to see prevail at those institutions, and especially the arrangements for the general education segment of the undergraduate course of study.

Here again, as in the matter of the exact balance between teaching or research to be expected or the specific type of scholarship involved in that balance, it is hard to believe that any single curricular model, however venerable its real or imputed ancestry, could really serve the needs or advance the missions of all our markedly varied colleges and universities. Of recent years, a core general education curriculum involving required courses pivoting on the Western cultural tradition and possessed of a "great books" component has been the model most persistently and publicly touted for that role. In *50 Hours: A Core Curriculum for College Students,* Lynne V. Cheney, chairman of the National Endowment for the Humanities, has outlined a balanced and unexceptionable version of such a curriculum spanning the humanities, social sciences and natural sciences, requiring a measure of foreign language study and also some exposure to a culture other than that of the West.[14] Her pamphlet should be very useful as a point of departure for countless curriculum committees when they are called upon to review the provision for general education at their respective institutions. Some, indeed, may be happy to adopt its proposals more or less *in toto*. And it is likely to appeal most strongly to those who need it most. I have in mind those institutions, many of them in the comprehensive sector, which either by virtue of their original mission or because of admissions pressures, have tilted most heavily in their undergraduate programs toward the vocational or pre-professional, and which lack the resources to mount an extended array of courses in the arts and sciences. Less reassuringly, it may also acquire a role not unlike that enjoyed by the famous Yale Report of 1828 during the decades after its publication. Of that report, which mounted a ringing defense of the old classical course of study, it has been said that it "may have provided a veneer of educational philosophy" for curricular arrangements that were in reality the outcome of lack of institutional resources or of "a psychology of poverty."[15]

Whether or not that turns out to be so, I believe that the type of required core curriculum Cheney is urging will have much less of an appeal to colleges and universities in which the arts and sciences play a more central role, which are fortunate enough to be able to mount a rich array of course offerings focusing both on the Western cultural tradition and on cultural traditions beyond the West, and where the great interpretative disputes of the day (without shouldering aside the teaching of the "classic" authors)[16] have become central to intellectual discourse on campus. Of course those institutions among them which possess a previous history of curricular commitment to general education are likely to respond more sympathetically than those which lack it. In the latter case I have in mind institutions which never adopted the core curricular approach and have been content, instead, to provide for the requisite breadth in their students' education via the mechanism of guided election or distribution requirements. It should be recognized that there is nothing "second class" about such an approach. It is, in fact, more common than its core curricular rival. If its great weakness is the absence of a unifying course experience which all students by virtue of the core requirement share in common, in small colleges at least, that lack is often compensated for by the fact that surprisingly large percentages of the total student body themselves elect, year in year out, to take certain much admired (or much needed) courses.[17] If a subsidiary weakness may be the absence of a programmed effort at synthesis or integration designed to help students transcend the disconnections and divisions among subject areas that academic specialization has conspired to aggravate, it is not at all clear that the core curricular approach does that much better. Despite endless discussion of the matter (and it is an important one) nothing even approximating a consensus has emerged on how to go about the desired exercise in integration.[18] And if and when it does, my own guess is that it will take the form, not of some specific curricular effort linked with the general education segment of the undergraduate course of study, but rather of a shift in the way in which the whole curriculum is approached and taught.[19]

Of the many institutions that follow the distribution-requirement approach to the non-major part of the curriculum, it is important to recognize, then, that some do so, not because at some point in the past they abandoned the core-curricular approach, but because they had never chosen to adopt it. The reason for that may well be (and Williams College is a pertinent example) that having never succumbed in the late-nineteenth century to the then fashionable allures of the new free-elective system, they were never, as a result, called upon to heal the wounds characteristically inflicted by that system by applying the reforming balm of general education in its core curricular version. And such institutions may serve to remind us yet once more of the marked degree to which the whole ethos of old colleges and universities—as manifested in their curricula no less than in their modes of governance and community life—are shaped by the dense particularities of their specific individual histories. Whether that fact, in a particular institution, is on balance a source of rigidity or strength is itself conditioned by what has gone before. But whatever the case, as any battle-scarred veteran of the curricular wars in such a setting can attest, whether one is simply trying to understand what is or attempting to change it for what one believes to be better, the particularities of the individual institutional history represent an impressively stubborn reality which has to be reckoned with.

If that recognition should dispose us to accept with a certain measure of calm the continuing presence in different settings of differing approaches to the undergraduate course of study, we should also recognize that there are some issues that will continue to press in on us with a considerable degree of urgency. Prominent among them, to turn now to my second point, is the matter of cultural inclusion—whether what is at issue is woman's studies, Afro-American studies, Asian and Latino studies, or other aspects of the transition to what is often referred to as "multiculturalism." The issue is a very important one and clearly warrants the extended discussion it has evoked. But that discussion has been unnecessarily muddied, I believe, by the running together of two distinct issues. Both involve the drive for "representation" in the undergraduate course of studies of the formerly invisible history, culture and experiences of groups now increasingly represented in the student population. But the first involves their inclusion by means of individual courses or instructional programs in the curriculum as a whole, with the subject-areas in question available for election by any students interested, whether they be freshmen or seniors, women, white males or members of a racial minority. The second, on the other hand, concerns the representative inclusion of such materials in general education courses that all undergraduates are required to take, usually in their freshman year. There is understandably some ambivalence about the former option—stemming largely from worries about the encouragement of separatism in the classroom, about the uncertainty of evaluative criteria characteristic of new fields of study, about the balkanization of the undergraduate course of study and its domination by concerns pivoting on gender, race and class, and about the general threat of "politicizing" the curriculum. But it is the latter that constitutes the truly neuralgic point in the current debate, generating heated demands for the abolition of core courses focused on the Western tradition, anguished cries that without them the Western cultural heritage will somehow not be mediated, drawing attention away from the balance of the curriculum as a whole and focusing it instead (and confusingly so) on an issue which is not directly pertinent to the curricular arrangements prevailing at the bulk of our colleges and universities.

Large numbers of those colleges and universities, after all (and as we have seen), provide for the general education of their students, not by the imposition of several core courses that all are required to take, but by requiring them instead to distribute their elections among groups of courses, in some cases fairly narrowly, in others quite broadly, defined. And for such colleges and universities the issue of cultural inclusion, while by no means an easy one, tends to come into focus in relation to the overall balance of the curriculum rather than in relation to the syllabuses of one or two introductory courses. For some of these institutions, anxious to ensure that all their students will benefit from the heightened representativeness of their curricula in an era of growing national diversity and increasing global interconnectedness, cultural inclusion has extended also to the recalibration of distribution requirements in such a way as to require of all students some exposure to a world culture other than the Western or to a domestic minority culture with its roots in one or other of those world cultures. In rather disingenuous fashion such institutions have sometimes been criticized for making that particular move while at the same time having "no Western civilization requirement."[20] But, of course, the move in question is predicated on the fact that their students are multiply exposed to the Western cultural experience via the vast majority of the courses they take in the humanities and social sciences, and *all* the courses they take in the natural sciences. For science as we know it, however universal its modern vogue, is after all the great and distinctive achievement of the Western intellectual tradition, and the achievement, at one remove or another, both by action and reaction, that has most profoundly shaped the modern sensibility.[21] So multiple, indeed, is the exposure of our students to things Western, that having examined or bumped up against so many Western "trees" in the course of their studies, they may fail to grasp the dimensions and distinguishing characteristics of the cultural wood of which those trees are a part, or, worse, fail to perceive that there *is* indeed such a wood, or, even, that they themselves are in it. Here, the desire of the critics to see the offering in things Western of some more broadly interpretative and less specialized courses akin to those offered in non-Western areas strikes me as wholly justified.[22]

Those critics, moreover, are themselves by no means adamantly opposed to an enhanced measure of cultural inclusion.[23] What outrages them, I sense, is less the demand for inclusion itself than the degree of heat and excess with which some of those affiliated with "the cultural left" (a very accommodating term) permit themselves to denounce the hegemonic oppressiveness of the Western cultural tradition.[24] More often than not literary theorists of one sort or another, the latter tend to betray a marked lack of interest in empirical data and show little sign of having undertaken any rigorous or extended effort in comparative cultural investigation or of having subjected their sweeping generalizations to the disciplined cross-civilizational analysis which alone could have warranted their framing.

Despite such excesses and the discordant din of battle over cores and canons which understandably accompanies them, it is my own sense that the debate about cultural inclusion has already been decided. It has, in effect, been decided in favor of those advocating enhanced inclusion. And quite properly so, given the historic movement of peoples in our era, the accompanying progress of global integration and the sweeping and ongoing transformation taking place in the composition of our own national population. That process is nudging the United States forward, however hesitantly, to meet its destination in the twenty-first century as "the first universal nation" of the world.[25] The outcome of the debate over cultural inclusion could scarcely have been otherwise, moreover, given the parallel transformation in the make-up of our overall student population (and in terms of gender as well as race), the dramatic rise of a feminist consciousness (one of the truly great, shaping developments of our times), and the indisputable enrichment of our understanding of the grandeurs and miseries of the human condition made possible by the contributions of scholars in global, cross-cultural, minority and women's studies.

Any more closed stance, it should be added, would be very much at odds with the whole genius and direction of the Western cultural tradition itself. That tradition, after all, when seen in historical and cross-cultural perspective, stands out in the end as a persistently syncretistic and open-ended one. However hesitant, hostile or conflicted its initial reaction, across the centuries it has ultimately proved able to assimilate the contribution of Jew as well as Greek, Celt and German as well as Roman, Arab as well as Asian, and, in the more recent past, African no less than Latin American.[26]

The challenge for the future, then, is how to get beyond the phase of anxious questioning and fruitless bickering in which we currently seem stuck and, while remaining faithful to the tried and true norms of institutional and academic process, to continue, as we shape and reshape the undergraduate course of study, with the ongoing task of cultural inclusion. Given the training of our current faculties, the problems concerning the availability in the future of the pertinent specialists, the limits on our institutional resources, the ever-present threat of intellectual and educational faddishness, and the disabling edginess of the politics of race and gender, that task is not going to be an easy one. No more so, indeed, than the historic challenge confronting the country as a whole as it struggles to measure up to the haunting vision of a great nation true to its own deepest and most compelling ideals, a nation harmonious in its differences, rich and proud in its diversity, just and compassionate in its social transactions. A nation faithful, at least in the profundity of its aspiration, to the dream of the "beloved community" which Martin Luther King and the leaders of the civil rights movement so eloquently evoked.

That much is clear, at least to me. Equally clear, to turn now to my third point, is the importance of grasping the direction and significance of the current wave of criticism. Leaning back against the ethos of academic specialization, research and intellectual discovery and calling for the unification of the undergraduate course of study around the mission of mediating to students the community's traditional heritage of ideas and cultural values—it should properly be situated, I believe, in the context of the age-old dialectic between the rival rhetorical and scientifico-philosophical versions of the liberal arts ideal.[27] So situated, and despite its own misleading self-representation, it emerges not as a clarion call summoning us back to the high ground of educational probity on which we were all once proud to take our stand, but which the deplorable events of the 1960s betrayed us into abandoning for the adventure in skeptical confusion that has culminated in our present plight. Instead, it reveals itself as another (if updated) effort to reassert in modified form some of the central values embedded in the old rhetorical understanding of liberal education at the end of a period during which the scientifico-philosophical version of the liberal arts ideal (Bruce Kimball's "liberal-free" ideal), with its stress on the free, skeptical and unending pursuit of truth by the individual critical intellect, has been dominant.

To say that is not to brush aside the case to be made for that rhetorical version. Much of the vitality and strength of the Western tradition of education in the liberal arts and its demonstrated ability periodically to renew itself has come from the conflictedness of its roots and the tension-ridden nature of its growth. During the modern university era, the tradition may conceivably have tilted too sharply and persistently toward the liberal-free ideal. It could be that "the individualism and free pursuit of truth of the philosophical mind" associated with that ideal may, in the end, "hazard self-indulgent and nihilistic education and culture, which can lead finally to [cultural] anarchy." And, if that is so, it might well indeed be time to call upon the traditional virtues of the rhetorical (*artes liberales*) ideal to restore a measure of needed balance.[28]

That, certainly, is the view that Bruce Kimball himself is inclined, albeit cautiously, to take. My own inclination, however, lies in a different direction. It does so in part because I find it impossible to ignore the fact that our very understanding of the centuries-long dialectic between the rhetorical and philosophical versions of the liberal arts tradition is itself the happy outcome of an energetic and painstaking historical investigation mounted by a succession of scholars, not least among them Kimball himself, and pursued in accord with the established norms of "scientific" scholarship and via a sustained exercise of the critical reason in the manner characteristically fostered by the liberal-free ideal. It is the sort of understanding, in effect, that it is hard to imagine having being nurtured by an educational approach shaped in accord with the rhetorical ideal.

Nor do I think we should overlook the twinge of dogmatism evident in the strictures of the neo-rhetoricians, the contemporary critics of curricular incoherence, who are prone to giving the impression that "faculties, deans, and presidents, could simply decide to walk out of the [educational] wilderness if they really wanted to," and that the problem, rather than reflecting intractable disagreement, is really "one of intellectual backbone," so that "the solution is a matter of willing, even wishing, the coherence to appear." As with Hutchins in the 1930s, the complexities and daunting dilemmas of modern life are brushed impatiently to one side, and our "colleges and universities" are exhorted "to commit themselves to something, rather than indulging in skepticism and relativism."[29] Nor, at a deeper level, should we miss the degree to which the characteristic concerns of the neo-rhetoricians themselves parallel (unconsciously reflect?) the great wave of questioning so evident in contemporary intellectual life in general. That questioning has been generated by the anxious preoccupation of our era with language, interpretation and the very grounding of knowledge, and it has posted a severe challenge to the scientifico-philosophical tradition that lies so close to the very heart of the university ethos itself.[30] That the inclination toward perspectivism and the skepticism concerning the determinacy of meaning to which the critics so vociferously object are themselves of "rhetorical" vintage, fostered by the great linguistic and interpretative turn in contemporary intellectual life, serves only to exacerbate the intellectual disarray which informs the educational uncertainties of the day and which, rather than any lack of resolve on the part of academics, seems destined to project those uncertainties on into the future. Doubtless we would all rejoice if transported by some act of redemptive deliverance into a state of intellectual and educational grace. But the clamor of exhortation and recrimination notwithstanding, if there is any obvious sacramental shortcut to that salvific state, it has yet to be identified. What is called for then, or so I conclude, is not some leap of faith or act of will committing our colleges and universities to the "traditional" educational verities, but a calm, consistent and persistent application to the adjudication of the claims advanced on behalf of the rhetorical tradition (and, in no lesser degree, to its own counter-claims)[31] of the questing, critical reason that lies at the heart of the liberal-free ideal. Here again, as on the vexed issue of cultural inclusion, I do not believe that the way forward into the future can lie via a retreat into the past, whether it is a past rightly or wrongly conceived. It will lie, rather, via a tenacious (and courageous) following of the course for which we have long since set our compass, and with which the university as an institution has historically been associated.

How exactly any of us as members of an academic community will go about pursuing that course will depend on the nature of the college or university to which we belong, on its distinguishing ethos and the nature of the mission it exists to serve, on the strength of the faculty with which we are associated, the quality of the students we are called upon to teach, and the nature and extent of the resources (intellectual as well as financial) that sustain us in our work. In that respect, as in others, of those to whom much has been given much is likely to be required. And given the intricacy of the intellectual currents to be negotiated, it seems reasonable to suppose that on this matter especially responsibility for leadership should properly fall on the most favored sectors of our higher educational system.

2. The selective liberal arts college, its traditional strengths and future destiny

In 1980 the Carnegie Council on Policy Studies in Higher Education published *Three Thousand Futures,* the final report in a series of topical reports it had issued over the course of the six years preceding. In that report, emphasizing the hard choices higher education would be destined to confront in the closing years of the century, the Council identified the research universities and selective liberal arts colleges as the institutions best positioned to preserve the integrity of their internal community life, the quality of their academic programs, and an appropriate balance among fields of study. In relation to the last point, and indicating concern about the shift over the course of the previous decade away from the liberal arts and in the direction of professional studies, the Council also concluded that upon those same institutions would probably fall "the greatest responsibility" for leaning against heightened vocationalism and for preserving an appropriate measure of curricular balance—the research universities by "maintaining graduate fields with low numbers of Ph.D. candidates," the selective liberal arts colleges (presumably) by retaining that serenely undiminished intensity of focus on instruction in the arts and sciences which some of their less-selective brethren, in common with many a comprehensive or community college, might be forced to relinquish.[32]

The assignment of such a role to the liberal arts colleges strikes me as entirely appropriate. And given Breneman's discovery that so many of the colleges in the Liberal Arts II sector had transformed themselves under admissions pressures into "small professional colleges,"[33] the shifting of the primary responsibility for maintaining curricular balance to the more selective among them seems equally warranted. The *statistical* significance of this small group of survivors (or direct lineal descendants) of the first colleges in North America is not very marked. Once providing the characteristic setting in which the bulk of American students received their undergraduate education, in our own era they have come to constitute a tiny minority among our institutions of higher education. If Breneman is correct in the case he makes for reducing the overall universe of such colleges to something in the neighborhood of two hundred, then they constitute little more than 5 percent of all such institutions of higher education, and educate probably fewer than 3 percent of all American undergraduates. As institutions of higher education, they now constitute an exception to the norm. And the type of undergraduate education they offer—in small face-to-face residential communities which maximize the degree to which the extracurriculum reinforces the curriculum—has equally become an exception to the norm.

But as the Carnegie Council does well to remind us, there are forms of significance more pertinent than the merely statistical. Fortune, certainly, has favored at least the most highly selective among these colleges. Whatever financial stringencies they confront, they are still, given their number and size, collectively the beneficiaries of an impressively large proportion of the resources available to higher education. Being humane in size and scale and better positioned than most to juggle successfully the bleak equations of quality and cost, their traditional ethos has been less exposed in times of economic and demographic turbulence to the corrosive impact of market forces. Their student bodies, highly talented and carefully selected, are matched in overall quality by those of no more than a handful of the nation's leading research universities. Their faculties are distinguished and well supported in their work. To the fulfillment of their mission they bring the strength imparted and the inspiration afforded by the great richness of their individual institutional histories. And that mission involves an undiffused intensity of focus on the education of undergraduates in the arts and sciences that has long since become wholly extraordinary, not only in Europe, but also here in the United States.

Just how extraordinary is evident from the difficulty which the leaders of the new-style American research universities experienced a century ago in accepting the colleges as part of the higher educational system at all, and the eagerness with which they sought to reclassify them, instead, as belonging to the upper echelon of the system of *secondary* education. But in that, we have seen, they were wrong. Although the immediate models of the first of the colonial colleges were the constituent colleges that together made up the universities of Oxford and Cambridge, the American liberal arts colleges are also the lineal descendents of the single college-universities that had emerged in the fifteenth and sixteenth centuries in Spain, Scotland and Ireland.[34] Proud bearers of an educational tradition more ancient than that which inspired the creation of the modern American university and one powerful enough to help shape the latter's twentieth-century development, the liberal arts college is not to be regarded as something less than a university of the modern American type, but as something *other* than that—perhaps even, in some of its dimensions, as something more. If it lacks the stimulus and enrichment afforded by the presence of professional schools and graduate programs, it lacks also the distraction they inevitably generate, and it is able to harness the entire resources of a university to the task of educating undergraduates. In such a setting the liberal arts subjects encounter no competitors for institutional support, the commitment to teaching is unquestioned, and research activity is nudged accordingly in the direction of "a distinctive and broader mode of scholarship."[35]

So far as the commitment to teaching and to the overall well-being of the College is concerned, the evidence is totally clear. Asked in the 1989 Carnegie Survey whether their interests lay primarily in teaching or research, an overall 70 percent of faculty nationwide indicated a primary interest in teaching. But a break-down by institutional sector reveals that that figure dropped to 58 percent if one included only the faculty at the four-year institutions in general, and to 33 percent if one focused on the research universities alone. Of those at the liberal arts colleges, however, 83 percent indicated that preference.[36] Seventy-six percent, moreover, agreed that teaching effectiveness should be the primary criterion for the promotion of faculty. (For faculty at all institutions the global percentage on the question was 62%, for faculty at the four-year institutions as a group, 47%, and for those at the research universities, 21%.)[37] Moreover, in comparison with faculty members at all other four-year institutions, those at liberal arts colleges indicated that their institutions, in granting tenure, placed much less weight on such "external" or "professional" factors as numbers of books or articles published, reputations of the presses or journals publishing their work, published reviews of their books, and research grants received.[38] Conversely, in granting tenure only the two-year colleges appear to accord greater weight to the observation of teaching by faculty or administrative colleagues, and no other type of institution (not even the two-year college) comes close to placing as much weight as does the liberal arts college on service within the campus community, or on such instruction-related factors as student evaluations of teaching, recommendations from current or former students, recommendations from colleagues on the faculty, syllabuses of courses taught, and academic advising of students.[39]

Given the extreme seriousness with which teaching is clearly taken, not only by faculty members themselves but also in the structure of institutional incentives, it is tempting to assume that research or scholarship could hardly bulk large in the lives of academics at such colleges. That is far, however, from being the case. In 1989, some 40 percent of the faculty at liberal arts colleges reported their sense that in their departments it would be difficult for a person to achieve tenure without publishing. Twenty-two percent even fretted the pressure to publish might be reducing the quality of teaching at their college.[40] And, as we have seen,[41] were we to narrow the institutional universe down to the leading liberal arts colleges, the research profile as measured simply by numbers of publications is much the same as that to be found at the second echelon universities where less emphasis is placed upon undergraduate teaching and less honor accorded to it.

If that scholarly profile, however, is judged by more nuanced and qualitative rather than simply quantitative criteria, it begins to look rather different. Given the intensity of teaching and governance demands, and in the absence of graduate students, research assistants, research libraries and large research laboratories, the pursuit at a liberal arts college of research in the sense of Boyer's "scholarship of discovery"[42] is in some degree an exercise akin to pushing water up hill. It is something that *can* be done and *is* in fact done, but only with determination and not with ease. Because of that, university people (and especially those in the natural sciences)[43] are prone to assume that research is alien to the environment of the liberal arts college and that those who teach in that environment do precisely that and nothing else. Of the most selective among those colleges that is certainly not the case today; nor at those colleges is the highly unusual balance they maintain between teaching and scholarship in any way a novelty. It showed up clearly in the data collected in 1969 during the first Carnegie faculty survey,[44] and it was certainly evident to me when I first began teaching in such a setting almost a decade before that.

What did not catch my attention then, however, though it has long since impressed itself on me and been a frequent topic of discussion with colleagues, is the degree to which scholarship pursued over a period of years in the setting of a selective liberal arts college tends inexorably to take on a somewhat distinctive intellectual profile—one akin, in fact, to "the scholarship of integration" as Ernest Boyer has described it.[45] When Williams College moved in 1985 to establish a Center for the Humanities and Social Sciences to promote faculty development and sustain faculty scholarship, it was in part with the explicit goal of stimulating and encouraging precisely that distinctiveness. The group of faculty proposing the move had argued that "in the absence of a specialized research library, of graduate and professional schools, of large departments with concentrations of contiguous research specialties, conditions of life and work at a liberal arts college understandably present some obstacles to the more specialized and technical varieties of scholarship—those, for instance, involving archival research, the editing of texts, or large-scale quantitative-empirical work." At the same time, they had claimed that those obstacles were offset by "the intellectual stimulus generated by the unspecialized and uninhibited promptings of bright undergraduate minds and by the wonderful ease of contact enjoyed in crossdisciplinary fashion with colleagues in a broad array of fields." They had urged, therefore, the creation of a Center that would seek "to capitalize on such advantages by consciously fostering the type of broad-gauged critical and interpretative scholarship that frequently links with undergraduate teaching and can readily be done in the context of a first-rate liberal arts college, with its inescapable need for breadth, for communication across disciplines, for continual recurrence to the basic problems." They had indicated a firm commitment to the view that "that type of scholarship, more integrative and reflective, less wedded to certain confined analytical techniques, interpretative and literary rather than simply formal, quantitative and abstract, represents an important and distinctive contribution to the advancement of knowledge and understanding." Such a contribution, they had concluded, "complements the more technical and specialized research that has come to dominate scholarly activity in so many of our large university departments, and it is one, we firmly believe, that it is our particular obligation to make."[46]

That being so, and having been one of the group making that particular case, I find it heartening now to learn, from the results of a broad-gauged study conducted during the years 1983–85 and published in 1987, that in attributing a certain distinctiveness to the scholarship pursued at our sort of institution, we were not in the grip of some sort of collective self-delusion. Combining quite extensive interviewing with an analysis of the 1984 Carnegie faculty survey data, and noting that "at selective liberal arts colleges... the fixation on discipline is attenuated by the belief in a broad, liberal approach to the world of knowledge" and that "the temperament which promotes integrative scholarship is at home" in such a setting, Kenneth P. Ruscio concluded that the type of scholarship produced at such colleges does, indeed, and in some of its key dimensions, bear a distinctive stamp.[47] Three things about it stand out. First, the degree to which it responds to, or is designed to serve, direct educational goals. "For the liberal arts professor, the standard for credible research is not only peer acceptability but also use of the research in the undergraduate classroom." In the natural sciences especially, research projects are often chosen and designed in order to make student involvement (via honors theses, for example) not only practicable but also educationally fruitful.[48] Second, "research in the selective liberal arts college is more individualistic than bureaucratic." That is to say, it tends to be "unlike the highly organized and entrepreneurial research" typically found at universities that "often requires an intricate administrative structure." Concomitantly, faculty pursuing research in the college setting report themselves to be under "less pressure... 'to carve out a niche in the profession'," and freer "to move around as the mood strikes."[49] Third, often perceiving their fields "to be preoccupied with narrow, specialized topics and marginal, incremental contributions to an arcane literature," faculty members at such colleges are prone to finding "the boundaries of specializations and the taxonomies of disciplines" to be "artificial and constraining." While "deeply engaged in scholarship, ... they feel less compelled to contribute to the discipline in the conventional manner, to be [in effect] 'taxonomically upstanding.' There is a tolerance for a broader range of activities under the heading of scholarship."[50]

Thus, while "by virtue of their continuing research activity," as Trow and Fulton wrote in 1975, academics teaching at the selective liberal arts colleges "are... reading the same research and scholarly literature as are those in the leading graduate departments," they are not *necessarily* committed (as those authors further supposed) to "raising the same kinds of questions" or teaching wholly "within the research currents of their discipline."[51] Instead, the nature of their academic environment, the quality of the students they teach, and the intensity of their own commitment to teaching those students well often have the effect across time of shifting the direction of their own scholarly engagement, nudging it closer to their teaching activity, broadening and (in the case of the most gifted, at least) deepening its scope.

These distinctive features are for the selective colleges an important source of strength and equip them well, I believe, to exert some leadership in coming to terms with the problems besetting the undergraduate course of study today. That strength has long been brought to bear on matters curricular during the intensely serious and frequently quite wearing and divisive debate into which the faculties of such colleges fling themselves, generation after generation, with seemingly undiminished ardor. And while even that intensity and seriousness of engagement has failed to produce the intellectual agreement which alone could justify the particular type of structured curricular coherence for which the most prominent critics yearn, that fact itself conveys a very powerful message. It may be, in effect, that in such a setting and at this particular juncture in history we would do well to focus our energies less on persistently inconclusive wrangling about the overall *content* of our curriculum than on the way in which we characteristically frame our courses and the manner in which we teach them.[52]

About overall content itself disagreements of one sort or another seem destined to persist, with cyclical movement in the direction, alternatively, of greater openness and greater prescription, and with the current movement being in the direction of greater prescription. Given the continuing richness at the selective colleges of course offerings pertaining to Western culture, including offerings quite traditional in nature, the pressure for broader cultural inclusion will continue, and that pressure is likely to be marked by (or to stimulate by way of reaction) periodic protests and upheavals that will divide student bodies, set faculty teeth on edge, put hard-pressed administrators sorely to the test, anger one segment or another of the alumni constituency, and catch the negative attention of members of the general public. That instances of intellectual shoddiness and egregious politicization will occur, even at institutions of the highest quality, I have little doubt. But the best (and ultimately the only) protection against such failings is the strong scholarly fibre, the intellectual confidence, and the pedagogic integrity of their faculties. And everything I know and sense, after thirty years of teaching in such a setting, suggests to me that such characteristics are present in abundance.

Despite my own long-standing preoccupation with the overall content of the curriculum, then, and despite the obsessive amount of public attention focussed on it of late, I conclude that as we at the liberal arts colleges assess the undergraduate course of study today we would do well to direct our attention elsewhere.

Two worries signaled by the critics strike me as warranted. The first concerns the drawbacks attendant on the vogue of tight academic specialization, especially when it leads to an excessively narrow framing of courses at the introductory level. The second concerns the comparative incoherence of the typical undergraduate course of study today, the exact configuration of which (the disciplinary frontiers drawn, the intellectual territories distributed, and the defensive bulwarks established) can only be explained by means of an exercise in historical reconstruction.

In connection with the first of these worries, I concur in the view of the critics that in our framing of courses we have tended to tilt too far of recent years in the direction of confined topics and heightened specialization. While a preoccupation with intellectual muscularity is entirely warranted, the courses in one or other of the natural sciences that we properly require of our non-science majors should not, for example, be so narrowly designed as to speak only to the needs of prospective majors in a given discipline. Nor, in our teaching of history, should we fail to balance the wide array of specialized courses we offer with more broad-gauged survey courses, or hesitate to face up to the bracing task at the undergraduate level of teaching world (i.e. global) history or be content to leave that most important of subjects to be studied by our students for the last time in their high school or even junior high school years. Again, given the propensity of academic specialists to make the most extraordinary and flimsily supported generalizations about the supposed virtues or defects of one cultural tradition or another, we should be working harder and more systematically in our teaching at the challenging task of sustained, comparative, cross-cultural study.

As for the second worry, I share the regret of the critics about the element of incoherence that has come to characterize what one observer has called our "'cafeteria counter' curriculum." What I do not share is the eagerness of the more conservative among those critics to advance as the only possible solution to the problem a position that smacks of what the same observer has labeled (no less pejoratively) as "educational fundamentalism."[53] That is to say, I do not believe that it is any longer possible to ground the desired coherence in some sort of agreed-upon unitary curricular content determined in accord with the universal norms and values of our inherited common culture. Indeed, it is already a long time since such a stance was truly viable, and we have seen that the seeming universalism and commonality that at one time underpinned a higher measure of cultural consensus than is available today was bought at the price of a degree of exclusion on the basis of gender, race, class and ethnicity that we are still struggling hard to put behind us.[54] Even if that were not the case, I believe that the sweeping and profound intellectual disagreements which dominate our era, touching the very grounding of knowledge and challenging the very possibility of determinate meaning, would themselves have rendered the pursuit of such a cultural consensus quixotic.

But the persistent strengths which we have seen to be characteristic of the selective liberal arts colleges and of their faculties equip them well, I think, to exercise some leadership by boldly taking up the task of addressing these stubbornly intractable disagreements directly in their pedagogy. And by saying that I am indicating my sense that, in this institutional sector if not necessarily in all, we would do well to explore the route to a heightened measure of curricular coherence proposed of recent years (and with great insistence) by Gerald Graff of the University of Chicago.

Graff's point of departure is the set of conclusions we have earlier seen him draw from his painstaking inquiry into the history of literary studies in the American academy from the early nineteenth century down to the recent past.[55] Far from being a story of "triumphant humanism, nationalism or any professional model," that history, it will be recalled, consisted in "a series of conflicts... classicists versus modern language scholars; research investigators versus generalists; New Humanists versus New Critics; academic critics versus literary journalists and culture critics; critics and scholars versus theorists."[56] If that fact has been in remarkable degree concealed from us it is in part because such conflicts have tended to be pursued "behind the scenes" in the professional journals and at scholarly gatherings, being typically "exemplified rather than foregrounded by the department and the curriculum." As a result, they have not "become part of the context of the average student's education or the average professor's professional life." Via "the field coverage model of departmental organization, which has conceived of literature departments as aggregates arranged to cover an array of historical and generic literary fields," a system of "patterned isolation" came to dominate, diminishing the need for debate among contiguous specialists and permitting "the job of instruction" to proceed "as if on automatic pilot." The great virtue of that model is that it has certainly facilitated the process of receiving and assimilating new ideas and approaches. That has been true even in the case of such "disruptive novelties . . . as contemporary literature, black studies, feminism, Marxism, and deconstruction," which have been absorbed without subjecting departments to "paralyzing clashes of ideology" or demoralizing students by exposing them to professional controversies rather than "the *results* of such professional controversies." The model's correlative vice, however, is that by substituting "administrative organization" for "principled thought and discussion," methodological and ideological disagreements dividing the faculty have been sidestepped, "potentially edifying conflicts" prevented "from becoming part of what literary studies were about," and "students and instructors . . . thus deprived of a means of situating themselves in relation to the cultural issues of their time."[57]

In Graff's view, the disadvantages of this mode of conflict avoidance (which is not, of course, limited to literary studies) clearly outweigh the advantages. The managing of novel approaches and ideas via "the 'add-on' principle of departmental and curricular change" has helped create the "cafeteria-counter" curricular configuration that recent conservative commentators are not alone in criticizing. The conflicts, disagreements and antagonisms do not go away; they are simply repressed. The curriculum develops into "a geological overlay of ideologies, many of which contradict one another, but since they exist in separation, the contradictions are not experienced by students as contradictions."[58] Critics have urged that a solution to the problem can be found by reorganizing the curriculum around a "restored consensus." But Graff correctly views such an approach as unviable, whether the restored consensus involved the notion of "a 'common culture' based on unitary truths and values" or some sort of "revolutionary ideological critique." Instead, the route back to a heightened measure of curricular coherence which he himself proposes involves a forthright acknowledgment of the existence and likely persistence of an array of intractable ideological conflicts. It involves, also, the recognition that such conflicts can be used to insert into the learning process a degree of intellectual tension that is educationally beneficial, and the decision, therefore, to foreground them in the curriculum, to "sharpen" them, "bring them out into the open"—in effect, to "teach the conflicts." "The important thing," he says, "is to shift the question from 'Whose overview gets to be the big umbrella?' in which form it becomes unanswerable, to 'How do we institutionalize the conflict of interpretations and overviews itself'?" To do that is neither to "turn conflict [itself] into a value, nor . . . to reject consensus where we can get it. . . . It simply takes our point of departure from a state of affairs that already exists." And that approach has in fact been adopted by a growing number of graduate programs in literature.[59]

This approach clearly has applicability in fields other than the study of literature. The big question, however, is whether it would turn out to be a viable approach if transferred from the graduate to the undergraduate course of study. Nobody who has taught undergraduates in a common syllabus course with a colleague from another discipline (and I myself have done so on more than one occasion) is likely to underestimate the difficulty of achieving a pedagogic balance that will serve to maximize the intellectual stimulus generated by the clash of competing perspectives without at the same time plunging the students into a state of frustrated confusion. If it can be done, it is certainly not easy to do it well. But we should not permit ourselves to miss the fact that a significant element of confusion is already present, even if, in common with the conflicts themselves, it remains latent. The humanities and social sciences are currently rife with great interpretative disputes. And those disputes which, while they certainly agitate and energize, conspire also to confuse, cannot simply be wished away. Nor will we serve our students well if, as we construct our curricula, we attempt to sidle around such disagreements. In the course of any given week, as they move in a liberal arts setting from courses in the natural sciences to classes in art, literature, the behavioral sciences, history or religion, I have the uneasy sense that many of our students are fated to traverse epistemological centuries, to maneuver among radically divergent theories of knowledge without being fully conscious of so doing, and without getting adequate help in the process. They deserve better of us than that. Ideas have consequences. So, too, does intellectual confusion.

In the context especially of the selective liberal arts college, then, the great pedagogic challenge as I see it for the immediate future will be that of inserting these contemporary disputes and dilemmas into the very heart of our teaching endeavor—whether through the design of individual courses or via team-teaching, exercises in "teacher-swapping" (whereby teachers periodically take each other's classes), or the punctuation of the work of several courses by assembling everyone together periodically for "a joint conference."[60] The ways in which the task can be accomplished will doubtless vary from department to department and college to college. It will call for energy, imagination, sensitivity, confidence, diplomacy, careful planning, a strong and collegial commitment to the values of intellectual tact and generosity, and a willingness to forgo the joys of competitive liminality—a phenomenon which has become of recent years a singularly unhelpful feature of intellectual discourse in some segments of the academy.

None of this will come easily to us. But the distinctiveness of the way in which our faculties go about their calling as teachers and scholars is well adapted to this particular task, and in some of our departments and programs we are likely to find the pre-conditions for the "teaching the conflicts" approach already present. Philosophy departments (or those at least not monolithic in the philosophical orientation of their members and still committed to sustaining a reasonably lively collegial life) have long since had to face up to the challenge of enabling their students to come to terms with radically divergent philosophical viewpoints. Religion departments, too, especially those that have not abandoned the difficult commitment to teaching a common syllabus introductory course, have had to be quite self-conscious about the project of acquainting their students with the differing (and often conflicting) paradigms theologians, historians, anthropologists, psychologists and sociologists have employed in attempting to come to terms with religious phenomena. And given the variety of ideological commitment and methodological tactic that distinguishes such pluralistic or loosely assembled disciplines as anthropology, psychology, political science and sociology, those fields afford ample opportunity for foregrounding the conflicts. At Williams, indeed, where anthropology and sociology have an unusual history of having started out as separate departments but subsequently coming together as one, the faculty has succeeded in shaping the two programs of study in such a way that anthropology and sociology majors share in common some courses that do indeed foreground the shifting paradigms and conflicting approaches which, across time, have inspired both to illuminate and to shadow our understanding of human societies. Because of the distaste for theoretical and metahistorical questions that seems to be firmly rooted in the temperament of so many historians, history departments, I suspect, are likely to find it much more difficult to adapt a pedagogic tactic that would involve confronting the latent conflicts which are almost as deeply embedded in the professional study of history as in that of literature. But those of us who are historians would do well to recognize that our very field, as demarcated and studied in the modern academy, is itself an historical product, explicable less by any logical criteria than (appropriately enough) by an exercise of historical understanding. Graff, indeed, makes this point well and makes it as part of a larger generalization applying to the whole panoply of academic disciplines. "A university," he says,

> is a curious accretion of historical conflicts that it has systematically forgotten. Each of its divisions reflects a history of ideological conflicts that is just as important as what is taught within the divisions yet is prevented from being foregrounded by the divisions themselves. The boundaries that mark literary study off from creative writing, composition, rhetoric, communications, linguistics and film, or those that divide art history from studio practice, or history from philosophy, literature and sociology, each bespeak a history of conflict that was critical to creating and defining these disciplines yet has never become a central part of their context of study. The same is true of the very division between the sciences and the humanities, which has been formative for both yet has never been an obligatory context for either.
> ... Falling into the creases as they do, interdisciplinary conflicts go unperceived by the students, who naturally see each discipline as a frozen body of knowledge to be absorbed rather than as social products with a history that they might have a personal and critical stake in.[61]

If foregrounding the conflicts would deepen and further the education of our students, I am inclined to believe that it would also be healthy for those of us who as faculty members were engaged in the struggle to make that pedagogic tactic work. We would certainly find it less easy to succumb to the ever-present temptation of assuming a unidirectional movement in the development of our own disciplines, one that has naturally culminated in the redemptive triumph of the position, viewpoint, methodology or intellectual tactic which we ourselves, in our particular generation, encountered in graduate school (whether it be Anglo-American analytic philosophy, poststructuralist criticism, "history from the bottom up," or feminist approaches to a whole range of disciplines). And if we had lost sight of the fact, we would also be likely to recover a sharper sense of the importance for fruitful academic discourse of civility and intellectual generosity than tends to be fostered when the dominant mode of intellectual exchange is a reassuring exercise in competitive agreement pursued within contiguous (but mutually exclusive) coteries of the like-minded.

About the recent vogue of solemnly bemoaning the alleged prevalence on our campuses of "political correctness" there is, doubtless, something quite overblown.[62] The term itself has had a rather complex history. Only a very few years ago it was functioning in student discourse as a useful and rather healthy piece of self-mockery. Too slender a reed, one might have thought, to sustain the status of "a philosophy" are even "a movement" which the media now seem determined to thrust upon it. But if I am sometimes tempted to think that the posture most politically correct in the current climate of opinion is likely to be one involving solemn denunciations of political correctness, I am also uncomfortably conscious of the fact that the academy has usually been rather better at marshalling its energy and courage to fend off *external* attempts to limit its freedom of thought and expression than it has at disciplining its own proclivity for giving a hard time to those within its own ranks who stubbornly adhere to ideas or viewpoints currently unfashionable in academic circles.

About that proclivity there is, alas, nothing new. The university is one of the great legacies of the European Middle Ages to the intellectual life of the modern world. And I have argued that, when compared with the instrumentalities of higher education in other cultures, its historical significance resides in part in its ability across time to secure for the teachers and scholars who compose it at least some precious measure of immunity, as they pursue their work, from the encroachment of outside forces on their freedom of intellectual maneuver.[63] As we have seen, that ability was evident as early as the thirteenth century at the University of Paris. But so, too, it should now be conceded, was a periodic willingness to discourage or suppress unfashionable ideas or initiatives within the ranks of its own instructional corps, and even on occasion to align with the external authorities (or to seek their intrusion) in an attempt to accomplish that same end.[64] While we should not exaggerate the frequency with which that willingness has manifested itself over the centuries, it is surely important to note that it has never been entirely absent from the academy.

What, then, is to be concluded? I have conceded the need for a greater measure of coherence in the undergraduate curriculum. And I have sketched out the case that can be made for attempting to insert that heightened coherence by deliberately foregrounding and building into the collective pedagogic tactic the great interpretative disagreements and ideological conflicts that have conspired over the years to diminish it. What I would add now, and by way of conclusion, is that an important related benefit of that attempt—and especially so at this particular moment in our cultural history—is the degree to which, by its very focus on disagreement, it will serve constantly to remind us, faculty and students alike, of the preconditions requisite if disagreement is indeed to be fruitful. It will serve, in effect, to nudge to the forefront of our collective consciousness the power and importance of an ideal with the ascendancy of which the history of Kimball's liberal-free understanding of the liberal arts tradition has been closely intertwined. It is an ideal that we in the academy in North America tend to take utterly for granted until we encounter its absence elsewhere in the world or are threatened by its loss in our own institutions of higher education. It is the ideal enshrined in the belief that the oldest, the finest, the noblest, the most enduring mission of service to the larger society that colleges and universities can properly be called upon to fulfill is that of providing a privileged forum, one buffered by the very tenacity of its own commitment to freedom of inquiry and freedom of expression from the more egregious intrusions of prejudice and intolerance; a sort of dialectical space wherein the complex and testing issues of the day can be vigorously debated and tenaciously explored in an atmosphere distinguished above all by its openness, its rationality, its civility, its generosity of spirit.

Dissident voices, I well realize, are likely to be raised from within the academy arguing that this ideal is itself ideologically conditioned and should not be accorded so absolute a privilege. And that discordant view deserves no less attentive a hearing than does any other. I conclude, however, that it deserves also a firmly negative response. What is being privileged, after all, is nothing other than the commitment to a certain "morality of process," without which the ability of a community of learning to examine competing intellectual claims and to adjudicate between them by anything other than an exercise of judgmental force would be severely compromised. The history of the rhetorical approach to a liberal education attests to the fact that the lack of such a commitment would not preclude the survival into the future of *some* version of the liberal arts tradition. But in its total absence, I would insist, the liberal-free understanding of that great tradition could not be expected long to endure. And it is in support of that version of the tradition that I take my stand.

EPILOGUE

Levavi oculos meos in montes, unde veniet auxilium mihi.

Psalm 120(121)

At more than one point in the pages preceding I have been at pains to take issue with the recent critics of American higher education. For that I make no apology. But as I steer this little book into what I can only hope will be a not unwelcoming harbor, perhaps I may be permitted to step back for a moment from the tangled disputes and edgy discontents which have occupied so much of my attention, and to look now to the higher and more common ground upon which all of those who value the age-old tradition of education in the liberal arts can, without discomfort, assemble.

From time to time one cannot help wondering if part at least of our current educational discontent does not stem from the displacement onto the academy of widespread anxieties and fears spawned by the historic changes sweeping across the world at large. Certainly, much of that discontent would appear to have been stimulated by the way in which the world of higher education has responded to some of those changes. And while to speak of change in general is to risk submersion in an ocean of cliché, it is surely important to make some effort to come to terms with the implications of the ways in which our world is being transformed. In some respects, of course, that effort represents even in the European or Western intellectual tradition so habitual and nagging a challenge that for the past two millennia and more philosophers have maneuvered to position themselves between the archetypal positions of Parmenides and Heraclitus. In other respects, however, as the very nature of change itself has come to be transformed, the challenge involved has become itself a markedly novel one. So novel, indeed, that only of recent years have some of our historians, breaking out finally from the pattern of thinking that had led them to see the course of history as unidirectional and irreversible, and startled, it may be, by the longer and richer perspectives that only comparative cross-cultural work and a knowledge of the more alien present or the more distant past can afford—only in recent years have some of our historians come fully to grasp the oddity, the singularity, the wholly unprecedented nature of the tempestuous changes that have swept across the globe in our lifetimes and of the dizzying pace at which those changes have been occurring.

At the economic and technological level the significance of these changes is quite transparent; we are all of us patient, product or producer of what Karl Polanyi dubbed long ago as "the great transformation."[1] For some 5,000 years and more the greater part of mankind sustained itself by farming the land or by herding domesticated livestock. By the end of the present century that may well cease to be so worldwide, just as it has long ceased to be so in our own country. Our age is already distinguished from all that have gone before by the size of the minority that does not find its livelihood in agricultural work, by the speed with which that minority has been growing, and by the essentially urbanized occupations by which it sustains itself. No one today is likely to gainsay the significance of this transition. No change in the social and economic life of mankind comparable in magnitude has occurred since the Neolithic invention of agriculture. And given the fact that that change moved into high gear only with the Industrial Revolution in the late eighteenth century and only in our own century spread in any marked degree beyond Europe, North America and Japan, it must clearly be judged revolutionary in its pace as well as its scope.

We have had ruefully to learn, moreover, that technological transformation and economic change are no respecters in their consequences of the anxious boundaries we raise in our instinctive efforts to preserve unaffected other realms of life. Even the most passionate of counter-modernizing movements, in the developed no less than the developing societies, have proved powerless to prevent the unrelenting process of functional rationalization that is part and parcel of modernization from invading every area of social life and progressively reshaping human consciousness itself. For modernization, it has been said, "operates like a gigantic steel hammer, smashing both traditional institutions and traditional structures of meaning." While affording the individual new freedoms and opportunities for choice, it also works to destroy "the security which, however harsh they may have been, traditional institutions provided for him" as well as that "cosmological security provided by traditional religious world views." Its classic and constantly repeated outcome is a condition in which the individual finds himself bereft of "meaning that will provide adequate direction for his life," as being "no longer 'at home' in society, in the cosmos, or ultimately with himself."[2] In the older developed societies, familiarity with this condition has conspired to dull its attendant pain. But its poignancy and the traumatic nature of its initial impact are well conveyed by the words of a man whom the anthropologist Colin Turnbull interviewed over a quarter of a century ago in what was then the Belgian Congo, and who reported that when he was growing up he had come to understand that by following the prescribed practices of his tribe

> ... [W]e were living the life that our fathers had lived before us, and their fathers before them, and that our children would live the same life after us, and their children after them. In this way our life was one, the past and the future, even in death.... Above all, I learned to feel close to the ancestors, and to know that we were one with them, although I still do not know where they lived or how....
>
> This is what we have lost, what we have had taken away from us. Now it is forbidden for us to talk to our ancestors ... we can no longer learn their will or call on them for help. We no longer have any reason for living, because we have been forced away from the ways of our ancestors, and we lead other men's lives, not the lives of our fathers.[3]

There are few, I realize, to whom such thoughts can come altogether as a novelty. What is novel instead, and ironically so, is the degree to which we threaten now to become domesticated in our homelessness, anesthetized by the presumption of perpetual growth, unconscious of the unprecedented nature of the transpositions through which our world has been reeling, unaware of the fact that what we are living through may well turn out to be, when viewed from the perspective of the long history of humankind, no more than a limited episode of cataclysmic upheaval sandwiched between millennia of stasis or gradual evolution. For the greatest transformation looming ahead of us may turn out to be, not more of the same, but a marked retardation, gradual or sudden, in the tempestuously accelerating pace of change that has dominated all our lives. Or so the critics of growth would suggest, promoters of an ecological awareness that would weigh with skeptical caution the ramifying costs of any too impetuous or intensive a mode of change, prophets, indeed, of an inevitable return to an economy of limits, to a condition of existence closer, it may be, in its stability, predictability and restraint, to the immemorial rhythms of life with which mankind was once both familiar and of necessity content.

It would take more foresight than I can muster and more confidence than I possess either to affirm the rectitude of that vision or to dismiss it as lacking wholly in plausibility. What I can affirm, however, and with no little conviction, is that there would be something seriously lacking in a college or university education which failed utterly to take perspectives of that kind into account. Over the past two decades in an anxious attempt to respond to the ambiguous imperatives of an uncertain economy and a rapidly changing job market, the world of higher education has produced a plethora of instant programs and disposable curricula—most of them vocational or pre-vocational in their orientation. But if it is a cliché to say that we must so educate the upcoming generations that they can readily cope with rapid change, it is clearly a cliché that calls for further specification. Man, Aristotle said, is the animal that desires to know. Or, as the sociologists of knowledge would now put it, human beings are animals that appear impelled by the very urgencies of their constitution and from the very well-springs of their creativity to infuse the universe with meaning and direction, to comprehend their own existential situation, and to frame for themselves moral goals.[4] In the face, then, of waves of change that break upon the very bastions of meaning that men and women have erected in their anxious quest to make themselves at home in a mysterious and frequently hostile world, one must question the adequacy of educational approaches that are willing to sacrifice to short-term vocational advantage the age-old struggle for some breadth of intellectual perspective and the attainment of interpretative depth. For there can be no real coping without some richness of understanding. There can be, that is, no *ultimately* practical preparation for living if it leaves one bereft of the wherewithal to comprehend one's situation from a vantage point less partial and a perspective less impoverished than that afforded by the task-oriented, means-end, functional rationality at which we so excel, which accounts for so many of our modern achievements, and which has come to dominate so very much of our day to day lives.

Of course, the chastening history of our own century has been such as to suggest the wisdom of restraint in the claims one makes for the efficacy of any educational pattern. But the longer history of education in our own culture has also been such as to suggest the openness, resilience, flexibility and power of that age-old tradition of education in the liberal arts that at its best is consciously geared to no less inclusive an activity than that of living itself. Rooted in a past already archaic when disaster overtook the classical civilization of the Mediterranean world, we have seen the liberal arts tradition to have proved itself resilient enough to survive that catastrophe, flexible enough to respond creatively to the shifting intellectual imperatives of the centuries that followed, open enough (despite its essentially literary origins) to embrace the enormous expansion in the natural and social sciences that has characterized the modern era, and, throughout all such transpositions, faithful enough to the central intuition from which it has always derived its compelling force. Simply this: that no education which truly aspires to be a preparation for living can afford to ignore the fundamental continuities that exist between the cultivation of specific areas of specialized knowledge, expertise or skill (without which we could scarcely endure) and that more fundamental and wide-ranging attempt to penetrate by our reason the very structures of the natural world, to evoke the dimensions and significance of the beautiful, to reach towards an understanding of what it is to be human, of one's position in the universe, and of one's relations with one's fellows, moral no less than material. Towards that attempt we seem impelled by the very fiber of our being. In its total absence, while doubtless we survive, we do so as something surely less than human.

The history, moreover, of that most American of educational institutions, the independent, free-standing liberal arts college, witnesses forcefully to the power of that central educational intuition when wedded to the other long-standing conviction that education is not a process that can wholly be confined to classroom, laboratory, studio or library, but one to which the diverse experience and richly variegated moments of life in a residential community must all combine to make their particular contribution. Extracurriculum as well as curriculum; play as well as work; fellowship as well as solitude; the foreign as well as the familiar; discomfort as well as ease; protest as well as celebration; prescription as well as choice; failure as well as success.

But if that intuition is to continue to inform our educational endeavors on into what promises to be an enormously challenging future, those of us privileged to pursue our callings in such an institutional setting must be ready, I believe, to accept a heightened measure of responsibility. The indisputable achievements of academic specialization notwithstanding, it is my conviction that in so favored a setting, where we do indeed benefit from "the particular type of intellectual stimulus generated by the unspecialized and uninhibited promptings of bright undergraduate minds and by the wonderful ease of contact enjoyed in cross-disciplinary fashion with colleagues in a broad array of fields"—in such a setting, we have less excuse than most to surrender, either in our teaching or in the scholarly activity that sustains it, to the tepid professionalism, the theoretical diffidence, the seeming inability even faintly to trust the larger hope that characterizes so much of our contemporary intellectual discourse and renders agreement on curricular matters so very hard to find. Such is the splintering and balkanization of intellectual activity, so dominant, if you wish, is the analytic rather than the synthetic mode, so prone indeed are our contemporaries to compartmentalize knowledge, to divide it into discrete disciplines and segregated subject areas, that it has become demoralizingly difficult to hold before one's eyes that beckoning vision of the unity of all human knowing that we may all well need if we are to succeed in according to our intellectual and educational activities the sort of seriousness and moral significance they properly deserve. Here, if anywhere surely, we are called upon as custodians in our generation of the liberal arts tradition firmly to lean into the prevailing intellectual wind.

Or so I would argue—not unmindful, I might add, of the discomfort such a posture may involve. Speaking in 1977 of what he called "the cultural sadness" of our era and approaching the matter from a scientific angle, Dr. Lewis Thomas, formerly president of the Memorial Sloan-Kettering Cancer Center, remarked in words that have since been much quoted:

> These are not the best of times for the human mind. All sorts of things seem to be turning out wrong, and the century seems to be slipping through our fingers here at the end, with almost all promises unfulfilled. ...[W]e do not know enough about ourselves. We are ignorant about how we work, about where we fit in, and most of all about the enormous, imponderable system of life in which we are embedded as working parts. We do not really understand nature, at all.... We are *dumb.*[5]

Perhaps so. Perhaps he is right. But perhaps also we would do well, under such unpromising circumstances and as we go about our educational business, to draw a moment of departing comfort from the words of Alfred North Whitehead (that other scientist turned philosopher)—words that relay harmonics of a larger hope, of that faith in reason, that trust (he says) "that the ultimate natures of things lie together in a harmony which excludes mere arbitrariness," that conviction that "detached details, merely in order to be themselves demand that they should find themselves in a system of things," that stubborn sense, even, "that our experience, dim and fragmentary as it is, yet sounds the utmost depths of reality."[6]

NOTES

INTRODUCTION

1. I would divide these publications into two groups. The first, a series of reports and analyses, all of them somewhat discouraging in tone but lacking the harder edge that characterizes the second group, which includes some works of markedly punitive and vituperative bent. The first group includes such works as William J. Bennett, *To Reclaim a Legacy: A Report on the Humanities in Higher Education* (Washington, D.C.: The National Endowment for the Humanities, 1984); Ernest L. Boyer, *College: The Undergraduate Experience in America* (New York, 1987); Lynne V. Cheney, *Humanities in America: A Report to the President, the Congress, and the American People* (Washington, D.C.: The National Endowment for the Humanities, 1988); *idem, Tyrannical Machines: A Report on Educational Practices Gone Wrong and Our Best Hopes for Setting Them Right* (Washington, D.C.: The National Endowment for the Humanities, 1990); Mark H. Curtis *et al., Integrity in the College Curriculum: A Report to the Academic Community* (Association of American Colleges; Washington, D.C., 1985). In the second group I would place such works as Allan Bloom, *The Closing of the American Mind: How Higher Education Has Failed Democracy and Impoverished the Souls of Today's Students* (New York, 1987); Dinesh D'Souza, *Illiberal Education: The Politics of Race and Sex on Campus* (New York, 1991); Roger Kimball, *Tenured Radicals: How Politics Has Corrupted Our Higher Education* (New York, 1990); Chester E. Finn, Jr., "Higher Education on Trial: An Indictment," *Current* (Oct. 1984), 14–24; *idem,* "The Campus: 'An Island of Repression in a Sea of Freedom'," *Commentary,* 86 (Sept. 1989), 17–23; Page Smith, *Killing the Spirit: Higher Education in America* (New York, 1990); Charles T. Sykes, *ProfScam: Professors and the Demise of Higher Education* (New York, 1990).

The gloomy phrases quoted below are drawn from works in both groups. With the possible exception of the last four authors listed above, none, I should concede, is more negative about the state of American undergraduate education than was Abraham Flexner *Universities: American, English, German* (New York, 1930), pp. 46–72. None, certainly, can match the vituperative exuberance Flexner brought to the subject some sixty years ago. It should be noted, however, that having belabored Columbia College, Chicago and Wisconsin mightily for their sins, he excluded from his strictures such institutions as Harvard College, Yale, Princeton, Swarthmore, Vanderbilt, Amherst, Williams, Bryn Mawr, Smith, and Wellesley. These, he conceded (p. 64), offered in his day "a varied and solid curriculum to undergraduate students who may care to be educated." Few of our latter-day critics would be so generous in their exclusion.

2. Boyer, *College*, p. 2.

3. Curtis *et al., Integrity in the College Curriculum*, p. 1.

4. Bloom, *The Closing of the American Mind*, pp. 25–26, 39, 141–44, 155; Bennett, *To Reclaim a Legacy*, pp. 16–20.

5. Curtis *et al., Integrity in the College Curriculum*, pp. 2–3; Bennett, *To Reclaim a Legacy*, p. 20.

6. Bennett, *To Reclaim a Legacy*, p. 16.

7. *Ibid.*, p. 19.

8. Bloom, *The Closing of the American Mind*, pp. 58, 346; Bennett, *To Reclaim a Legacy*, p. 20.

9. Curtis *et al., Integrity in the College Curriculum*, p. 1.

10. Frederick Rudolph, *The American College and University: A History* (New York, 1965), p. 22, well reminds us that, although there were nine American colleges in 1776 they accounted among them for no more than 3,000 living graduates, and that "the largest graduating class of Harvard *before* the American Revolution was the Class of 1771, with sixty-three graduates, a number that would not again be approached for forty years."

11. See below, Chapter I, pp. 2–25.

12. See the useful chapter "The Undergraduate Curriculum Around the World," in Arthur Levine, *Handbook on Undergraduate Curriculum* (San Francisco, 1978), pp. 442–79 (good bibliography, pp. 479–83).

13. On which see below, Chapter II, pp 67–72.

14. On which see below, Chapter II, pp. 41–45.

15. See the useful brief statements by Nannerl O. Keohane, "Creativity, the Classics, and the Corporations," *Liberal Education*, 74 (No. 1, 1988), 33, and Bruce A. Kimball, "The Ambiguity of *Logos* and the History of the Liberal Arts," *ibid.*, 11–15. For an extended discussion of this whole issue, see below, Chapter II, pp. 45–66.

16. Page Smith constitutes an honorable exception to this generalization. See *Killing the Spirit*, esp. pp. 28–48, 304–5.

17. Thus Lawrence Stone in Lawrence Stone, ed., *The University in Society, I. Oxford and Cambridge from the 14th to the Early 19th Century* (Princeton, 1976), p. vii, where he continues: "We can now dimly see the shape of a vast seismic shift in west European cultural arrangements over the last four centuries. First came a period of astonishing growth after the middle of the 16th century, so that by 1640 in England, Germany, and Spain (and also, as Professor Kagan is discovering, in France and Italy) a staggering number of students were pouring into the universities. This boom was followed everywhere by a long period of decline and low enrollment which lasted from the middle of the 17th century until the first decade of the 19th. Then came

another period of huge expansion, first immediately after the Napoleonic Wars and then again after 1860."

18. On this see Derek Bok, *Higher Learning* (Cambridge, Mass., 1986), pp. 8–34. For a less optimistic appraisal of those characteristics, see David Riesman, *On Higher Education, The Academic Enterprise in an Era of Rising Student Consumerism* (San Francisco-Washington-London, 1980).

19. Bok, *Higher Learning*, p. 39.

20. Thus Kimball, *Tenured Radicals*, p. 38. He also (p. 37) improperly characterizes the ACLS report as exhibiting "an extraordinary contempt for the nonacademic public."

21. Thus Robert Scholes, for example, in his "Aiming a Canon at the Curriculum," *Salmagundi*, 72 (Fall 1986), 101–17 (at 102–4), while responding to E.D. Hirsch and commenting also on the Bennett report, does not hesitate to denounce "the establishment of a canon in humanistic studies" as "fundamentally undemocratic" or (improbably) to evoke the specter of Hitler and the *Führerprinzip*. If we can believe Roger Kimball (never prone, admittedly, to cherish understatement), similar sentiments were expressed at a Columbia seminar "Innovation in Education." See his report on the seminar in "Guns and Other 'Hermeneutical Acts' at Columbia," *The New Criterion*, 6 (No. 9, May 1988), 77–79.

22. Thus Curtis *et al.*, *Integrity in the College Curriculum*, p. 24; cf. p. 2.

23. Thus Bennett, *To Reclaim a Legacy*, p. 20.

24. Thus J. Hillis Miller, "Agreement Needed" (reviewing Joseph P. Blidiensderfer, "Report of Proceedings of a Conference of University Administrators of General and Liberal Education," Norman, Oklahoma, 1944), *Journal of Higher Education*, 16 (1945), 277–78. Among the questions involved, he lists: "What is the definition of liberal education? What is the relationship between the cultural and the utilitarian in liberal arts study? How may we distinguish between liberal education and general education? . . . etc.

25. James Bryant Conant, *The Child, the Parent and the State* (Cambridge, Mass., 1959), p. 1. "In such a mood," he adds, "I am ready to define education [simply] as what goes on in schools and colleges."

26. Bok, *Higher Learning*, p. 44. He makes that observation having just set forth (pp. 40–44) as clear and succinct a statement of the points at issue as any I have seen. "There are," he says, "three perennial issues in discussion about the liberal arts curriculum. The first of these is how much to prescribe and how much to leave to the freedom of students. Those who argue for detailed requirements claim that college students are too young to know what subjects are truly important and too disposed toward courses of immediate or practical relevance. Those who favor more electives believe that students are much too varied in their interests to be forced into a single curricular mold. . . . The second curricular issue is how to achieve breadth in each student's education. Through decades of discussion three major camps have pressed their rival claims. One group emphasizes the transmission of a defined

body of learning, often captured in a list of the great works of human thought. . . . Another school of thought stresses an acquaintance with the principal ways by which the human mind apprehends the world—methods of understanding and inquiring about literature, art, moral philosophy, history, economy, and society, as well as physical and biological phenomena. . . . The third camp advocates achieving breadth by simply requiring students to take a certain number of courses in each of several diverse categories, such as social science, natural sciences, and humanities. . . . The last of the curricular questions is how to achieve integration—how to teach students to synthesize what they have learned, to connect different modes of analysis and bodies of thought to illumine issues of human importance. . . . In fairness, however, we need to recognize that no one has yet progressed very far in creating a body of insights, generalizations, and concepts that will help students understand how to integrate the learning from different disciplines and modes of inquiry."

Preparing themselves in 1943 for the ending of the Second World War and the entry of the veterans into institutions of higher education, the members of the American Association of Colleges' Committee on the Re-Statement of the Nature and Aims of Liberal Education expressed similar sentiments. "Liberal education," they wrote, "as a creative enterprise of free men, is in perennial need of re-examination and reform. The tendency of all institutions, including educational institutions, is to lose sight of their ultimate objective, to adopt mechanical procedures, and to succumb to the inertia of static rigidity. This tendency can be combatted only by periodic reappraisal."—see James P. Baxter, 3rd., "Commission on Liberal Education Report," *Association of American Colleges Bulletin,* 29 (1943), 269–99 at 295–6 (the report itself 275–79). It should be noted that, at the time, the debate about undergraduate education in America was even more intense than it has been in the past few years.

27. Boyer, *College,* p. 26, estimates that there are "probably fewer than 50 colleges in the United States today that can be considered highly selective, admitting less than half the students who apply. At least one third are virtually open door." Riesman, *On Higher Education,* p. 124, estimates that only about 10 percent of American students attend colleges with sufficiently large applicant pools to permit a degree of selectivity. Frederick Rudolph, *Curriculum: A History of the American Undergraduate Course of Study Since 1936* (San Francisco-Washington-London, 1977), pp. 11–12, emphasizes the related point that "not until after World War II, in an environment that for the first time permitted colleges in any number to be selective in their admissions policies, were students who represented 'the academic culture'—the curriculum, the intellectual life—setting the tone of undergraduate society . . . ."

28. For an exploration of this more general theme, see Francis Oakley, *The Medieval Experience: Foundations of Western Cultural Singularity* (Toronto, 1988). Cf. Daniel O'Connor and Francis Oakley, eds., *Creation: The Impact of an Idea* (New York, 1969).

CHAPTER I

1. That is, the philosophic and scientific studies that came to be pursued by individual scholars outside the authorized structures of organized higher education. See Marshall G.S. Hodgson, *The Venture of Islam*, 3 vols. (Chicago and London, 1974), I, 473–95.

2. The roots of the system can be traced back even further to the Former Han dynasty (201 B.C.E.–8 C.E). I base my observations on Wolfgang Franke, *The Reform and Abolition of the Traditional Chinese Examination System* (Cambridge, Mass., 1960), Ichisada Miyazaki, *China's Examination Hell: The Civil Service Examinations of Imperial China*, trans. Conrad Schirokauer (New Haven and London, 1976), and John W. Chaffee, *The Thorny Gates of Learning in Sung China: A Social History of Examinations* (Cambridge, 1985).

3. Thus Franke, *Reform and Abolition*, p. 14, though he notes the concomitant growth in the "academies" of alternate centers of learning and academic instruction. Cf. Chaffee, *The Thorny Gates of Learning*, pp. 88–94.

4. As also, for that matter, in Tokugawa Japan—see R.P. Dore, *Education in Tokugawa Japan* (Berkeley and Los Angeles, 1965). At the start of the era (early 17th century), the populace was largely illiterate and higher learning at a very low ebb. By the eighteenth century, though higher education was "still largely a world of private academies where a single teacher instructed his personal disciples" (Dore, p. 23), Edo (Tokyo—by then possibly the world's largest city) had emerged as a lively center of scholarly activity. And, on the eve of the Meiji Restoration in 1868, Confucian scholarship had long been liberated from the temples, the Hayashi School of Edo had been established as the national center for the study of Sung Confucianism, and great secular schools had emerged which incorporated into their curriculum elements of Dutch learning in the fields of medicine, astronomy and metallurgy.

5. H. I. Marrou, *A History of Education in Antiquity*, trans. George Lamb (New York, 1956), p. 307; cf. pp. 340–41.

6. Thus R.R. Bolgar, *The Classical Heritage and Its Beneficiaries* (Cambridge, 1954), pp. 33–34, speaking here specifically of the schools of the Roman imperial era.

7. See A.D. Nock, *Conversion: The Old and the New in Religion from Alexander the Great to Augustine of Hippo* (Oxford, 1933), pp. 164–86. Cf. H.I. Marrou, *Saint Augustin et la fin de la culture antique* (Paris, 1938), pp. 161–73. M.L. Clarke, *Higher Education in the Ancient World* (London, 1971), pp. 59–61, while not appearing to disagree with the general point, does evince a measure of tepid skepticism about the religious status of the Academy during Plato's lifetime.

8. Marrou, *History of Education in Antiquity*, pp. 317–23; Clarke, *Higher Education in the Ancient World*, pp. 119–20. Marrou notes (p. 317), however, that Christians did set up religious schools on the rabbinical model

"whenever the Church was set up in a 'barbarian' land, i.e. one that had not assimilated classical culture."

9. Marrou, *History of Education in Antiquity*, p. 340.

10. See *ibid.*, pp. 9 and 341.

11. *Ibid.*, pp. 340–49.

12. *Institutiones divinarum . . . lectionum*, 30; J.P. Migne, ed., *Patrologiae Cursus Completus . . . series latina*, 221 vols. (Paris, 1844 ff.), 70:1144D; cited in E.K. Rand, *Founders of the Middle Ages* (New Haven, 1957), p. 143.

13. On which, see Charles Homer Haskins, *The Renaissance of the Twelfth Century* (Cambridge, Mass., 1927), pp. 368–69.

14. See, for example, Marrou, *History of Education in Antiquity*, pp. 307, 340–41; Clarke, *Higher Education in the Ancient World*, p. 130; Miyazaki, *China's Examination Hell*, p. 116; Chaffee, *The Thorny Gates of Learning*, pp. 6, 30–32, 103–4. Cf. George Makdisi, *The Rise of Colleges: Institutions of Learning in Islam and the West* (Edinburgh, 1981), p. 293, for a brief discussion of those authors who attempt to equate *madrasa* and university.

15. John W. Baldwin, *The Scholastic Culture of the Middle Ages: 1100–1300* (Lexington, Mass., 1971), p. 40.

16. Baldwin, *The Scholastic Culture*, p. 42.

17. Frederick Rudolph, *Mark Hopkins and the Log: Williams College, 1836–1872* (New Haven and London, 1956), pp. 9–10.

18. As in the case of other types of guild only the masters enjoyed full membership of the university (or, at least, did so in those universities established on the Parisian model.) The bachelors were those who had made their way to an intermediate [or journeyman] status. The terms "master" and "doctor" were at the outset used interchangeably in all faculties. Eventually the terms "doctor" and "professor" came to be used only of those who possessed the status of master in the "superior" faculties of medicine, the two laws (canon and civil) and theology. See Hastings Rashdall, *The Universities of Europe in the Middle Ages*, ed. F.M. Powicke and A.B. Emden, 3 vols. (Oxford, 1936), I, 19–20.

19. In the thirteenth century, the norm was four to five years in arts and an additional eight to twelve years in law or theology.

20. Haskins, *The Renaissance of the Twelfth Century*, pp. 370–71.

21. For a recent discussion of which see the interesting papers collected in Khalil I. Semaan, ed., *Islam and the Medieval West: Aspects of Intercultural Relations* (Albany, 1980).

22. For the simple equation of *madrasa* with university see the works cited in Makdisi, *The Rise of Colleges*, p. 337 n. 4.

23. *Ibid.*, pp. 22, 27–32, 293. Makdisi, who bluntly rejects the equation of college and university (the *madrasa* "was an entirely different type of organization"), restates his central thesis in succinct form in his "On the Origins and Development of the College in Islam and the West," in Semaan, ed., *Islam and the Medieval West*, 22–49.

24. Makdisi, *The Rise of Colleges*, pp. 224–25.

25. Thus Henry Cattan, "The Law of Waqf," in Majid Khadduri and Herbert J. Liebesny, eds., *Law in the Middle East* (Washington, D.C., 1955), I, 202–22 (at 213–18); similarly Makdisi, "Origin and Development of the College," 39. In my view, the argument does not succeed in edging beyond the terrain of intriguing parallelism and temporal priority.

26. Contrary to popular mythology, colleges were not unique to Oxbridge but were a commonplace of life in the medieval universities.

27. In this and in what follows, I hew to Makdisi's analysis in *The Rise of Colleges*, pp. 224–29, rather than to the standard interpretation in Rashdall, *Universities of Europe in the Middle Ages*, III, 192–95.

28. Makdisi, "Origin and Development of the College," 41; *The Rise of Colleges*, p. 235.

29. Rashdall, *Universities of Europe in the Middle Ages*, II, 104–5, 283, 320–21.

30. See Samuel Eliot Morison, *The Founding of Harvard College* (Cambridge, Mass., 1935), pp. 122–23; cf. Connecticut Law Reports, *Yale University vs. The Town of New Haven*, 71 Conn. (Jan. 1899), 316–39. My attention was drawn to this intriguing case by Makdisi, *The Rise of Colleges*, pp. 229–30.

31. For a brief synoptic account, see Willis Rudy, *The Universities of Europe 1100–1914: A History* (Cranbury, N.J., 1984), pp. 40–100.

32. Lawrence Stone, ed., *The University in Society*, 2 vols. (Princeton, 1974), I, vii. Cf. his essay in that volume, "The Size and Composition of the Oxford Student Body 1580–1910," 3–110, and Richard L. Kagan, "Universities in Castile 1500–1810," *ibid.*, II, 355–405.

33. With the coming of the French Revolution the traditional French system of universities was destined to be dismantled and eventually replaced by specialized schools and Napoleon's Université de France. In the territories of the Holy Roman Empire, fourteen of the old universities ceased to exist during the revolutionary wars—see Charles M. McClelland, "The Aristocracy and University Reform in Eighteenth-Century Germany, in Lawrence Stone, ed., *Schooling and Society: Studies in the History of Education* (Baltimore and London, 1976), p. 146. Also McClelland's *State, Society and University in Germany: 1700–1914* (Cambridge, 1980), pp. 101–2.

34. Nicholas Phillipson, "Culture and Society in the 18th Century Province: The Case of Edinburgh and the Scottish Enlightenment," in Stone, ed., *The University in Society*, II, 410–11, 448. Also David B. Horn, *A Short History of the University of Edinburgh: 1556–1889* (Edinburgh, 1967), pp. 40–61.

35. For which see McClelland, *State, Society, and University in Germany*, pp. 30–98.

36. McClelland, "The Aristocracy and University Reform in Eighteenth-Century Germany," 170 and 166.

37. Thus McClelland, *State, Society, and University in Germany*,

pp. 172–73. "One is hard pressed," he continues, "to find any eighteenth-century professors who took research as seriously and passionately as many of the great discoverers and writers of the 1830s onwards." McClelland, pp. 101–89, gives a good account of the importance of Berlin and the emergence of the "research ethic."

38. For some aspects of this educational diaspora, see Eric Ashby, *Universities: British, Indian, African—A Study in the Ecology of Higher Education* (Cambridge, Mass., 1966).

39. Thus, whereas in the Soviet Union of 1950 some 1.2 million students were enrolled in the universities, polytechnics and specialized institutes of which the higher education sector is composed, and 4.6 million in 1973, in the China of 1978 the fewer than 600,000 students enrolled amounted to less than three-quarters of the number enrolled prior to the Cultural Revolution. See Arthur Levine, *Handbook on Undergraduate Curriculum* (San Francisco-Washington-London, 1978), pp. 444 and 475.

40. *Ibid.*, pp. 455, 462, 472.

41. Philip G. Altbach, "Problems of University Reform in India," in Philip G. Altbach, ed., *University Reform* (Cambridge, Mass., 1974), 67.

42. Stephen d'Irsay, *Histoire des universités françaises et étrangères des origines à nos jours*, 2 vols. (Paris, 1933), II, 7–8; Ashby, *Universities: British, Indian, African*, pp. 8–12, where he discusses the transplantation of the Spanish university model in Latin America.

43. Morison, *The Founding of Harvard College*, pp. 160–209.

44. See the second part of the anonymous pamphlet, "New England's First Fruits" (1643), in Morison, *The Founding of Harvard College*, Appendix D, pp. 432–36. Cf. Frederick Rudolph, *Curriculum: A History of the American Undergraduate Course of Study Since 1636* (San Francisco-Washington-London, 1977), pp. 31–39.

45. On which, see below, Chapter II, pp. 59–61.

46. Donald H. Tewksbury, *The Founding of American Colleges and Universities Before the Civil War* (New York, 1932), pp. 32–35.

47. Frederick Rudolph, *The American College and University: A History* (New York, 1965), p. 47.

48. For example, by Richard Hofstadter and Walter P. Metzger, *The Development of Academic Freedom in the United States* (New York, 1955), pp. 209, 223–25; Hofstadter, *The Development and Scope of Higher Education in the United States* (New York, 1952), pp. 19–20. For a critique of this "Whiggish" version of the history of American higher education, see James Axtell, "The Death of the Liberal Arts College," *History of Education Quarterly*, 11 (Winter 1971), 339–52.

49. Quoted in Rudolph, *American College and University*, pp. 68 and 443. Rudolph also draws attention (pp. 330 and 443) to the similar and widely shared appraisal by Professor Burgess of Columbia in 1884: "I confess that I am unable to divine what is to be ultimately the position of Colleges which cannot become Universities and which will not be Gymnasia. I cannot see

what reason they will have to exist. It will be largely a waste of capital to maintain them, and, largely a waste of time to attend them. It is so now."

50. Thus Makdisi, "Origin and Development of the College," 28–29: "Americans familiar with education in Europe are aware of the fact that our colleges have little or nothing in common with European colleges. Our historians have to point out to us that the colleges of Oxford and Cambridge served as models for our early collegiate history. But the Oxonian type of college remains unique: it is a constituent part of the university and does not grant degrees. The Parisian college is not a college at all in our sense of the word. A *collège* and a *lycée*, both of which offer the same level of instruction, are below the college level in the United States."

51. Rudolph, *American College and University*, pp. 24, 165–68.

52. Connecticut Law Reports: *Yale University vs. The Town of New Haven*, 71 Conn. (January 1899), 323–27.

53. Cited in Rudolph, *American College and University*, p. 272.

54. Lawrence R. Veysey, *The Emergence of the American University* (Chicago and London, 1965), p. 166 and n. 145, where he adds (noting that at that time Catholic University also catered only to graduate studies): "that is, the only such university without a pervasive religious affiliation." Hall, himself a Williams graduate, had previously taught at that college, and Bliss Perry, recalling his own student days there, comments with admiration on "the brilliant lectures in the history of philosophy" he had given to the seniors. See Perry, *And Gladly Teach: Reminiscences* (New York, 1935), p. 61.

55. For which see below, Chapter II, pp. 61–63.

56. Rudolph, *American College and University*, pp. 266–67; Veysey, *Emergence of the American University*, pp. 70–71.

57. Axtell, "Death of the Liberal Arts College," 345.

58. *Ibid.*, 347–48. Axtell also does well to remind us that before 1885 or 1890 the differences between the old colleges and the new universities were much smaller than we tend often to assume. Of the 26 institutions in 1881 which had enrollments of 200 students or more, 17 were colleges. "Amherst was as large as Wisconsin and Virginia, Williams was larger than Cornell and Indiana, and Bowdoin was the near-equal of Johns Hopkins and Minnesota."

59. Levine, *Handbook on Undergraduate Curriculum*, pp. 588–92.

60. *Ibid.*, pp. 608–28. He notes (p. 608) that the Report proposed the expansion of community colleges; the end of curricular, religious, and racial barriers to higher education, mass access to college; the availability of a minimum of two years of college for all capable Americans; the initiation of a strong general education component in the curriculum; and the mixing of general education with education for work." Noble ideals all!

61. Including in that generalization, of course, the wrenching impact during the late 1970s and the 1980s of the cessation of the growth. For some observations on this point and on the unparalleled diversity of our student population (in terms of race, gender, ethnicity, age and social class), see Francis

Oakley, "Apocalypse Now in U.S. Higher Education," *America,* 160 (No. 12, 1989), 286–87, 308.

62. "The Size and Composition of the Oxford Student Body 1580–1910," in Stone, ed., *The University in Society,* I, 4.

63. The phrase is Makdisi's, *The Rise of Colleges,* p. 282.

64. *Ibid.,* pp. 40–44, 235–37; cf. his "Origin and Development of the College," 42–43.

65. The so-called "closing of the gate of ijtihad" linked with the creation in the thirteenth century of the salaried governmental post of mufti. See Makdisi, *The Rise of Colleges,* pp. 290–91.

66. On which, see below, Chapter II, p. 66.

67. See Francis Oakley, *The Western Church in the Later Middle Ages* (Ithaca and London, 1979), p. 46.

68. Rudy, *The Universities of Europe,* p. 73.

69. See James K. Pollock, *The Government of Greater Germany* (New York, 1940), pp. 169–70.

70. Rudolph, *American College and University,* pp. 166–67. The membership of the faculty, that is to say, ceased to be coterminous with the membership of the corporation, which came to be comprised, instead, of outsiders. Cf. Eric Ashby, *Any Person, Any Study: An Essay on Higher Education in the United States* (New York, 1971), p. 21, speaking of the two university systems: "The fundamental difference between America and Britain [resides] in the de jure status of both faculty and students. In Britain faculty and students are members of the corporation. In America the corporation is the trustees."

71. In a letter to James Marsh in 1829, quoted in Rudolph, *The American College and University,* p. 172. Nearly fifty years later in his inaugural address at Williams College (July 27, 1872), President Paul Chadbourne complained that members of the faculty "are often spoken of as working *for the College.* They ARE THE COLLEGE, so far as it is an active agency." In *Williams College Inauguration: of Pres. P.A. Chadbourne* (Williamstown, Mass., 1872), p. 33. Like recent critics of the academy unmindful of the more distant past, Robert Nisbet, *The Degradation of the Academic Dogma* (New York and London, 1971), pp. 102–3, claims that it was only in the 1950s that the faculty member, from being "member of the university" passed to being a mere "employee." He adds: "The transition I refer to was symbolized perfectly . . ., when, starting around 1950 one began to hear the word 'hire' [as opposed to 'appoint'] used more and more commonly around university halls."

72. For *Lehrfreiheit* and *Lernfreiheit* (i.e. "the absence of administrative coercions in the learning situation") and for the German influence on the American university scene, see Hofstadter and Metzger, *Development of Academic Freedom in the United States,* pp. 367–412.

73. Cited in Rudolph, *The American College and University,* p. 187. See also *idem, Mark Hopkins and the Log,* pp. 190–200.

74. *Idem, The American College and University,* p. 209. Detailed ac-

count in Leon Burr Richardson, *History of Dartmouth College*, 2 vols. (Hanover, 1932), I, 287–346.

75. Makdisi, *The Rise of Colleges*, p. 230.

76. *Trustees of Dartmouth College vs. Woodward*, in Frederick C. Brightly, ed., *Reports of Cases Argued and Adjudged in the Supreme Court of the United States* [Wheaton, 4] (Washington, D.C., 1883), XVII, 572–74.

77. Brightly, ed., *U.S. Reports*, XVII, 634, 637–39, 640–41.

78. Rudolph, *The American College and University*, pp. 211–12.

79. Though few European critiques can compete in degree of derisive condescension with our own home-grown diatribes.

80. On which see the helpful appraisal by Derek Bok, *Higher Learning* (Cambridge, Mass., 1986), pp. 3–34.

CHAPTER II

1. Frank H. Turner, *The Greek Heritage in Victorian Britain* (New Haven and London, 1981), p. 446.

2. *Ibid.,* pp. 305–7.

3. Bruce A. Kimball, *Orators and Philosophers: A History of the Idea of Liberal Education* (New York, 1986), pp. 3–4. "It is paradoxical," Kimball adds (p. 2), "that, precisely on a topic where academicians are forever eager to appeal to history, many erect ahistorical and relativistic conceptions of 'liberal education' as cairns to mark the trail." As a result (p. 9), "a brief overview of writings about 'liberal education' and about its history reveals contradiction and confusion; and the more that is written, the more confounded things become."

4. Perhaps the oddest version of this gambit is Bloom's location of this golden age in the 1950s.

5. Thus Joseph R. Levenson, *Confucian China and its Modern Fate*, 3 vols. (London, 1958–65), II, vi, vii—the whole work presents a splendidly nuanced analysis.

6. R. P. Dore, *Education in Tokugawa Japan* (Berkeley and Los Angeles, 1965), pp. 23, 26–29, 31.

7. Marshall G. S. Hodgson, *The Venture of Islam*, 3 vols. (Chicago and London, 1974), I, 473–75.

8. This whole arrangement was sustained in China, of course, by the all-important examination system focused on the canon of Confucian texts. From the eighth century onward it was the Board of Rites which possessed the authority over the examination system, and Wolfgang Franke, *The Reform and Abolition of the Traditional Chinese Examination System* (Cambridge, Mass., 1960), notes (p. 5) that "[T]he Board of Rites was in charge of the official cult of ritual observances in honor of Confucius and the state ceremonies based on Confucian doctrines. This subordination of the examination system to the authority responsible for the Confucian cult and the upholding of Confucianism served to strengthen the ties between the two: at the same

time it stressed the union of spiritual and secular authority fundamental to the traditional Chinese 'state'."

9. Perhaps one may be permitted to note the odd asymmetry between the current sensitivity to the charge of "Orientalism" and the ease with which a unitary "Occident" is identified. The Bible, after all, is the achievement of a West Asian culture. Classical Greece and Rome and medieval Byzantium were Mediterranean rather than European cultures. And Europe itself, at least as anything more than a geographical expression, is a product of the Latin Middle Ages. To lump them all together as "Western" serves to generate its own problems.

10. See James Bowen, *A History of Western Education*, 3 vols. (London, 1972–81), I, 5–62.

11. On which, see below, §2, pp. 45–59.

12. For some general thoughts on this, see Francis Oakley, *The Medieval Experience: Foundations of Western Cultural Singularity* (Toronto, 1988), pp. 108–70.

13. Matthew Arnold, *Culture and Anarchy: An Essay in Political and Social Criticism* (New York, 1883), ch. 4, pp. 110, 112. Stressing that Arnold's understanding of the Greeks stemmed "in large measure, from the image of Greece communicated by Herder, Humboldt, Goethe, and Heine," Turner, *The Greek Heritage in Victorian Britain*, pp. 23, 21, warns that "his Hebrews were not Jews but contemporary English Protestant Nonconformists. His Greeks were not ancient Hellenes but a version of humanity largely conjured up in the late eighteenth century German literary and aesthetic imagination."

14. Turner, *The Greek Heritage in Victorian Britain*, esp. pp. 154–70, 265–74, 299–300, 314–21, 372–73, 430, 447–51.

15. On which, see Jaroslav Pelikan, *The Emergence of the Catholic Tradition* (Chicago, 1971), pp. 27–41.

16. R. R. Bolgar, *The Classical Heritage and Its Beneficiaries* (Cambridge, 1954), p. 50, asserts that "Jerome and Augustine were the men who decided the educational future of the West." And, again, p. 57: "St. Jerome, St. Augustine, St. Gregory the Great in the West, St. Basil of Caesarea and St. Gregory Nazianzan in the East, these were the oracles to which the future was to turn for guidance."

17. Tertullian, *On Prescription Against Heretics*, ch. 7; cited in Étienne Gilson, *Reason and Revelation in the Middle Ages* (New York, 1938), pp. 9–10.

18. As Bolgar, *The Classical Heritage*, p. 368, correctly notes: "... [T]he efforts made by the Christian Churches to restrict the unfettered use of pagan material were no less important for the cultural and social programme of Europe than the contrary efforts of the Humanists to make that material a part of the European heritage." I argue this case in relation to science and law in my *Omnipotence, Covenant, and Order: An Excursion in the History of Ideas from Abelard to Leibniz* (London, 1984), and, in more general terms, in *The Medieval Experience*, pp. 156–70.

19. Though it is worth noting that among the philosophical proposi-
tions condemned by the Bishop of Paris in 1277 as yielding too much ground
to Aristotelian rationalism were several that can be attributed to Thomas
Aquinas, whose superbly architectonic philosophico-theological synthesis was
later to become almost synonymous with Roman Catholic orthodoxy—see
Oakley, *The Medieval Experience,* pp. 164–65.

20. Bolgar, *The Classical Heritage,* pp. 356–59; cf. Anthony Grafton
and Lisa Jardine, *From Humanism to the Humanities: Education and the
Liberal Arts in Fifteenth- and Sixteenth-Century Europe* (Cambridge, Mass.,
1986), p. 197.

21. Frederick Rudolph, *Curriculum: A History of the American Undergraduate Course of Study since 1636* (San Francisco-Washington-London,
1977), p. 56; *idem, The American College and University: A History* (New
York, 1965), p. 141; *idem, Mark Hopkins and the Log: Williams College,
1836–1872* (New Haven, 1956), p. 57.

22. H. J. Marrou, *A History of Education in Antiquity,* trans. George
Lamb (New York, 1956), pp. 99–101.

23. Grafton and Jardine, *From Humanism to the Humanities,* pp. xiv–
xv. It has "clouded our intellectual judgment," they continue, "of the progress
and importance of the liberal arts from the days of Guarino down to T. S.
Eliot, Leavis and the twentieth-century guardians of European 'civilisation'."
Eliot's essay, "What Is a Classic?," for example, "bears all the hallmarks of
humanist ideology and mystification."

24. Though he does so with an appropriate measure of caution—see
Levenson, *Confucian China and Its Modern Fate,* I, 18–19. For the ideal itself,
see Sheldon Rothblatt, *Tradition and Change in English Liberal Education:
An Essay in History and Culture* (London, 1976).

25. Formally entitled *General Education in a Free Society,* the Redbook
was the outcome of two years' work by the Harvard Committee on the
objectives of general education in a free society—*General Education in a Free
Society: Report of the Harvard Committee* (Cambridge, Mass., 1950), p. 44
(see the whole of ch. 2 devoted to "Theory of General Education," pp. 42–
78).

26. Arnold, *Culture and Anarchy,* ch. 2, pp. 40–41; ch. 4, pp. 125–
27.

27. Thus, of the ideal advocated by the Harvard *Redbook,* Rudolph
has said: "In urging revitalization of general education, Harvard proposed to
democratize what had once been the education of a gentleman and an aris-
tocrat and make it the education essential to the responsibilities of every
citizen." But "Yale in 1828 and Harvard in 1945 did not speak the language
of the country which they addressed. . . . General education . . . was not the
expression of the dominant culture. It spoke for a counterculture that acted
as if it were *the* culture, it was an expression of the 'establishment'."—*Curriculum,* pp. 259–61.

28. Gerald Graff, *Professing Literature: An Institutional History* (Chi-

cago and London, 1989), pp. 81–85. Bliss Perry, who went from Williams to teach at Princeton and Harvard, well conveys the "feel" of the generalist approach in his book of reminiscences, *And Gladly Teach* (Boston, 1935).

29. Terry Eagleton, *Literary Theory: An Introduction* (Oxford, 1983), pp. 22, 26.

30. *Ibid.*, p. 49. See the whole discussion, pp. 17–53. For some judiciously critical remarks concerning Eagleton's whole approach, see Graff, *Professing Literature*, pp. 11–14.

31. Kimball, *Orators and Philosophers*, pp. 2–3.

32. *Ibid.*, p. 14.

33. *Ibid.*, pp. 13, 15–16, 20–22; cf. Marrou, *A History of Education in Antiquity*, p. 177. He adds (p. 196): "the essential ambiguity of the word [*paideia*] is worth remembering. It meant both education and culture." For the origins of the term *tekhnai eleutherioi* see also Henri Marrou, "Les arts libéraux dans l'antiquité classique," in *Arts libéraux et philosophie au moyen âge: Actes du quatrième Congrès internationale de philosophie médiévale* (Montreal and Paris, 1969), pp. 11, 30–31.

34. Bolgar, *The Classical Heritage and Its Beneficiaries*, pp. 42 and 35; cf. Paul Oskar Kristeller, *Renaissance Thought II: Papers on Humanism and the Arts* (New York, 1965), pp. 172–74. Henri Marrou, however, would push the point of definitive curricular agreement back to an earlier period—see his *Saint Augustin et la fin de la culture antique* (Paris, 1938), pp. 211–19.

35. In what follows I do no more than reproduce in outline form the argument Kimball develops in his *Orators and Philosophers*, pp. 16–19, 31–41. Cf. Marrou, *A History of Education in Antiquity*, esp. pp. 61, 87–90, 161–64, 169, 194–96, 205–7, 210–12, 223–24.

36. Conceding (p. 82) that "in a general sense" and "from the technical point of view Isocrates simply continued the teaching of the Sophists," Marrou adds, however, that the rhetorical education Isocrates offered aspired to be more than a training in oratory. His orator is "led to choose . . . subjects which are most in conformity with virtue." What gives words weight is "the personal authority which is conferred upon . . . [them] . . . by a virtuous life." "Thus in the hands of Isocrates rhetoric is gradually transformed into ethics"—*A History of Education in Antiquity*, pp. 88–89.

37. Kimball, *Orators and Philosophers*, p. 5.

38. Marrou, *A History of Education in Antiquity*, p. 206. See above, Chapter I, p. 13 and n. 7.

39. Marrou, *A History of Education in Antiquity*, pp. 194, 89. For, Cicero, Aulus Gellius, the terms *studia humaniora, studia humanitatis* and what they denoted, see Paul Oskar Kristeller, *Renaissance Thought: The Classic Scholastic, and Humanist Strains*, rev. ed (New York, 1961), pp. 3–23, 95–111, 131–39.

40. Thus Bolgar, *The Classical Heritage*, p. 252.

41. Marrou, *A History of Education in Antiquity*, p. 161. Pointing out the great lengths to which "the Hellenistic age carried its official canonization

of the classics," he adds: "A classical culture can be defined as a unified collection of great masterpieces existing as the recognized basis of its scale of values."

42. Kimball, *Orators and Philosophers*, pp. 36–38, where he elaborates this typology.

43. The reference is to Quintilian, *Institutio oratoria*, I, prœmium, 9–10.

44. Werner Jaeger, *Paideia: The Ideals of Greek Culture*, 3 vols. (Oxford, 1939–45), III, 46.

45. Marrou, *A History of Education in Antiquity*, p. 210.

46. Thus Grafton and Jardine, *From Humanism to the Humanities*, pp. xii–xiii, where they deplore the tendency of such scholars as Eugenio Garin to depict "the downfall of scholasticism as the natural triumph of virtue over vice." "[T]he triumph of humanist education cannot simply be explained by reference to its intrinsic worth or practical utility. On the contrary, the literary education of the humanists displaced a system far better adapted to many of the traditional intellectual and practical needs of European society. . . . The liquidation of this intellectual system was clearly the murder of an intact organism, not the clearing away of a disintegrated fossil." Cf. Kristeller, *Renaissance Thought: The Classic, Scholastic and Humanist Strains*, esp. pp. 113–19, for the claim that in Italy scholasticism actually developed as a growing concern side by side with humanism.

47. Rothblatt, *Tradition and Change*, pp. 43–45. Cf. Richard Foster Jones, *Ancients and Moderns: A Study of the Rise of the Scientific Movement in Seventeenth-Century England* (Berkeley and Los Angeles, 1965); David Spadafora, *The Idea of Progress in Eighteenth-Century Britain* (New Haven and London, 1990), pp. 21–84.

48. William Irvine, *Apes, Angels and Victorians: The Story of Darwin, Huxley, and Evolution* (New York, London, Toronto, 1955), p. 285.

49. An argument which he set forth in his *Education of a Christian Prince*, trans. Lester K. Born (New York, 1936).

50. For which, see Rothblatt, *Tradition and Change*, esp. pp. 26–30, 59–60.

51. Thus Kimball, *Orators and Philosophers*, p. 207: "The humanism of the *antiqui* [of the Italian Renaissance], derived from Cicero and Quintilian, was transmitted to the rest of Western Europe during the fifteenth and sixteenth centuries. It was this outlook, amplified by notions of 'courtesy' and Christian ethics, that was eventually transmitted to the American colonies in the archetype of the Christian gentleman." See also, pp. 107–10.

52. For his account of the emergence of this ideal, see Kimball, *Orators and Philosophers*, ch. 5, pp. 114–56. The typology of the liberal-free ideal is set forth on pp. 119–22.

53. Quotations from Kimball, *Orators and Philosophers*, pp. 115–16, 119.

54. See above, Chapter I, pp. 21–22.

55. See above, Chapter I, pp. 22–23; Rothblatt, *Tradition and Change*, p. 76. Kimball, *Orators and Philosophers*, pp. 130–31, is somewhat skeptical about the claims made for the "progressive" nature of the education offered by the Dissenting Academies.

56. Sheldon Rothblatt goes into the matter in considerable detail in "The Student Sub-Culture and the Examination System in Early 19th-Century Oxbridge," in Lawrence Stone, ed., *The University in Society*, 2 vols. (Princeton, 1974), I, 247–303.

57. Rothblatt, *Tradition and Change*, p. 130. He adds ("The Student Sub-Culture," 303): [T]he introduction of competitive examinations produced what were the most conspicuous pedagogical features of pre-Victorian Oxbridge, a weak professoriate, a high degree of college autonomy, and an extensive network of private teaching. It should not be surprising, therefore, that the central purpose of the great reforms of 1856 to 1880 was to correct those deficiencies, in fact to undo some of the damage which arose paradoxically as a consequence of the most notable development in English higher education in over a century."

58. See above, Chapter I, pp. 22–23. Rothblatt, *Tradition and Change*, pp. 164–67, argues that it is warranted to use the phrase "knowledge revolution" to catch the significance of "the transformation that occurred within the universities of Europe when they dropped the museum concept of a university—a place to store and admire the marvellous achievements of the past—and adopted a dynamic and open-ended conception of knowledge."

59. *Ibid.*, pp. 157, 197.

60. Arnold, *Culture and Anarchy*, ch. 1, pp. 6–7.

61. *Ibid.*, ch. 4 and Conclusion, pp. 124, 205. Cf. Jones, *Ancient and Moderns*, pp. 268–71, for the Puritan onslaught on the old classical curriculum.

62. Irvine, *Apes, Angels and Victorians*, comments, p. 283: "These two men offer the happy spectacle of antagonists who never fully realized how deeply they were at variance."

63. Thomas Henry Huxley, "Science and Culture" (an address delivered at the opening of Mason College, Birmingham, in 1880), in Cyril Bibby, ed., *T.H. Huxley on Education* (Cambridge, 1971), pp. 181–82. In an earlier address, "A Liberal Education: Where to Find It," *ibid.*, p. 81, Huxley had delivered himself of the following striking claim: "That man has had a liberal education ... whose intellect is a clear, cold, logic engine, with all its parts of equal strength, and in smooth working order; ready, like a steam engine, to be turned to any kind of work, and spin the gossamers as well as forge the anchors of the mind." Kimball discusses the exchange in *Orators and Philosophers*, pp. 171–73.

64. Huxley, "Science and Culture," p. 182: "I am too well acquainted with the generosity of spirit, the true sympathy with scientific thought, which pervades the writings of our chief apostle of culture to identify him with these opinions; and yet one may cull from one and another of these epistles to the

Philistines, which so delight all who do not answer to that name, sentences which lend them some support."

65. Perry, *And Gladly Teach*, pp. 78–79.

66. Matthew Arnold, "Literature and Science," in his *Discourses in America* (New York, 1902), pp. 72–137. I cite from pp. 82, 94–95, 105–7, 112, 121–22, 129.

67. Kimball, *Orators and Philosophers*, p. 171. He discusses the exchange at greater length in his "Matthew Arnold, Huxley and Liberal Education: A Centennial Retrospective," *Teachers College Record*, 86 (No. 3, 1985), 475–87. Cf. Irvine, *Apes, Angels and Victorians*, pp. 283–86.

68. As described in the anonymous pamphlet entitled "New England's First Fruits" (1643), reprinted in Samuel Eliot Morison, *The Founding of Harvard College* (Cambridge, Mass., 1935), App. D., pp. 420–46 (at 432–36). Cf. Rudolph, *Curriculum*, pp. 31–32.

69. Or, it was so at least in 1816 when President Zephaniah Swift Moore outlined the College's Course of Study—see Williams College Library, Archives and Special Collections, Misc. Mss., vol. 15, p. 48. The Course of Instruction set forth in the 1839–40 catalogue betrays little sign of change, although the range of both the Greek and Latin authors assigned had been expanded—*Catalogue of the Corporation, Officers and Students of Williams College, 1839–40* (Troy, N.Y., 1839), pp. 15–17.

70. Rudolph, *The American College and University*, pp. 32–3.

71. *Ibid.*, pp. 125–67; *idem, Curriculum*, pp. 81–83.

72. Rudolph, *The American College and University*, pp. 140–41; *idem, Curriculum*, pp. 39–42, and, for Mark Hopkins, *idem, Mark Hopkins and the Log*, esp. pp. 46–52. Perry, *And Gladly Teach*, pp. 60–64, gives an affectionate portrayal of the way in which Hopkins taught the capstone course when he was 78.

73. Thus Rudolph, *The American College and University*, pp. 130–31, 134–5; cf. idem, *Curriculum*, p. 75.

74. As the Report said: "The two great points to be gained in intellectual culture, are the *discipline* and the *furniture* of the mind: expanding its powers and storing it with knowledge." Reprinted in part in R. Hofstadter and W. Smith, *American Higher Education: A Documentary History*, 2 vols. (Chicago, 1961), I, 278. Kimball, *Orators and Philosophers*, p. 151, notes that the same notion occurred "no less prominently in the 1850s reports at Oxford and Cambridge than in those at Yale in 1828."

75. For some differing assessments, see Richard Hofstadter and Walter R. Metzger, *The Development of Academic Freedom in the United States* (New York, 1955), pp. 209–22; Richard Warch, *School of the Prophets: Yale College, 1701–1740* (New Haven and London, 1973); Rudolph, *Curriculum*, pp. 37–98; Kimball, *Orators and Philosophers*, App. I, pp. 243–54.

76. Levine, *Handbook on Undergraduate Curriculum*, p. 559, labels Cornell as "the jewel of the land-grant movement."

77. Though less congenial, it seems, to others. Irvine, *Apes, Angels and*

Victorians, p. 297, tells us that some saw the combination of Huxley's presence and the omission of any opening prayer as intolerable. President Gilman received a letter that said "It was bad enough to invite Huxley. It were better to have asked God to be present. It would have been absurd to ask them both."

78. Graff, *Professing Literature*, pp. 81–97, 126–28; also Michael R. Harris, *Five Counterrevolutionaries in Higher Education: Irving Babbitt, Albert Jay Nock, Abraham Flexner, Robert Maynard Hutchins, Alexander Meiklejohn* (Corvallis, 1970). Harris (p. 44) characterizes Irving Babbit (teacher of both Foerster and T. S. Eliot) as "pre-eminent among...the New Humanists." For Sherman, see Jacob Zeitlin and Homer Woodbridge, *Life and Letters of Stuart P. Sherman*, 2 vols. (New York, 1929). Graff notes (p. 90) that even generalists like Carter of Williams, "who strongly regretted the trivialization of literature by pedantic scholarship," were careful to avoid giving offence to their scholarly colleagues. See, for example, Franklin Carter, "The Study of Modern Languages in Our Higher Institutions," *Transactions and Proceedings of the Modern Languages Association*, 2 (1886), 3–21.

79. Over the centuries, the rival rhetorical and philosophical educational ideals had succeeded in making a marked impact upon each other. Marrou, *A History of Education in Antiquity*, pp. 210–11, has said that "[t]he opposition between the two hostile forces caused a creative tension, an influence that worked both ways, and, as always happens in the course of a prolonged struggle, the two adversaries ended up by taking a good deal of colour from each other." He adds (p. 212): "There was not only hostility between the two types of culture, but an inextricable interweaving, knitting the classical tradition into an ever-closer unity."

80. See Levine, *Handbook on Undergraduate Curriculum*, p. 506.

81. *Ibid.*, pp. 336–40.

82. Kimball, *Orators and Philosophers*, p. 224, citing Paul L. Dressel and Margaret F. Lorimer, *Attitudes of Liberal Arts Faculty Members Toward Liberal and Professional Education* (New York, 1960), pp. 37, 51.

83. Although the two great bastions of the core curriculum, Columbia College and the University of Chicago, both sought for some years to do without the undergraduate major at all.

84. See Levine, *Handbook on Undergraduate Curriculum*, pp. 3–53. He points out (p. 28) that "the major or concentration is now viewed as probably the most successful part" of the undergraduate course of study. Cf., for a not dissimilar appraisal, *Missions of the College Curriculum: A Contemporary Review with Suggestions*. A Commentary of the Carnegie Foundation for the Advancement of Teaching (San Francisco-Washington-London, 1977), pp. 186–99.

85. Rudolph, *Curriculum*, pp. 236–39, 241, 252–64, 276–80; Graff, *Professing Literature*, pp. 133–35, 162–79.

86. Graff, *Professing Literature*, p. 162, sees the Second World War as having "brought the crisis of education to a head" and the general education

movement as having been "institutionalized" only after the war. "The general education movement was a response to two kinds of fears: that because of increasing disciplinary specialization and emphasis on vocational training, knowledge was becoming fragmented, and that because of deepening conflicts of ideology, the unity of Western culture was disintegrating into a chaotic relativism."

87. Kimball, *Orators and Philosophers*, p. 234.

88. See Bennett, *To Reclaim a Legacy;* Cheney, *Humanities in America.*

89. Kimball, *Orators and Philosophers*, pp. 157–241, teases out, in formidable detail, the increasingly intricate interweaving of the two ideals as the century has progressed.

90. Paul O. Kristeller, "Liberal Education and Western Humanism," in *Seminar Reports*, 5 (No. 1, Fall 1976), 15–25 (see especially 15–16, 21 and 23–24). Kimball's brief discussion in *Orators and Philosophers*, pp. 235–36, drew this interesting essay to my attention.

91. Charles Frankel, "Intellectual Foundations of Liberalism," in *Seminar Reports*, 5 (No. 1, Fall 1976), 3–14. See especially 4–5 and 8, where he continues: "What separates liberalism, in its own view, from conservatism, and what protects it, in its own self-image, from radicalism's effort to dismiss it as just another ideology, is its conviction that there are ways and means by which the human mind can improve its understanding of the universe and, therefore, introduce some rational framework within which it can sift and criticize ideas."

92. Frankel, "Intellectual Foundations of Liberalism," 10–11, 12, 14. In response to a question Frankel conceded (p. 13) the novelty of the situation now confronting liberal education. "Until relatively recently, liberal culture and liberal education have been instruments for loosening the traditional culture, reducing its rigidities, eliminating its excessively mechanistic qualities. ... Today, however, liberal culture is in a relatively new condition. It has always been an adversary culture, existing in a context in which traditionalism and religious or moral orthodoxy have been the order of the day. But what happens when the regnant orthodoxy becomes the orthodoxy of individualism and eccentricity? ... When liberal culture becomes the dominant culture, the problem it faces is to look at its own self-parody, its own rigidifications, and to return to its contextual method of criticism."

93. Charles Francis Adams, Jr., *A College Fetich* (Boston, 1883), pp. 16–19.

94. Perry, *And Gladly Teach*, pp. 38–41.

95. Bolgar, *The Classical Heritage*, pp. 35–45; Marrou, *A History of Education in Antiquity*, pp. 176–85, 281–82. Note, later on, the gap that must have existed between the ambitious nature of the Greek program set forth in the Jesuit *Rationes studiorum* of 1586, 1591 and 1599 and what could possibly have been accomplished—see Bolgar, pp. 358–60.

96. Bolgar, *The Classical Heritage*, pp. 67–78.

97. Graff, *Professing Literature*, pp. 1–2.

98. *Ibid.*, p. 14.

99. *Ibid.*, pp. 248–49. It should be added that Graff is by no means disposed to minimize the radicalism of the deconstructive stance—at least to the extent to which it is firmly grounded in its philosophical presuppositions. On which, see his *Literature Against Itself: Literary Ideas in Modern Society* (Chicago and London, 1979). It may be that the position he adopts in *Professing Literature* is predicated on a measure of skepticism about the degree to which his literary colleagues have succeeded (or even wish to succeed) in appropriating those philosophical assumptions.

100. Grafton and Jardine, *From Humanism to the Humanities*, p. 1.

101. *Ibid.*, pp. 1–3 (italics theirs).

102. *Ibid.*, pp. 18–22. They note (p. 20) that "even a student who spent several years attending Guarino's lectures on rhetoric would probably have studied only the equivalent of a few hundred modern pages of text *in all.*" R. R. Bolgar, "Classicist Reading in Renaissance Schools," *Durham Research Review*, 6 (1955), 18–26, concludes that the grammar schools of sixteenth-century England covered a surprisingly limited and fragmentary curriculum. Boys read about as much of the Greek and Latin classics as would be required today, respectively, for O-level Greek and A-level Latin in the G.C.E. See Gerald Strauss, "Liberal or Illiberal Arts?", *Journal of Social History*, 19 (No. 2, 1985), 361–67, for a similarly critical view of the classical regimen pursued in the German *gymmasia* of the sixteenth and subsequent centuries. In an important recent book, Paul F. Grendler, *Schooling in Renaissance Italy: Literacy and Learning, 1300–1600* (Baltimore and London, 1989), pp. 406–10, mounts a spirited defence of the classical education of the era, but he does not really address the enormous gap between ideal and reality which is the point at issue here.

103. *Ibid.*, pp. 27–28.

104. Grafton and Jardine, *From Humanism to the Humanities*, pp. xiv–xv.

105. *Ibid.*, pp. xii–xiv: "The triumph of humanist education cannot simply be explained by reference to its intrinsic worth or practical utility. On the contrary, the literary education of the humanists displaced a system far better adapted to many of the traditional intellectual and practical needs of European society. Scholasticism was very much a going concern in the fourteenth and fifteenth centuries."

CHAPTER III

1. Charles J. Sykes, *ProfScam: Professors and the Demise of Higher Education* (New York, 1990), pp. 259, 262–63. Similarly, *Page Smith, Killing the Spirit: Higher Education in America* (New York, 1990), p. 221, where he speaks of the "small, private, once-denominational colleges and community colleges where there is a strong tradition of placing the needs of students rather than the ambitions of professors at the center of the institutions."

2. Frederick Rudolph, *The American College and University: A History* (New York, 1965), pp. 47, 486.

3. Susan G. Broyles, ed., *Dictionary of Postsecondary Education*, 2 vols, (U.S. National Center for Education Statistics: Washington, D.C., 1990), I, xv and xxvi (Tables 1 and 12). Under the rubric of "postsecondary institution" the *Directory* lists "universities, colleges at the 4-year and 2-year levels, professional schools, community colleges, technical institutes, business schools, and occupationally oriented vocational schools." Under the heading of "Higher Education Institutions," it lists those institutions "accredited at the college level by an agency or association recognized by the Secretary, U.S. Department of Education"—see pp. vii and viii.

4. See *A Classification of Institutions of Higher Education: 1987 Edition* (Carnegie Foundation for the Advancement of Teaching: Princeton, N.J., 1987), Table 4, p. 5; Thomas D. Snyder, ed., *Digest of Educational Statistics* (U.S. Department of Education: Washington, D.C., 1988), Table 163 (figures based on the 1986–87 academic year). For that same year, the American Council on Education, Division of Policy Analysis and Research, comes up with a figure of 3,483 "institutions of higher education," but includes in that number some 263 proprietary (for profit) institutions. See Cecily A. Ottinger, ed., *Higher Education Today: Facts in Brief* (Washington, D.C., 1989), p. 33. For the year 1987–88, the *Digest of Educational Statistics: 1989 Edition* (U.S. Department of Education: Washington, D.C., 1989), Table 196, p. 217, gives a total of 3,587 institutions, but warns of lack of comparability with earlier data because the number of branch campuses reporting separately has increased.

5. See *A Classification of Institutions of Higher Education: A Technical Report Sponsored by the Carnegie Commission on Higher Education* (Berkeley, 1973). For the most recent version of this, see Carnegie Foundation for the Advancement of Teaching. *A Classification of Institutions of Higher Education: 1987 Edition* (Princeton, N.J., 1987), which is up to date for conditions prevailing in the academic year 1985–86.

6. William G. Bowen and Julie Ann Sosa, *Prospects for Faculty in the Arts and Sciences: A Study of Factors Affecting Demand and Supply, 1987 to 2012* (Princeton, N.J., 1989), pp. 191–92.

7. See Carnegie Foundation for the Advancement of Teaching, *A Classification of Institutions of Higher Education: 1987 Edition*, pp. 7–8.

8. The liberal arts being defined as including, in addition to the fine arts, foreign languages, literature and the social sciences, mathematics, the biological and physical sciences and psychology, as well as area and interdisciplinary studies

9. *A Classification of Institutions of Higher Education: 1987 Edition*, Table 4, p. 5.

10. David W. Breneman, "Are We Losing Our Liberal Arts Colleges?," *The College Board Review* (No. 150, Summer 1990), 16–21, 29.

11. *Ibid.*, 29, where Breneman adds: "I do not know the time pattern

of these changes, i.e., how many colleges shifted their emphasis within the last 10 to 15 years."

12. See *A Classification of Institutions of Higher Education: 1973 Edition*, Table 1, p. 7. The 1987 edition gives adjusted and corrected totals of 430 (1987) and 575 (1970)—see Table 1, p. 3.

13. If one accepts Breneman's downward revision of the number of liberal arts colleges to 212, then the drop to 6.3 percent in the percentage they represent of the institutional total overall is even more dramatic.

14. For the two-year colleges back to 1936, see Ottinger, ed., *Higher Education Today: Facts in Brief*, p. 31. For the other figures, see *A Classification of Institutions of Higher Education: 1987 Edition*, Tables 2 and 4, pp. 4–5; *Digest of Education Statistics: 1989*, Table 196, p. 217.

15. W. Vance Grant and Thomas D. Snyder, eds., *Digest of Educational Statistics: 1985–86*, 2 vols. (U.S. Department of Education: Washington, D.C., 1986), I, 2.

16. Thomas D. Snyder, ed., *Digest of Education Statistics: 1989*, (U.S. Department of Education: Washington, D.C., 1989), Table 3, p. 10.

17. *Ibid.,* Table 186, p. 203.

18. *Ibid.,* Table 149, p. 168.

19. I draw these figures from Bowen and Sosa, *Prospects for Faculty in the Arts and Sciences*, pp. 43–45, p. 206 (Table D. 1).

20. *Three Thousand Futures: The Next Twenty Years for Higher Education*, Final Report of the Carnegie Council on Policy Studies in Higher Education (San Francisco and London, 1980), p. 19 n. 6, reports that between 1960 and 1979 the number of students living on campus dropped from about 60 percent of the total student body to about 20 percent.

21. Bowen and Sosa, *Prospects for Faculty in the Arts and Sciences*, p. 44, Fig. 4.1; Ottinger, ed., *Higher Education Today: Facts in Brief*, p. 31

22. Bowen and Sosa, *Prospects for Faculty in the Arts and Sciences*, p. 32, Table 3.1; Ottinger, ed., *Higher Education Today: Facts in Brief*, p. 45

23. *Digest of Education Statistics: 1989*, Table 153, p. 172; Ottinger, ed., *Higher Education Today: Fact in Brief*, pp. 45 and 51.

24. *Digest of Education Statistics: 1989*, Table 175, p. 193; Table 150, p. 169. Cf. Ottinger, ed., *Higher Education Today: Facts in Brief*, p. 43.

25. *Digest of Education Statistics: 1989*, Table 196, p. 217; Table 148, p. 167.

26. Bowen and Sosa, *Prospects for Faculty in the Arts and Sciences*, pp. 30–31.

27. See above, n. 24, and for the comparisons with the situation in 1960, *Three Thousand Futures*, pp. 53–54.

28. *Three Thousand Futures*, p. 53, predicting also that the percentage of students who were commuters would rise as high as 85 percent by the year 2000. Bowen and Sosa, *Prospects for Faculty in the Arts and Sciences*, pp. 34–39, predict that part-time enrollments will reach 45.8 percent of the total but settle back to 44.4 percent by the year 2002. Their projections also indicate

that the percentage of students belonging to the over 24 years old group will rise to 49 percent by 1996 but then fall back to the level of the mid-1980s. Debra A. Gerald, Paul J. Horn and William J. Hussar, eds., *Projections of Education Statistics to 2000* (U.S. Department of Education: Washington, D.C., 1989), pp. 17–18, 21–25, Figs. 13, 14 and 17.

29. *Three Thousand Futures*, p. 54.

30. Cf. the pertinent essay by Richard A. Easterlin in Arthur Levine *et al.*, *Shaping Higher Education's Future: Demographic Realities and Opportunities, 1990–2000* (San Francisco and Oxford, 1989), pp. 135–41.

31. *Three Thousand Futures*, pp. 85–86. Cf. the useful brief discussion of national educational policy as it has shaped undergraduate studies in the People's Republic of China, France, the Federal Republic of Germany, Great Britain, Japan, Sweden and the Soviet Union, in Arthur Levine, *Handbook on Undergraduate Curriculum* (San Francisco—Washington—London, 1978), pp. 442–83.

32. Sarah E. Turner and William G. Bowen, "The Flight from the Arts and Sciences: Trends in Degrees Conferred," *Science*, 250 (26 Oct. 1990), 517–21 (at 517). For an illustration of that claim for the 1950s and 1960s, see J. B. Lon Hefferlin, *Dynamics of Academic Reform* (San Francisco, 1969), esp. 54–72.

33. Though, at the undergraduate level, it is certainly possible for course enrollments in a field of study to go up even while majoring is falling. Thus, at Williams, while the number of art majors declined from 83 to 59 during the period 1973–76 to 1985–86, the number of course enrollments went up during the same period from 1,327 to 1,553. Classics, on the other hand showed across those years the reverse pattern of an increase in the number of majors coupled with a decrease in the overall number of course enrollments. See James B. Wood, *The Williams Curriculum, 1973–75: An Overview of Curricular Discussions and Actions During the Presidency of John W. Chandler* (unpublished, 1985), Tables VIII and X, pp. 111–12, 115–16.

34. Alexander W. Astin and Kenneth C. Green, "The American Freshman: Twenty Year Trends: 1966–1985," in Alexander W. Astin, Kenneth C. Green, and William S. Kern. *The American Freshman: Twenty Year Trends* (Cooperative Institutional Research Program: Los Angeles, 1987), pp. 7–28 (at 7). Also Alexander W. Astin, William S. Kern, Ellyne R. Berg, *The American Freshman: National Norms for Fall 1989* (Cooperative Institutional Research Program: Los Angeles, 1989).

35. Astin *et al.*, *The American Freshman: National Norms for Fall 1989*, pp. 50–51.

36. Provided by the Higher Education General Information Surveys (HEGIS), now called the Integrated Postsecondary Education Data System (IPEDS), and, since 1962, annually published in summary form in the *Digest of Education Statistics*. Using these data, along with those provided by the Survey of Doctorate Recipients as well as the Survey of Earned Doctorates, and supplementing them "with more detailed breakdowns of degrees conferred

by sector of higher education and field of study for the period since 1976,"
Bowen and Sosa produced the analysis and projections drawn upon below—
see *Prospects for Faculty in the Arts and Sciences*, pp. 45–65, and Appendix
A, pp. 187–90.

37. Astin and Green, "The American Freshman: Twenty Year Trends
1966–1985," 15–16 (italics theirs).

38. Leading Astin and his colleagues to conclude that "the great surge
of popularity of business majors and careers that we witnessed during the
1970s and 1980s has ended"—Astin *et al., The American Freshman: Norms
for Fall 1989*, pp. 5–6, 50–51; Astin and Green, *The American Freshman:
Twenty Year Trends*, 14–16, 90–92. It also seems reasonable to conclude that
the drop in student interest in majoring in the humanities (and arts and sciences
in general) has now also reached its term.

39. I follow here their very helpful analysis in *Prospects for Faculty in
the Arts and Sciences*, pp. 46–57. For their sources, see above, n. 36.

40. Bowen and Sosa, *Prospects for Faculty in the Arts and Sciences*,
pp. 47–49, 54; Turner and Bowen, "The Flight from the Arts and Sciences,"
517–20.

41. See, for example, William J. Bennett, *To Reclaim a Legacy: A Report
on the Humanities in Higher Education* (Washington, D.C., 1984), pp. 1–2;
Lynne V. Cheney, *Humanities in America: A Report to the President, the
Congress, and the American People* (Washington, D.C., 1988), pp. 4–5. For
the statistics see Bowen and Sosa, *Prospects in the Arts and Sciences*, pp. 51–
57.

42. Bowen and Sosa, *Prospects for Faculty in the Arts and Sciences*,
Appendix A, pp. 187–89.

43. For this argument and the data cited in its support, I am indebted
to Turner and Bowen, "The Flight from the Arts and Sciences," 517–21. The
authors note, for example (Table 1, p. 518), that in 1954 such institutions as
Fairleigh Dickinson University, San Jose State College and Ball State University
awarded in the arts and sciences as a percentage of all the B.A. degrees they
conferred no more, respectively, than 29 percent, 25.1 percent, and 2.5
percent.

44. Thus Turner and Bowen, 517–18, citing J.B. Lon Hefferlin's study
of curricular change between 1962 and 1966—*Dynamics of Academic Reform*
(San Francisco, 1969). Identifying a "trend toward a more academic focus . . .
particularly evident in the vocational fields," Hefferlin reports (pp. 60, 63 and
67) that "the dominant trend in course expansion and reform during the
period from 1962 and 1967 was away from service. . . . During the past five
years, many formerly struggling institutions have had the opportunity—thanks
to the supply of students—to move toward academic respectability. . . . Former
vocational colleges have at long last embraced general education. For a bachelor's degree the tiny teachers colleges, technological schools, and Bible colleges are now enforcing a common standard that consists of required foreign
languages, humanities, and the sciences. And more state universities are im-

posing these requirements on all of their students and not simply on those in the liberal arts."

45. Turner and Bowen, 518, Table 1. Similarly, across the same span of time, the arts and sciences' share of B.A.s conferred at Fairleigh Dickinson had gone from 29.0 percent to 41 percent and then back down to 19.6 percent; at San Jose State from 25.1 percent to 43.5 percent and then back down to 26.2 percent.

46. Turner and Bowen, 518. Note that Fairleigh Dickinson, which had conferred only 245 B.A.s in 1954, conferred 2,276 in 1970, while the number conferred at San Jose State had risen over the same years from 864 to 4,136. By 1986 those numbers had fallen back, respectively, to 1,602 and 3,458.

47. Thus Turner and Bowen, 521, n. 4.

48. They do so by the complex calculation pursued in Turner and Bowen, 518–19 and Table 2.

49. Turner and Bowen, 519–20.

50. Thus Turner and Bowen, 520: "In both business and education . . . , the shifting patterns of degrees conferred have been dominated by the movements of women into and out of these fields . . . , with pronounced effects on interest in the humanities."

51. For these figures, see Bowen and Sosa, *Prospects for Faculty in the Arts and Sciences*, pp. 55–57, Tables 4.2 and 4.3.

52. See Turner and Bowen, 518, Table 1. Differences by institutional sector help account for the skepticism about the decline in humanities enrollments evinced by the authors of the response to the critics put out by the American Council of Learned Societies—see George Levine *et al.*, *Speaking for the Humanities*, pp. 21–23. Most of those authors teach at Research I Universities.

53. A point which Bowen and Sosa make (*Prospects for Faculty in the Arts and Sciences*, p. 48 and note 2) in relation to the drop of student interest in engineering. The scientific research sector in the United States has become increasingly dependent for the continuing progress of its work on its success in importing foreign expertise. Should that falter (and there are some straws in the wind suggesting that it may), it is not at all clear where the necessary talent is going to come from.

54. See David Davis-Van Atta, Sam C. Carrier, and Frank Frankfort, *Educating America's Scientists: The Role of the Research Colleges* (A Report for the Conference "The Future of Science at Liberal Arts Colleges" held at Oberlin College, June 9–10, 1985: Oberlin, Ohio, 1985), esp. pp. 7–15 (and affiliated tables). Also David Davis-Van Atta and Sam C. Carrier, *Maintaining America's Scientific Productivity: The Necessity of the Liberal Arts Colleges* (Report for the 1986 Conference "The Future of Science at Liberal Arts Colleges" held at Oberlin College, 9–10 June, 1986: Oberlin, Ohio, 1986), esp. pp. 6–12 (and affiliated tables).

55. Davis-Van Atta and Carrier, *Maintaining America's Scientific Pro-*

ductivity, p. 9, while conceding that "the total volume of baccalaureate degree production in the basic sciences by the 50 liberal arts colleges is less than that of the [top 20] universities, it is on the same order of magnitude. In 1983, the 20 universities conferred 6,783 bachelors in basic sciences; the 50 colleges produced 4,170.

56. Davis-Van Atta, Carrier, and Frankfort, *Educating America's Scientists*, pp. 7, 18 (Table I), 26 (Table VII); Davis-Van Atta and Carrier, *Maintaining America's Scientific Productivity*, pp. 9–10, p. 21 (Table I–1). In the former report, the authors add (pp. 12–13) that there is nothing new about the state of affairs: "The liberal arts colleges as a group have long been known to be the highest per capita producers of graduates going on to earn doctorates in scientific fields." As long ago as 1951, they point out, H. B. Goodrich, R. H. Knapp, and George A. W. Boehm, "The Origins of U.S. Scientists," *Scientific American*, 185 (No. 1, 1951), 15–17, had noted that "of the 50 leading institutions in this respect (i.e., those that turn out the largest proportion of graduates who become scientists), 39 are small liberal arts colleges. Only three large universities appear on this list of leaders, and only two technical institutions . . . ."

57. Davis-Van Atta *et al.*, *Educating America's Scientists*, pp. 35–40.

58. Mark Hopkins was president of Williams College from 1836 to 1872. See Frederick Rudolph, *Mark Hopkins and the Log: Williams College, 1836–1872* (New Haven and London, 1956), p. 227. The statement was made at a meeting of alumni in New York and in response to a critical report on the state of the College delivered by a faculty member (John Bascom, later to be president of the University of Wisconsin). Rudolph comments that, however exactly Garfield phrased his claim, it "placed on record his firm conviction that the inspired teaching of Mark Hopkins was at least equivalent to the libraries, laboratories, and other buildings which a critic like Bascom desired. It is doubtful, however, whether he intended to convey the impression, which some of his listeners gathered, that Williams College needed only Mark Hopkins in order to justify itself." Robert Maynard Hutchins, however, appears later on to have understood it more or less in the latter way. To him, this "nauseating anecdote about Mark Hopkins" was a manifestation of "anti-intellectualism," of "the great-man theory of education," according to which, he says, "you pay no attention to what you teach, or indeed to what you investigate"—*The Higher Learning in America* (New Haven and London, 1936), pp. 27–28.

59. Susan H. Russell *et al.*, *Faculty in Higher Education Institutions, 1988* (U.S. Department of Education: Washington, D.C., 1990).

60. For example, the public doctoral sector includes publicly-controlled institutions categorized by the Carnegie Foundation as specialized medical schools and, therefore, classified separately.

61. Clearly, if we were to accept Breneman's case for reclassifying most of the Liberal Arts II colleges as comprehensive institutions (see above, n. 10) this last figure would be much lower.

62. Russell *et al.*, *Faculty in Higher Education Institutions: 1988*, Tables 2.1 and 2.2; pp. 9–10.

63. *Ibid.*, Tables 2.7, 2.1, 2.3 and 2.4; pp. 9–12.

64. *Ibid.*, Table 2.5; p. 13.

65. *Ibid.*, Table 4.1; p. 45. See also pp. 39–40.

66. *Ibid.*, Table 4.3; p. 47. See also pp. 41 and 91.

67. *Ibid.*, Table 4.1; p. 45. See also p. 40.

68. *Ibid.*, Tables 4.4 and 4.6; pp. 44 and 50. See also, pp. 41–43 and 91.

69. *Ibid.*, Table 3.1; p. 25. See also, pp. 19–22 and 91.

70. *Ibid.*, Tables 3.1 and 3.3; pp. 25 and 28. See also, pp. 19–22 and 91.

71. The 1969 study used a questionnaire mailed to over 100,000 faculty member at 303 colleges and universities of various types around the country. The questionnaire and tabulations from the weighted data generated by the survey are to be found in Everett Carll Ladd, Jr. and Seymor Martin Lipset, *The Divided Academy: Professors and Politics* (New York, 1975), Appendix A and C, pp. 315–28, 341–69. Results of the 1989 survey are tabulated in Ernest J. Boyer, *Scholarship Reconsidered: Priorities for the Professoriate* (Carnegie Foundation for the Advancement of Teaching: Princeton, N.J., 1990), Appendix A, pp. 85–126. The "Technical Notes" in Appendix B indicate (p. 127) that whereas the 1989 and 1984 data "represent full-time campus faculty members," the 1969 figures "refer to all respondents." In addition to Ladd-Lipset and Boyer, see Martin Trow and Oliver Fulton, "Research Activity in American Higher Education," in Martin Trow, ed., *Teachers and Students: Aspects of American Higher Education* (New York, 1975), pp. 39–83; Everett Carll Ladd, Jr., "The Work Experience of American College Professors: Some Data and an Argument," *Current Issues in Higher Education,* AAHE (1979), 3–12; Howard R. Bowen and Jack H. Schuster, *American Professors: A National Resource Imperiled* (New York and Oxford, 1986).

72. Ladd and Lipset, *The Divided Academy*, p. 4.

73. Boyer, *Scholarship Reconsidered*, Appendix A, Tables A-26, A-20, A-19, A-23. See below, Chapter 4, pp. 112–20.

74. See Ladd and Lipset, *The Divided Academy*, pp. 348–49 and 352–53.

75. *Ibid.*, pp. 1–2 and Table 1. Their figures are drawn from *Historical Statistics of the United States* (1960, p. 210) and *Statistical Abstracts of the United States* (1973, p. 731) and include visiting and temporary faculty. They are, therefore, somewhat more "global" than those reported in the 1988 survey.

76. There are some problems with the comparability of the 1963 and 1988 numbers. I draw the 1963/1980 contrast from *Three Thousand Futures*, p. 82, where the basis for the count is not indicated. The figures reported in Russell *et al.*, *Faculty in Higher Education: 1988*, Table 2.5, p. 13, which are broken down, however, into full-time and part-time, give the following approximate counts: (a) Faculty at liberal arts colleges—full-time, 1 in about

12.5; part-time, 1 in 13.5; (b) Faculty at two-year colleges—full-time, 1 in 5.3; part-time, 1 in 2.

77. Bowen and Sosa, *Prospects for Faculty in the Arts and Sciences*, pp. 16–17; see especially Figure 2.1 and Table 2.1. Note that the authors (p. 127) view the 1987 age distribution as "more normalized."

78. That is, the decline between 1970–71 and 1983–84 "was so great that it eliminated entirely the gains in real salaries that had been achieved in the 1960s."—See Bowen and Sosa, *Prospects for Faculty in the Arts and Sciences*, pp. 145–47, and especially Table 8.1 for detailed comparisons with other occupations. Cf. Bowen and Schuster, *American Professors: A National Resource Imperiled*, ch. 6 (by W. Lee Hansen), pp. 80–112.

79. 32,278 were awarded in 1987. For these figures and what follows I am indebted to Bowen and Sosa, *Prospects for Faculty in the Arts and Sciences*, pp. 90–117.

80. *Ibid.*, pp. 92–93.

81. *Ibid.*, pp. 104–8.

82. *Ibid.*, pp. 93–94.

83. Bowen and Sosa, *Prospects for Faculty in the Arts and Sciences*, pp. 164–65, 168, 177–81; William G. Bowen, Graham Lord, and Julie Ann Sosa, "Measuring Time to the Doctorate: Reinterpretation of the Evidence," *Proceedings of the National Academy of Science*, 88 (Feb. 1991), 713–17. Cf., for earlier estimates, Bowen and Sosa, pp. 164–65, 168, 177–81.

84. For example, Michael J. Sovern, "Higher Education: The Real Crisis," *New York Times Magazine* (Jan. 22, 1989), 24–25, 56. In that article Sovern, president of Columbia University, asserted that "Colleges and universities all over the country are facing a massive wave of retirements." As Bowen and Sosa, *Prospects for Faculty in Arts and Sciences*, p. 15, indicate, their own findings "do not support this generalization."

85. Bowen and Sosa, *Prospects . . .* , pp. 6–7. Here they cite the perceptive comment made in 1974 by Allen M. Cartter, "The Academic Labor Market," in Margaret S. Gordon, ed., *Higher Education and the Labor Market* (New York, 1974), 282–83: Projections "may illustrate the consequences of current trends and thus serve to alter the course of events. In a meaningful sense, successful projections may be those that turn out to be poor predictions of actual events."

86. Bowen and Sosa, *Prospects for Faculty in the Arts and Sciences*, pp. 13–14, 135–37. While the current recession and the loss of fiscal equilibrium in so many of the states may serve to delay the onset of such drastic shortages, they seem unlikely in the long run to prevent them.

87. *Ibid.*, p. 12.

88. *Three Thousand Futures*, p. 54. It continues: "This is a fundamental, almost radical change in higher education.

CHAPTER IV

1. See Ernest C. Boyer, *College: The Undergraduate Experience in America* (New York, 1987), and *idem, Scholarship Reconsidered: Priorities of the*

Professoriate (Carnegie Foundation for the Advancement of Teaching: Princeton, N.J., 1990). In both works, he makes very extensive and supple use of statistical data.

2. *Three Thousand Futures,* p. 54.

3. See the helpful discussion and affiliated bibliography in Arthur Levine, *Handbook on Undergraduate Curriculum* (San Francisco-Washington-London, 1978), ch. 15: "The Undergraduate Curriculum around the World," pp. 442–83. On December 9, 1989, Gérard Courtois reported in *Le Monde,* for example, that the French universities were "grinding to a halt" and that faculties were being "swamped with ever-increasing numbers of students" and that "facilities and resources [had] not kept pace with this upward pressure." (Reprinted in *Manchester Guardian Weekly,* 142, No. 1 (Jan. 7, 1990), 16.)

4. Thus Derek Bok, *The President's Report 1988–89: Harvard University,* p. 2, where he notes the startling contrast between foreign admiration for American higher education and domestic criticism. "Far from praising our universities, critics in this country have attacked them more savagely during the past ten years than at any time in my memory."

5. Henry Rosovsky, *The University: An Owner's Manual* (New York and London, 1990), pp. 29–30, where he says: "By two thirds (perhaps three quarters) of the best, I mean that surveys of world universities rank a majority of American *public* and *private* institutions at the top"—a conclusion which he does not regard as inconsistent with the fact "that we are also home to a large share of the world's worst colleges and universities."

6. Thorstein Veblen, *The Higher Learning in America: A Memorandum on the Conduct of Universities by Business Men* (Academic Reprints, Stanford, 1954)—originally published in 1918; Abraham Flexner, *Universities: American, English and German* (New York, 1930); Robert Maynard Hutchins, *The Higher Learning in America* (New Haven and London, 1936); Robert Nisbet, *The Degradation of the Academic Dogma: The University in America, 1945–1970* (New York and London, 1971); Allan Bloom, *The Closing of the American Mind: How Higher Education Has Failed Democracy and Impoverished the Souls of Today's Students* (New York, 1987); Page Smith, *Killing the Spirit: Higher Education in America* (New York, 1990).

7. Veblen, *The Higher Learning in America,* pp. 22–24.

8. The words are those of David Riesman in his introduction to the 1954 reprint of Veblen's *The Higher Learning in America,* p. xi. He notes too (pp. xii–xiv) that Veblen believed that "the universities could run themselves, once outside interference was removed, precisely as he thought the economy could run itself, as a technical engineering problem, once the vested interests were liquidated. Here again, he fell back on a kind of Rousseauistic 'state of nature' thinking which regarded scholars as uncontaminated 'scientific men' who would naturally pursue the truth that lies at the margin of the already known, if only the conventional academic constraints could be removed."

9. Clark Kerr, "The Moods of Academia," in John F. Hughes, ed., *Education and the State* (Washington, D.C., 1975), pp. 267–68. I draw this lugubrious list from Kerr's article.

10. Bok, *The President's Report 1988–89: Harvard University,* p. 2. He notes, too, that the very sweeping nature of such accusations itself can generate highly defensive reactions, making it difficult to identify, much less admit, the irritating grain of truth that helped stimulate them and to which the academy would do well to pay attention.

11. David Riesman, *On Higher Education: The Academic Enterprise in an Era of Rising Student Consumerism* (San Francisco-Washington-London, 1980), p. 43.

12. Carnegie Foundation for the Advancement of Teaching, *Mission of the College Curriculum: A Contemporary Review with Suggestions* (San Francisco-Washington-London, 1977), pp. 164–85.

13. Charles J. Sykes, *ProfScam: Professors and the Demise of Higher Education* (New York, 1990), p. 103.

14. *Ibid.,* p. 54, where he adds: "In the modern university, no act of good teaching goes unpunished." This in a chapter entitled "The Crucifixion of Teaching" and following a previous one entitled "The Flight from Teaching."

15. William James, "The Ph.D. Octopus," in *William James: Writings, 1902–1910* (New York, 1987), 1,111–118, H. W. Whicker, "Doctors of Dullness." *North America Review,* 228 (1929), 115–19,—cited in Frederick Rudolph, *The American College and University: A History* (New York, 1965), p. 401; Flexner, *Universities: American, English, German,* pp. 82–83, 102–4; Jacques Barzun, *Teacher in America* (Boston, 1945), pp. 195–208; Page Smith, *Killing the Spirit,* pp. 177–98.

16. Smith, *Killing the Spirit,* p. 199.

17. A. C. Crombie, *Medieval and Early Modern Science,* 2 vols. (New York, 1959), II, 103–19.

18. Lynne V. Cheney, *Tyrannical Machines: A Report on Educational Practices Gone Wrong and Our Best Hopes for Setting Them Right* (Washington, D.C: The National Endowment for the Humanities, 1990), p. 30. At the same time she also notes an 800 percent increase in the number of books and articles published on Virginia Woolf, a figure which presumably reflects the rise of feminist criticism and a shift in the focus of scholarly interest.

19. Martin Trow and Oliver Fulton, "Research Activity in American Higher Education," in Martin Trow, ed., *Teachers and Students: Aspects of American Higher Education* (New York, 1975), pp. 57–58.

20. *Ibid.,* pp. 42–47.

21. *Ibid.,* pp. 42–45 and Table 2–2. In classifying institutions, Trow and Fulton do not use the Carnegie Classifications but divide institutions of higher education into three broad categories: universities (with a substantial emphasis on graduate work), four-year undergraduate colleges, and two-year colleges. They then break down both the university and the college category on the basis of differential quality, each into three further classes designated as high, medium, low. They set forth the grounds for these distinctions in Appendix A, pp. 366–70.

22. *Ibid.,* p. 46, Table 2–3.

23. *Ibid.,* pp. 49 and n. 13, 74 and 79.

24. *Ibid.,* pp. 66–75. Thus (p. 67): "To take one specific example of formal administrative activity, we find that at leading universities a frequent publisher is almost twice as likely to be or to have been head of the department as are inactives." At the same time (pp. 79–80), whereas "in the weaker universities and in the better colleges there is a division of labor within the faculty between those who do research and those who do not," in the leading universities "the division of labor between research and other functions of higher education is a division of the time and energy of individual academic men and women."

25. They refer to Talcott Parsons and Gerald Platt, *The American Academic Profession: A Pilot Study* (Washington, D.C., 1968).

26. See above, Chapter III, pp. 97–98 and nn. 73 and 74.

27. Everett Carll Ladd, Jr., "The Work Experience of American College Professors: Some Data and an Argument," *Current Issues in Higher Education,* AAHE (1979), 3–12 (at 3–5, 7–11; cf. Tables 1, 1A, 2, 3, 4, 5, 9, 10 and 11). Cf. the similar conclusion drawn by Howard R. Bowen and Jack H. Schuster, *American Professors: A National Resource Imperiled* (New York and Oxford, 1986), pp. 15–19.

28. See, for example, Mark H. Curtis *et al., Integrity in the College Curriculum* (Association of American Colleges: Washington, D.C., 1985), p. 6.

29. Boyer, *Scholarship Reconsidered,* Appendix A, Table A-38. In fact, those at the two-year colleges appeared somewhat *more* strongly committed to their disciplines than did those in the other institutional sectors. Eighty-one percent said their discipline was "very important" to them, as opposed to 77 percent at the research universities.

30. *Ibid.,* Table A-40; Cf. p. 56.

31. *Ibid.,* Tables A-1 and A-32. For the comparison between 1969 and 1989, see pp. 11–12, where he adds: "The change at comprehensive colleges—from 6 per cent to 43 per cent—is especially noteworthy since these institutions have virtually no doctoral programs and only limited resources for research."

32. On this, see the interesting observations by Bok, *The President's Report 1988–89: Harvard University,* pp. 4–5, and by Ladd, "The Work Experience of American Professors," 5, where he comments that "[i]n many cases," even apart from extrinsic incentives, "it seems that the faculty members themselves, however much they prefer teaching, find it hard to resist the notion that research really is a higher calling."

33. Ladd, "The Work Experience of American Professors," 5. He adds: "It may be that research properly construed—meaning scholarly activity aimed at the creation of new ideas, new knowledge, and new art forms and the like—makes demands and requires skills such as permanently restrict participation in it to a distinct minority of faculty."

34. Boyer, *Scholarship Reconsidered,* pp. 12 and 55, and Appendix A, Table A-23. The third chapter of the book, pp. 27–41, speaks well to the whole issue.

35. Thus Lynne V. Cheney, *Humanities in America: A Report to the*

President, the Congress, and the American People (Washington, D.C.: The National Endowment for the Humanities, 1988), pp. 4–5. Cf. William J. Bennett, *To Reclaim a Legacy, A Report on the Humanities in Higher Education* (Washington, D.C: The National Endowment for the Humanities, 1984), pp. 2, 6–8, 13, 17–20.

36. Roger Kimball, *Tenured Radicals: How Politics Has Corrupted Higher Education* (New York, 1990), p. xvii. Cf. Bennett, *To Reclaim a Legacy,* pp. 16–17, for a similar assertion. Also Sykes, *ProfScam,* p. 180.

37. See above, Chapter III, pp. 87–91.

38. Kimball, *Tenured Radicals,* p. 36, commenting on George Levine *et al., Speaking for the Humanities* (ACLS Occasional Paper No. 7: New York, 1989), esp. pp. 21–24, 35–37.

39. See above, Chapter III, pp. 88–89.

40. William G. Bowen and Julie Ann Sosa, *Prospects for Faculty in the Arts and Sciences: A Study of Factors Affecting Demand and Supply, 1987–2012* (Princeton, N.J., 1989), pp. 53–57. In breaking down the figures by field of study and institutional sector they lump together the humanities and social sciences (excluding psychology). In so doing, they note that "the curve for the social sciences resembles the curve for the humanities."

41. See, for example, Bennett, *To Reclaim a Legacy,* p. 22; Kimball, *Tenured Radicals,* pp. xiii–xiv.

42. John Henry Newman, *The Idea of a University,* ed. I.T. Ker (Oxford, 1976), pp. 117, 121–23, 147.

43. See above, Chapter II, pp. 61–66.

44. Frederick Rudolph, *Curriculum: A History of the American Undergraduate Course of Study since 1636* (San Francisco-Washington-London, 1977), pp. 205–8, 227–32.

45. *Ibid.,* p. 191.

46. Williams College was one of these. Hence its catalogue is at pains to insist that "not having abandoned itself to the elective principle in the nineteenth century, Williams did not need to rescue itself with the general educational principle of the twentieth century."

47. Ernest Boyer, *College: The Undergraduate Experience in America* (New York, 1987), pp. 92–101, 112.

48. Curtis *et al., Integrity in the College Curriculum,* p. 24.

49. Thus Bennett, *To Reclaim a Legacy,* pp. 7 and 22. Though by no means lacking in ambiguity, it is the clearest and most forthright of these statements.

50. Lynne V. Cheney, *50 Hours: A Core Curriculum for College Students* (National Endowment for the Humanities: Washington, D.C., 1989), p. 22; Bennett, *To Reclaim a Legacy,* p. 4. It should be noted that among the critics Page Smith, *Killing the Spirit,* pp. 148–49, registers a forceful dissent, dismissing the "Great Books of the Western Tradition" approach as "presentist" and even implicity "racist."

51. On which, see Francis Oakley, *The Medieval Experience: Foundations of Western Cultural Singularity* (Toronto, 1988).

52. See the essays collected in Daniel O'Connor and Francis Oakley, eds., *Creation: The Impact of an Idea* (New York, 1969); Francis Oakley, *Omnipotence, Covenant, and Order: An Excursion in the History of Ideas from Abelard to Leibniz* (Ithaca and London, 1984).

53. Hutchins, *The Higher Learning in America*, p. 66. Although such latter-day sympathizers with the Hutchins approach as Bennett and Cheney deny any wish to impose a common curricular model on all American colleges and universities, they clearly regard a curriculum pivoting on the study of Western civilization and on the direct study of the great texts and works of art as the model which all should emulate.

54. See above, Chapter II, pp. 49–59, and below, Chapter V, pp. 149–51.

55. Hutchins, *The Higher Learning in America*, p. 66. Harry D. Gideonse, *The Higher Learning in a Democracy: A Reply to President Hutchins' Critique of the American University* (New York, 1947), p. 3. See the interesting reflections of Edward Shils, "Robert Maynard Hutchins," *The American Scholar*, 59 (No. 2, 1990), 211–35. Cf. Bruce A. Kimball, *Orators and Philosophers: A History of the Idea of Liberal Education* (New York and London, 1986), pp. 179–86.

56. This last was the stated objective of John Erskine in his great books "General Honors" course at Columbia College after the First World War—see Gerald Graff, *Professing Literature: An Institutional History* (Chicago and London, 1987), pp. 133–36. Worries about this sort of "presentism" remain alive and well and lead Page Smith, despite his own critical stance, to reject the general education or core-curricular approach to undergraduate education—*Killing the Spirit*, pp. 148–51. Twelve years ago, when I myself chaired a committee at Williams which proposed the requirement of two core "great works" courses in the freshman year, we were forced to grapple with all of the arguments in question. In the end, they proved to be too persuasive to our colleagues and we failed to carry the day.

57. With the exception of Allan Bloom, *The Closing of the American Mind*, pp. 344–47.

58. See Kimball, *Tenured Radicals*, xiv, xvii; Bloom, *Closing of the American Mind*, p. 327. He devotes a whole chapter of the book (pp. 313–35) to "The Sixties."

59. Bennett, *To Reclaim a Legacy*, p. 19.

60. In 1986, he could warn in a speech that "nowadays...campus radicals...see the university as a kind of fortress at war with society, an arsenal whose principal task is to raise revolutionary consciousness, frustrate the government, discredit authority and promote a radical transformation of society." Cited in Peter Novick, *That Noble Dream: The 'Objectivity Question' and the American Historical Profession* (Cambridge and New York, 1988), p. 463.

61. Thus Gerald Graff, *Literature Against Itself: Literary Ideas in Modern Society* (Chicago and London, 1979), p. 24—though it should be noted that Graff is speaking here of the way in which the cultural left tends persistently to identify "realistic and objectivistic ways of thinking about language

and thought . . . with things nobody would be associated with if he could help it: with amoral science, positivism, mechanism, venal commercial calculation; etc." But his observation appears applicable equally to the tactics of the more splenetic of critics on the right.

62. Novick, *That Noble Dream*, pp. 606–7.

63. *Ibid.*, p. 462.

64. Bennett, *To Reclaim a Legacy*, pp. 1 and 30.

65. Cheney, *Humanities in America*, pp. 11–15.

66. Kimball, *Tenured Radicals*, p. xi. Cf. Dinesh D'Souza, *Illiberal Education: The Politics of Race and Sex on Campus* (New York, 1991), pp. 59–93.

67. For the pertinent definitions and a useful anthology of recent philosophical writing on the issue, see Jack W. Meiland and Michael Krausz, eds., *Relativism: Cognitive and Moral* (Notre Dame and London, 1982). As the title suggests, the editors distinguish between forms of relativism pertaining to our ways of knowing and those pertaining to the standards of morality in terms of which we judge our actions. It should be noted, however, that the general issue is complex enough to call for further (and more subtle) distinctions. Thus, for example, in his contribution to the discussion in the volume of cognitive relativism, Maurice Mandelbaum distinguishes between "Subjective, Objective, and Conceptual Relativism"—see pp. 34–61.

68. Bennett, *To Reclaim a Legacy*, pp. 16 and 20; Kimball, *Tenured Radicals*, pp. 157–58, 160, 162, 164; D'Souza, *Illiberal Education*, pp. 179, 189–92. Cf. Cheney, *Humanities in America*, pp. 7, 12 and 14.

69. Bloom, *The Closing of the American Mind*, pp. 25–26, 39, 141, 143–44, 155, 379.

70. Roland Barthes, "From Work to Text," cited in Oakley, *Omnipotence, Covenant, and Order*, p. 26—see also pp. 22–27, where the deconstructive "turn" is briefly discussed (along with Michel Foucault, whom Bloom also labels, but incorrectly, a deconstructionist).

71. Bloom, *The Closing of the American Mind*, p. 379.

72. M.H. Abrams, "How To Do Things with Texts," *Partisan Review*, 46 (No. 4, 1979), 568. The essay as a whole mounts a powerful critique not only of the textual strategies pursued by Derrida but also of those recommended by two American "new readers" of less philosophical bent, Stanley Fish and Harold Bloom.

73. Note the rueful response of Richard Rorty to "the widespread acceptance" among the conferees at a 1988 conference "Liberal Arts Education in the Late Twentieth Century" of the view that contemporary American society is "mainly unreasonable"—see his "Two Cheers for the Cultural Left," in Darryl L. Gless and Barbara Herrnstein Smith, *The Politics of Liberal Education* (Special issue of *The South Atlantic Quarterly*, 89 (No. 1, 1990), 222–33). John Searle, "The Storm over the University," *The New York Review of Books* (6 Dec. 1990), 34–42 (though somewhat unfairly taking a few overheated passages to be characteristic of the volume as a whole) comments that the contributions to those proceedings "express a mode of literary and

political sensitivity that has become fairly widespread in some university departments of the humanities." "The views expressed," he observes, "show a remarkable consensus in their opposition to the educational tradition and in their hostility to those who, like Bloom, have supported a version of the tradition." I would judge less persuasive Tzvetan Todorov's charge that "the authors" of the ACLS's response to the conservative critics "gladly confess to the crime of which they are accused." Certainly, they do not "explain that there is no such thing as truth or objectivity, that there are only points of view and particular interests"—"Crime Against Humanities," *The New Republic* (July 3, 1989), 28. What the authors of that response (all of them professors of literature) may properly be accused of, however, is their treatment of the crucial topic of "ideology and objectivity" with a singularly unhelpful measure of philosophical imprecision, see George Levine *et al.*, *Speaking for the Humanities* (ACLS Occasional Paper, No. 7: New York, 1989), pp. 9–12.

74. As Bloom himself appears to imply—*The Closing of the American Mind,* pp. 333–35.

75. Gilbert Allardyce, "The Rise and Fall of the Western Civilization Course," *The American Historical Review,* 87 (1982), 695–724, at 716–17, where he cites one opponent on the Harvard faculty as having argued: "To center a course exclusively on the Western tradition would merely help perpetuate the old myth of civilization as a monopoly of the regions bordering on the Atlantic." Cf. Novick, *That Noble Dream,* pp. 312–14.

76. Novick, *That Noble Dream,* pp. 311–14, where, while affirming the "grain of truth" in Allardyce's account, he provides a less pointed and more judicious appraisal.

77. *Ibid.,* pp. 249, 198–200.

78. T.C. Smith, "The Writing of American History in America, from 1884 to 1934," *American Historical Review,* 40 (1934–35), 439–49.

79. Meiland and Krausz, eds., *Relativism: Cognitive and Moral,* pp. 6–7. For a lucid account of the development of relativism in the nineteenth century, see Patrick Gardiner, "German Philosophy and the Rise of Relativism," *The Monist,* 64 (No. 2, 1981), 138–54.

80. Meiland and Krausz, eds., *Relativism: Cognitive and Moral,* pp. 7–8.

81. Novick, *That Noble Dream,* pp. 134–35, 137, 268–69.

82. I follow here the intriguing formulation of the issue offered by George Steiner, *Real Presences,* The Leslie Stephen Memorial Lecture (Cambridge, 1986), pp. 1–3.

83. Thus Graff, *Literature Against Itself,* p. 32. The continuity of the modernist and postmodern temper is one of the central themes of this stimulating book. For a useful attempt to dissipate some of the confusion surrounding "postmodern" and affiliated terms, see Allan Megill, "What Does the Term 'Postmodern' Mean?," *Annals of Scholarship,* 6 (No. 2–3, 1989), 129–51.

84. See esp. Charles Taylor, *Sources of the Self: The Making of the*

Modern Identity (Cambridge, Mass., 1989); Alasdair MacIntyre, *Whose Justice? Which Rationality?* (Notre Dame, Ind., 1988).
    85. "The Storm over the University," p. 34.

CHAPTER V

    1. It is most egregiously evident in the books of Charles Sykes, but, in this respect the writings of Roger Kimball and Chester Finn afford him some strong competition. See above, Chapter I, n. 1.
    2. Henri Marrou, *A History of Education in Antiquity,* trans. George Lamb (New York, 1956), pp. 95–226.
    3. Edmund Burke, *Reflections on the Revolution in France* (New York, 1961), pp. 45, 110.
    4. See Francis Oakley, *The Western Church in the Later Middle Ages* (Ithaca and London, 1979), pp. 213–16.
    5. Frederick Rudolph, *Curriculum: A History of the American Undergraduate Course of Study from 1636* (San Francisco-Washington-London, 1977), p. 232; cf. pp. 42, 69, 144, 146.
    6. Samuel Eliot Morison, *Three Centuries of Harvard: 1636–1936* (Cambridge, Mass., 1936), pp. 260–61. For this and further exemplification of past teaching deficiencies at Harvard, see Derek Bok, in Derek Bok *et al., The Improvement of Teaching* (ACLS Occasional Paper, No. 16: New York, 1991), pp. 1–3.
    7. The phrase is that of Jonathan C. Messerli, *Horace Mann: A Biography* (New York, 1922), p. 47—cited in Rudolph, *Curriculum,* p. 24. The words quoted earlier are drawn from Frederick Rudolph, *The American College and University: A History* (New York, 1965), p. 144.
    8. In this I concur in Derek Bok's judgment—*The Improvement of Teaching,* p. 3.
    9. See above, Chapter IV, pp. 112–20.
    10. Ernest Boyer, *Scholarship Reconsidered: Priorities of the Professoriate* (Carnegie Foundation for the Advancement of Teaching: Princeton, N.J., 1990), pp. 54–55.
    11. Reminding us that the term "research" found its way into "the vocabulary of higher education" only in the 1820s in England and in 1906 in the United States, Boyer claims that "scholarship in earlier times referred to a variety of creative work carried on in a variety of places, and its integrity was measured by the ability to think, communicate, and learn." Nowadays, however, "basic research has come to be viewed as the first and most essential form of scholarly activity, with other functions flowing from it."—*Scholarship Reconsidered,* pp. 15–16.
    12. *Ibid.,* p. 16 (italics his).
    13. In the last three paragraphs I have drawn on Boyer, *Scholarship Reconsidered,* pp. 18–25, 53–64. On p. 64, he sums up his case as follows: "Here, then, is our conclusion. In building a truly diverse higher learning

system, let's have great research centers where undergraduate education *also* will be honored. Let's have campuses where the scholarship of teaching is a central mission. Let's have colleges and universities that promote integrative studies as an exciting mission through a core curriculum, through interdisciplinary seminars and team teaching. And let's also have colleges and universities that give top priority to the scholarship of application, institutions that relate learning to real life—in schools, in hospitals, in industry, and in business—much as the land-grant colleges worked with farmers."

14. Lynne V. Cheney, *50 Hours: A Core Curriculum for College Students* (Washington, D.C: The National Endowment for the Humanities, 1989).

15. Rudolph, *Curriculum,* pp. 74–75. Cf. Rudolph, *The American College and University,* p. 135: "The privileged orders were pleased that Yale chose to withstand the demands for a more popular and practical education. ... And these ... were the people who ran the colleges, people who also knew that the American college was running on a shoestring and that the old course of study, while the best, was also the cheapest."

16. Despite the odd impression to the contrary that the critics somehow contrive to give, there seems little reason to fear that the teaching of Homer or Plato or Shakespeare or Milton is likely soon to perish from the land.

17. Of recent years, for example, approximately three-quarters of the student body at Williams have elected to take English 101 (The Study of Literature), three-fifths to take Economics 101 (Introduction to Economics), and half to take Art History 101–102 (Introduction to Art History), Political Science 102 (International Relations), and Psychology 101 (Introductory Psychology).

18. Derek Bok, *Higher Learning* (Cambridge, Mass., 1986), p. 44, comments: "If talk of achieving a synthesis has receded within the large universities, it is not because professors consider the goal unimportant, but because they are not sure how to pursue it or which general concepts of integration they can offer their students."

19. See below, pp. 159–65.

20. Thus Lynne V. Cheney, *Humanities in America: A Report to the President, the Congress, and the American People* (Washington, D.C: The National Endowment for the Humanities, 1988), p. 13, alluding specifically to Mount Holyoke College.

21. Thus Herbert Butterfield, *The Origins of Modern Science,* rev. ed. (New York, 1965) in the course of a series of lectures delivered at Cambridge University in 1948 with the object of stimulating interest in the history of science, observes (pp. 7–8): "Since that [scientific] revolution overturned the authority in science not only of the middle ages but of the ancient world— since it ended not only in the eclipse of scholastic philosophy but in the destruction of Aristotelian physics—it outshines everything since the rise of Christianity and reduces the Renaissance and Reformation to the rank of mere episodes, mere internal displacements, within the system of medieval Christiandom. Since it changed the character of men's habitual mental operations

even in the conduct of the non-material sciences, while transforming the whole diagram of the physical universe and the very texture of human life itself, it looms so large as the real origin of the modern mentality that our customary periodisation of European history has become an anachronism and an encumbrance."

22. See, for example, Cheney, *Humanities in America*, pp. 8–10, 11–15, 31–32; *50 Hours*, pp. 11–15, 18–25 (though here she is proposing required core courses).

23. See, for example, Cheney, *50 Hours*, pp. 17–25; William J. Bennett, *To Reclaim a Legacy: A Report on the Humanities in Higher Education* (Washington, D.C.: The National Endowment for the Humanities, 1984), p. 9; Page Smith, *Killing the Spirit: Higher Education in America* (New York, 1990), pp. 147–51. Speaking specifically of history, Smith says (p. 150): "[T]he point is that all academic efforts to give a comprehensive view of the history of mankind must from this point on eschew the merely Western and take in the whole range of human history. ... Each new phase of history requires that our past history be rewritten to incorporate the new experience. ... [W]e must 'enlarge our past' in order to make room for the future. So it is not surprising that many students, and not just minority students, see the present campaign for Western Civilization as a required part of the curriculum as a step backward and one with unfortunate, if doubtless unconscious, racial overtones."

24. See the comment by John Searle, "The Storm over the University," *The New York Review of Books* (December 6, 1990), 34–42.

25. The words are those of Ben J. Wattenberg in *The New York Times* (11 March, 1991), p. 1, commenting on the results of the 1990 national census, which revealed that between 1980 and 1990 the number of Americans tracing their roots to one or other minority group had grown from one in five almost to one in four. "This is the dawning of the first universal nation," he said. "It's going to cause some turmoil, but on balance it's an incredibly poetic fact."

26. In this connection, and so far as the issue of "the canon" is concerned, it should not be forgotten that even the canon of great classical works has been open-ended and in constant change across the centuries. The earliest and most dramatic extension occurred in the first century C.E., when the initially Greek canon of classical works began to be opened up to include the more distinguished products of the new literature being produced in Latin by the Romans. We should note, too, that what people have been willing to regard as "classical" has shifted across time, and, so far as Greek and Latin literature is concerned, is more narrowly circumscribed now than it was at times in the past. Again, we should not miss the fact that some works that all would agree to be works of great distinction were not always regarded as "canonical"—or were so regarded at one time and later ceased to be. Nowadays, Plato's *Republic* would appear on everyone's list. But for long centuries it was not the *Republic* that was honored as Plato's greatest dialogue but the

Timaeus (a work read today by hardly anyone other than historians of ancient or medieval philosophy). When Raphael, painting *The School of Athens*, wished to identify Aristotle and Plato by placing a distinguishing book in their hands, while he depicted Aristotle as holding the *Ethics*, the book he placed in Plato's hand is labeled *Timeo*. For some helpful remarks on the classical canon and the matter of canon formation, see George A. Kennedy, "Classics and Canons," in Darryl J. Gless and Barbara Herrnstein Smith, *The Politics of Liberal Education*—a special issue of *The South Atlantic Quarterly*, 89 (No. 1, 1990), 217–25.

27. For which, see above, Chapter II, pp. 49–59.

28. Thus Bruce Kimball, *Orators and Philosophers: A History of the Idea of Liberal Education* (New York and London, 1986), pp. 237–41, where he adds: "[T]he oratorical mind and *artes liberales* ideal emphasize the investigation of the best of traditions and the public expression of what is good and true, rather than the discovery of new knowledge. The fact that the investigation and expression were no less important and creative than the discovery is not appreciated today. What has been emphasized instead in the twentieth century is that the oratorical concern with expression and tradition—with language and texts—tempts dogmatic conservation in education and culture, tending in the long run toward authoritarianism. The liberation from such dogmatism and oppression is what the university builders and then the progressivists celebrated in the late nineteenth and early twentieth centuries." In similar (if much less nuanced) vein, Lawrence R. Veysey, *The Emergence of the American University* (Chicago, 1965), p. 338, speaks of "the redefinition" since 1900 "of the liberal arts curriculum away from the genteel tradition, towards identification with critical intellect and creativity."

29. The words, ironically, are Bruce Kimball's—see his "Historical and Cultural Dimensions of the Recent Reports on Undergraduate Education," *American Journal of Education*, 96 (No. 3, 1988), 307–8 (italics mine). See above, Chapter IV, pp. 127–35.

30. For this suggestion I am again indebted to Kimball's interesting article, "Historical and Cultural Dimensions of the Recent Reports on Undergraduate Education," 305–13.

31. On this last specific point the response of Charles Frankel to a question put to him by David Sikorsky is directly pertinent—see Charles Frankel, "Intellectual Foundations of Liberalism," *Seminar Reports* (No. 1, 1976), 12–14.

32. Or have already done so—see *Three Thousand Futures: The Next Twenty Years for Higher Education*, Final Report of the Carnegie Council on Policy Studies in Higher Education (San Francisco and London, 1980), pp. 100, 114–15.

33. See above, Chapter III, pp. 77–78.

34. See above, Chapter I, pp. 26–28.

35. See Kenneth P. Ruscio, "The Distinctive Scholarship of the Selective Liberal Arts College," *Journal of Higher Education*, 58 (No. 2, 1987), 205–

22. He notes the degree to which faculty members in such a setting pursue research that is more individualistic and less bureaucratically structured. They are less concerned in their scholarly efforts with disciplinary boundaries and are more prone to seeing "their research as a benefit to students as well as a contribution to their peers outside the college."

36. Boyer, *Scholarship Reconsidered*, Appendix A, Table A-26. Note that if faculty at the liberal arts colleges were divided into those at the more and those at the less selective colleges the last percentage would almost certainly be lower at the more selective. In analyzing comparable data from the 1969 Carnegie Survey, and dividing the liberal arts colleges into three groups in terms of their quality (though selectivity does not appear to have been a dominant criterion used in assessing quality), Trow and Fulton found that 74 percent of the faculty in the highest quality group indicated a primary interest in teaching—see Martin Trow and Oliver Fulton, "Research Activity in American Higher Education," in Martin Trow ed., *Teachers and Students: Aspects of American Higher Education* (New York, 1975), Table 2-2, p. 44.

37. Boyer, *Scholarship Reconsidered*, Appendix A, Table A-23.

38. *Ibid.*, Tables A-5, A-10, A-17, A-9.

39. *Ibid.*, Tables A-7, A-12, A-6, A-13, A-11, A-15, A-18.

40. *Ibid.*, Tables A-1 (here the global figure is 54%; that for 4-year institutions in general, 77%; and for research universities, 95%); A-32 (here the global figure is 35%; that for 4-year institutions in general 46%; that for research universities 53%).

41. See above, Chapter III, pp. 97–98. Trow and Fulton, "Research Activity in American Higher Education," 43, where they point out that "while all the four-year colleges show a primary commitment to teaching, the high-quality colleges have as many 'researchers' on their faculties as do the weaker universities." Cf. *ibid.*, 79–80. Also C. Jencks and David Reisman, *The Academic Revolution* (New York, 1968), p. 24.

42. See above, p. 142.

43. Prone to be faithful in this to the rather condescending attitude of the late nineteenth-century presidents. See above, Chapter I, pp. 26–27.

44. See Trow and Fulton, "Research Activity in American Higher Education" pp. 43–44, and Table 2–2, 79–80.

45. See above, pp. 142–43.

46. *A Proposal for the Establishment at Williams College of a Center for the Humanities and Social Sciences,* June, 1984, pp. 5–6. In further describing the mission of the proposed Center, the proposal went on to say (p. 6) that "while not questioning the importance of topics of investigation that fall comfortably within one or other of the arts, humanities or social science disciplines as conventionally defined, the Center is committed to the view that there are equally important topics which, because they do not fit easily or completely within any of those disciplines, or because they straddle the ill-defined frontier between the humanities and social sciences, remain unstudied or inappropriately studied. At a time, then, when so many of the established

disciplines continue the process of narrowing their boundaries in order to achieve a sharper intellectual focus, to give priority to a particular methodology, or to pursue a more rigorous treatment of their subject matter, the Center seeks especially to identify and support those ares of inquiry which may have suffered from or been marginalized by that very process. ... And in choosing to give special prominence to such areas of inquiry the Center has committed itself also (and necessarily) to the attempt to identify and substitute for the technical or even hermetic vocabularies that currently threaten to fragment the humanities no less than the social sciences the rudiments, at least, of a viable common discourse."

47. Ruscio, "The Distinctive Scholarship of the Selective Liberal Arts College," 205–22.

48. *Ibid.*, 218. As a result, "the marginal contribution to the literature is not pursued; the emphasis is on major, reflective publications; the insightful synthesis ranks alongside the purely original formulations; and student involvement is encouraged."

49. *Ibid.*, 210–11.

50. Ruscio, "The Distinctive Scholarship of the Selective Liberal Arts College," 213–15, where he cites one faculty member as celebrating the fact that in his institutional setting "I could follow precisely where my curiosities led without having to answer to anybody or to feel that I was professionally imperilling myself." The general point rings very true to my own experience and to that of many of my colleagues over the years at Williams.

51. Trow and Fulton, "Research Activity in American Higher Education," 79.

52. In this respect, I find myself in sympathy with the judgment rendered by Derek Bok, *Higher Learning,* p. 71: "In evaluating the state of undergraduate education, one must be careful not to exaggerate the significance of the curriculum. It is important to conduct a review at suitable intervals in order to achieve *some* reasonable set of requirements and *some* clear set of educational goals that will unify and inspirit the faculty. But curricular debates only involve the arrangement and rearrangement of individual courses and do not touch upon the ways in which professors organize their material, teach their classes, and examine their students." In any case, standing back from the curricular nuts and bolts, stating that "it does not seem to me very difficult to describe some of the necessary conditions for being a well-educated person," and then going on to describe those conditions in a few, succinct paragraphs, John Searle was able to catch the spirit common, I believe, to most faculty at our leading colleges and universities. See Searle, "The Storm over the University," *The New York Review of Books* (December 6, 1990), 42.

53. Thus Gerald Graff, "Teach the Conflicts," *The South Atlantic Quarterly,* 89 (no. 1, 1990), 52–53. See above, pp. 150–51, and also Chapter IV, pp. 122–27.

54. Cf. Graff, "Teach the Conflicts," 53, "[T]he educational fundamentalists fail to confront the question of whose common culture it is to be.

Educational fundamentalists look back fondly to a past when there was still enough consensus over the content of higher education that this question did not have to arise. They conveniently ignore the fact that the past consensus was made possible only by the narrow and exclusive social base from which educators and educated then were drawn. It is not too hard to get a consensus if you start by excluding most Jews, blacks, immigrants, women, and others who figure to make trouble." In any case, he adds, "even this delimited consensus had become fragile as early as the 1870s when the modern university began to take shape."

55. See above, Chapter II, pp. 46–47.

56. Gerald Graff, *Professing Literature: An Institutional History* (Chicago and London, 1989), p. 14.

57. *Ibid.,* pp. 6–9, 225.

58. Graff, "Teach the Conflicts," 57–58.

59. Graff, *Professing Literature,* pp. 15, 258; "Teach the Conflicts," 52, 64.

60. These are the tactics Graff suggests—see his "Teach the Conflicts," 61–66, and his "Teach the Conflicts: An Alternative to Educational Fundamentalism," in Craige ed., *Literature, Language and Politics* (Athens and London, 1988), pp. 107–8.

61. Graff, *Professing Literature,* pp. 257–58.

62. As a recent survey conducted by the American Council on Education certainly suggests—see *The Chronicle of Higher Education,* August 7, 1991, A23.

63. See above, Chapter I, pp. 32–34.

64. Charles Homer Haskins, *The Rise of Universities* (Ithaca, 1957), pp. 51–57. Haskins notes that "freedom was general, save in philosophy and theology. In law, in medicine, in grammar and mathematics, men were normally free to lecture and dispute as they would"—though, at Oxford, one poor master was deposed (i.e. fired) for proposing "the abolition of the cases of latin nouns and the personal endings of verbs." For the theologians and the degree to which the masters themselves served as judges in matters pertaining to "freedom of thought and expression within the university community," see William J. Courtenay, "Inquiry and Inquisition: Academic Freedom in Medieval Universities," *Church History,* 58 (1989), 168–81.

EPILOGUE

1. Karl Polyani, *The Great Transformation* (New York, 1944).

2. Peter L. Berger, *Pyramids of Sacrifice: Political Ethics and Social Change* (Garden City, N.Y., 1976), p. 23.

3. Colin Turnbull, *The Lonely African* (New York, 1962), pp. 237–39. Berger, *Pyramids of Sacrifice,* pp. 192–93, drew my attention to this intriguing account.

4. See Peter L. Berger and Thomas Luckmann, *The Social Construction of Reality: A Treatise in the Sociology of Knowledge* (Garden City, N.Y., 1967).

5. Lewis Thomas, "Address to the American Association for the Advancement of Science," cited from Jeremy Bernstein, "Biology Watcher," *The New Yorker,* Jan. 2, 1978, 45–46.

6. Alfred North Whitehead, *Science and the Modern World* (New York, 1948), pp. 19–20.

INDEX